THE HENNESSY
COGNAC GOLD CUP
THE DEFINITIVE HISTORY

THE HENNESSY COGNAC GOLD CUP

THE DEFINITIVE HISTORY

STEWART PETERS

TEMPUS

FRONTISPIECE – What's Up Boys (red) and Hindiana go to post for the 2001 race in front of a packed grandstand.

FRONT COVER – Trabolgan (left) and L'Ami jump the final fence in 2005.
BACK COVER – Action from the 2003 race.

First published 2006

Tempus Publishing Ltd
The Mill, Brimscombe Port
Stroud, Gloucestershire GL5 2QG
www.tempus-publishing.com

British Library Cataloguing in Publication Data.
A catalogue record for this book is available from the British Library.

ISBN 0 7524 3790 9

Typesetting, design and origination by Tempus Publishing.
Printed in Great Britain

FOREWORD

Like all fans of National Hunt racing, the Hennessy Cognac Gold Cup is one of the races that I look forward to most during the season. Not only is it one of the most valuable and important chases, but it is also a race that boasts great tradition. The Hennessy meeting always has a special feel to it, and a quick glance through the list of previous winners of the big race is enough to inspire anyone.

As a jockey, I was fortunate enough to have a number of great rides in the Hennessy. My first came on Approaching in 1983. Approaching was a veteran by that stage, but he had won the race in 1978 and still had a touch of class, giving me a fine ride round and eventually finishing fifth.

Then came my consecutive wins for Devon trainer David Barons in 1986 and 1987. In 1986 I rode Broadheath, a strong bay, well-built and with a tremendous heart. Broadheath was a horse that preferred genuinely good ground, but he showed his adaptability that day by winning on draining ground on the soft side. He had made a mistake three out that could have knocked the stuffing out of him, but the horse was very courageous and determined and fought really well to win, giving me the biggest win of my career at that point.

A year later I was on board Playschool, a horse that David had bought in New Zealand. Playschool was not as big or robust as Broadheath, but had more class. He was a relentless galloper, capable of running his rivals into the ground. Playschool had been a brilliant novice, but had been slightly overshadowed at the time by Kildimo, a very good horse trained by Toby Balding, who had beaten him in the Sun Alliance Chase at Cheltenham, and therefore Kildimo was favourite at Newbury. Playschool though was a beautiful jumper when finding his rhythm, as he did in the Hennessy. He never stopped galloping and won comfortably. He was one of the best I ever rode and had superb stamina, winning a Welsh Grand National next

Paul Nicholls, who won the Hennessy as a jockey in 1986 and 1987, later became one of the sport's leading trainers.

followed by an Irish Gold Cup. He was favourite too for the Gold Cup at Cheltenham, but I eventually pulled him up after he ran no sort of race. Something must have been wrong and David was convinced he was 'got at', yet tests proved nothing and it remains a mystery. Still, he was brilliant on his day and was a marvellous Hennessy winner.

As a trainer, my team has enjoyed some wonderful days at Newbury, and none could be better than when Strong Flow won the Hennessy in 2003. He was only a six-year-old and had relatively little jumping experience, and there was always the worry that the inexperience could have gone against him in such a big race. There was a big field in 2003

Paul Nicholls as a jockey with his 1987 Hennessy winner Playschool.

including Hedgehunter, who won the Grand National very easily the season after, but Strong Flow was given a great ride by Ruby Walsh and, despite one awful mistake early on, the horse was breathtaking and ended up thrashing the rest and winning by fourteen lengths. To see a young horse like that realise the talent that you know he has inside him is something that fills me with immense pride.

Strong Flow's win aside, I have had many good horses run in the Hennessy. Deep Bramble was my first runner back in 1994, and some of my favourites like Earthmover and Ad Hoc have run with great credit in the race. Whitenzo was third in 2002 and could have been closer but for

a late jumping error, while Royal Auclair showed what a fine horse he has been, finishing third under a big weight in 2004, a season in which he later finished fourth in the Gold Cup and second in the National.

The Hennessy has given me some wonderful experiences as both a jockey and a trainer, and I think that this book by Stewart Peters relives perfectly all the key moments in the history of one of the great races in our sport.

Paul Nicholls

THE AUTHOR

For me, the Hennessy Cognac Gold Cup marks the true beginning of the National Hunt calendar. Of course, the season has officially been up and running for a number of months by the time it rolls around, with the Open Meeting at Cheltenham a major attraction some two weeks before Newbury. But the Hennessy always provides that extra feeling of spine-tingling excitement that can only be derived from top-class steeplechases, and there is no doubting it is the biggest attraction in the jumping game prior to Christmas. Such is the importance of the race, it often becomes a focal point for the remainder of the season, offering up clues for the major end-of-season festivals at Cheltenham and Aintree.

In writing this book, I needed only to look at the horses that have graced the race since its inception in 1957 to provide me with all the inspiration necessary. Many of the early editions were stocked full of the very best chasers in the land, winners of genuine brilliance such as Mandarin, Mill House and Arkle, while the trend of ultra-competitive Hennessys has continued right through to the present day. Even the 'also rans' have been of tremendous quality, truly great names like Pas Seul, The Dikler, Red Rum and The Fellow all featuring in the archives of the race.

Indeed, in more recent times, some of my favourite horses have run in the Hennessy. I shall never forget the young One Man announcing his arrival on the chasing scene with such elegance in 1994 or the way in which Suny Bay recovered from the most horrendous of early blunders to annihilate the 1997 field. As I say, the inspiration for this book comes from those that have defined the race's history. It has been a privilege to watch and write about them.

Stewart Peters

Marlborough (2) and Frosty Canyon in action in the 2002 race.

Stewart Peters is a freelance sports writer and leading author of horse racing history. He has been a lifelong fan of racing, in particular National Hunt, and has previously written successful books about the Cheltenham Festival, Aintree Grand National and Epsom Derby.

The Queen Mother in the paddock at the 1992 Hennessy meeting.

SETTING THE SCENE

Hunting through my files for the pictures for Stewart Peters' book has brought back a great many happy memories of racing at Newbury, in particular the Hennessy Cognac Gold Cup, which I first covered in 1969. Edward Courage, who owned and trained Spanish Steps, was anxious that I should be there to take pictures of his horse in action, and I have never missed a Hennessy since.

There is no doubt that the Hennessy Cognac Gold Cup is one of the major highlights of the National Hunt season. It was also a great favourite of Queen Elizabeth The Queen Mother, who took delight in making the most of presentations to the winning connections, even at the great age of 101.

Newbury is the professional's racecourse. There is never a bad race at Newbury, either on the flat or over the sticks and it is an excellent course for photography, especially in the spring.

Race days for my wife and I don't begin and end at the racecourse. The journeying plays an important part and the drive from our home to Newbury takes us either through or close to the 'Valley of the Racehorse', Lambourn, and the many training establishments in a part of the country that is lovely at all times of the year.

Bernard Parkin, Royal Racing Photographer

Bernard Parkin was, for many years, Racing Photographer to Queen Elizabeth The Queen Mother and currently serves Her Majesty The Queen in the same capacity. In addition to having covered every Hennessy since the year Spanish Steps triumphed in 1969, he is also the official Racecourse Photographer for Cheltenham Racecourse. This is the third book in which Peters and Parkin have worked together, the pair previously collaborating on highly successful titles Festival Gold – Forty Years of Cheltenham Racing *and* The Grand National – The History of the Aintree Spectacular.

INTRODUCTION

The Hennessy Cognac Gold Cup has long been established as one of the most prestigious races in the National Hunt calendar. First run at Cheltenham in 1957, the race was transferred permanently to Newbury three years later and now continues as the Berkshire course's most important race of the jumping season, always attracting a high-class field and enormous betting interest. A Grade Three handicap steeplechase with prize money in excess of £120,000, the Hennessy is the sport's leading pre-Christmas event.

Usually run on the last Saturday of November, to be present at Newbury on a crisp afternoon with the depths of winter lurking in the background offers a rare feeling of excitement for the racing months ahead, combined with a sense of tradition and importance sparked by the wonderful chapters that have made up the history of the Hennessy.

Helping to make the Hennessy Cognac Gold Cup such a fine race is the course itself. Aintree's Grand National course has its unique, giant fences; Cheltenham has its deeply undulating circuit and Kempton Park its tight, lightning-quick track, all of which provide their own separate challenges. Newbury is tough but fair, and regarded as one of the finest jumping tracks in the country; wide with long straights, easy bends and very few minor undulations, the emphasis is on jumping and galloping.

Run over a distance of just over three miles two furlongs, the fences at Newbury provide a strong test for participants. Twenty-one are jumped in the Hennessy, comprising of sixteen plain fences, four open ditches and the water jump once, run over two laps of the course. Starting opposite the stands near the entrance to the three-quarters-of-a-mile-long back straight, horses are able to get into an early rhythm and find a position as they jump the five fences down the back, with the early stages calling for safe, accurate fencing.

The Hennessy Cognac Gold Cup trophy.

Turning left-handed at the end of the back straight, the field negotiate the cross fence and then swing into the home straight for the first time. Watching from the stands, it is one of the most inspiring sights in racing to see the runners draw ever closer, soaring over the four big black fences in the home straight and, by the time the field take the spectacular water jump in front of the stands, the always packed-solid Newbury crowd lend rich vocal encouragement to proceedings. The sight of the field streaming over the water jump is a glorious one, and has been acknowledged by the Newbury executive in recent years with the building of a small viewing stand on the inside of the course, where samples of the sponsor's product can be enjoyed.

Roared on by the crowd, the second circuit begins with increased expectancy, and one can sense the tension and excitement combining irresistibly, fuelled by the prospect of the drama that is to unfold. It is when the field are duelling in the back straight for the final time that the race really takes shape, as contenders move forward to mount their challenges,

The Newbury grandstands following
Hennessy day 2004.

while some are unable to maintain the intensity level and begin to fade. By the time the cross fence is reached for the final time, any horse not within striking distance of the lead is unlikely to feature in the finish.

Then, for the final time, those left in contention attack the finishing straight; plain fence, open ditch, then two plain fences to finish, with the crowd on their feet as the leaders fly the last, the jumping of the horses vital by this stage. The run to the finishing line from the final fence is 255 yards, while runners must also carve right-handed to avoid the water jump, meaning those on the inside must be wary of being cut off by a challenger on the stands side. Having run well over three miles at a fast pace, a horse must show its reserves of stamina to achieve victory and, on crossing the line, each and every winner of the Hennessy fully deserves their moment of glory and a place on the famous roll of honour.

Now in its fiftieth year, the race has enjoyed some wonderful renewals throughout its history, with some of the most recognisable names in National Hunt racing having tasted success. With sponsorship provided by James Hennessy & Co., the world-famous cognac family, it was perhaps fitting that the very first owner to win the race was a member of the sponsoring family, Madame Killian Hennessy, whose brilliant horse Mandarin took the inaugural event in 1957. Mandarin was a perfect flag-bearer for the fledgling race as the horse enjoyed a most memorable career, cementing himself as one of the modern greats by winning a second Hennessy in 1961 and adding the cherished Cheltenham Gold Cup a year later.

A glance at the Hennessy roll of honour leaves one inspired, and the race's early years saw such championed horses as Kerstin, Mill House, Rondetto and Spanish Steps take the honours, while unquestionably the finest chaser

Grange Brake (green), Coome Hill (centre) and Lo Stregone jump the water in the 1996 race.

of his or any other generation, the legendary Arkle, won the Newbury race on two mesmerising occasions in the mid-1960s, and was only denied a third title following an almighty battle with the little grey horse Stalbridge Colonist in one of the Hennessy's most captivating finishes ever.

In more modern times, Cheltenham Gold Cup winners Bregawn and Burrough Hill Lad exuded their class by winning the Hennessy with devastating conviction, while the 1990s saw an unforgettable sequence of much-loved grey horses coming out on top, including Teeton Mill, Suny Bay and the wonderful athlete that was One Man.

The Hennessy has seen many outstanding winners of the race, with young, improving horses traditionally faring very well, yet it is not just the equine stars that have made the race such a force. Many of the top trainers and jockeys have enjoyed success in the race. The great Fulke

Walwyn sent out the Hennessy winner an incredible seven times, with Neville Crump, Tom Dreaper, Josh Gifford, Michael Dickinson, Fred Winter, Jenny Pitman and Martin Pipe to name but a few all training the winner at least once, while names such as Pat Taaffe, Stan Mellor, Richard Pitman, John Francome, Peter Scudamore, Norman Williamson and Ruby Walsh enrich the winning jockeys' list. Then there are those, namely Andy Turnell and Paul Nicholls, who managed the rare achievement of success in both spheres.

The story of the Hennessy Cognac Gold Cup is full of brilliant horsemen and women and stocked deep with some of the finest horses to have graced the sport. It is hoped that the future of the great Newbury race brings with it as many breathtaking races and engrossing storylines as the chapters that have made its history.

MANDARIN

The first running of the Hennessy Gold Cup took place not at the course that would become the race's eventual home – Newbury – but at Cheltenham. As it is now, that first running was a handicap and was run over three miles one furlong. With sponsorship from James Hennessy & Co., the world-famous cognac family, the prize money for the inaugural race was good, at just over £5,000. Together with the money, the winning connections would receive the 'Hennessy Gold Cup', a trophy with a value of £200. Detrimental to the race's debut was the fact that the Hennessy clashed with two other important races of the time, the well-established flat race the November Handicap, run at Manchester, as well as the three-mile Emblem Handicap Chase.

Mandarin and jockey Gerry Madden, the first Hennessy winners.

In spite of those two races, the first ever Hennessy attracted a fine field of nineteen runners, clustered with top-class chasers, and was graced with the presence of the reigning Cheltenham Gold Cup winner Linwell. A ten-year-old brown gelding, Linwell had won a thrilling Gold Cup at Cheltenham in March, narrowly defeating the mare Kerstin. For that fine performance he had been allotted top weight of 12st 2lbs in the Hennessy. Linwell was a small horse but possessed a brilliance that revolved around superb jumping ability and a courageous heart. In addition, Linwell was partnered in the race by one of the strongest jockeys of the era, Michael Scudamore.

The honour of being the first ever Hennessy favourite fell to the grey horse The Callant, a nine-year-old trained by Stewart Wight. The Callant was something of a Cheltenham specialist, having twice won the Foxhunter Chase over four miles at the course. His stamina for a race such as the Hennessy was guaranteed, his speed appeared sufficient for the shorter distance and the horse generally seemed an ideal candidate for the race,

even taking into account his hefty weight of 11st 12lbs. Enhancing his claim was the fact that, on his most recent run, The Callant had defeated the Gold Cup runner-up Kerstin over three miles at Ayr.

At only six years of age, the Fulke Walwyn-trained Mandarin was the youngest horse in the race, and was owned by a member of the sponsoring family, Madame Killian Hennessy. On his only previous run of the season, Mandarin had finished out of the frame at Newbury. However, that race was over two miles, a distance far shorter than the horse desired. Mandarin was a talented and potential-rich individual, and had displayed great promise when finishing second by a neck in the previous season's Whitbread Gold Cup at Sandown. It was this race that seemed to stick in the minds of the betting public, and Mandarin began the race a well-backed 8/1 joint second favourite with Linwell.

Other horses to receive considerable attention in the first Hennessy were Much Obliged, Lochroe, Bremontier and Hall Weir. Much Obliged, trained by Neville Crump in Yorkshire, had won his fair share of big races the season before, including the Mildmay Memorial Chase and the Whitbread Gold Cup, both at Sandown, but had been unplaced on two starts during the current season at Hexham and Wetherby. Lochroe was a classy nine-year-old trained by Peter Cazalet but was a horse with suspect stamina and his better performances had come on far flatter tracks than Cheltenham's undulating course. Bremontier had no such stamina worries, having won the Scottish Grand National in April and having also won very easily at Catterick recently, while the consistent and highly regarded Hall Weir, trained by Frank Cundell, had run well at Cheltenham on previous visits, such as when running Linwell close at the November meeting in 1956.

Several horses did their chances no good at all before the race had even started. The first to display a cause for concern was the Whitbread winner Much Obliged, who sweated up tremendously during the race preliminaries. The concern was justified in the race itself as Much Obliged found himself a long way behind after one circuit and was never able to get into contention. Springsilver also had his followers worried as he fell on the run to the start. Although the loose horse was eventually caught by his jockey, the mishap meant a delay to the start. Unfortunately for Springsilver, it would not be the last fall he would endure as he also capsized in the race. Whether the delay affected the 20/1 shot Lough Ennel or not is open to debate, but the horse virtually ruined his chance at the start, whipping round and losing lots of ground as the runners were sent on their way, and he too would later fall.

Of those that remained calm, the prospect of Hennessy glory was alive and well, and it was the seven-year-old Newlands Prince that led the field, tracked by the big, robust Bob Tailed 'Un, The Callant, Gay Donald, Vigor, Mandarin, Hall Weir, Dilston and, for a short while, Much Obliged.

The pace set by Newlands Prince was strong and, by the seventh fence, the horse had drawn clear of the pack. Despite jumping slightly to his right he was fencing with gusto, and the horse still held an advantage with a

Cheltenham racecourse in 1957.

mile to run, closely followed by The Callant and Mandarin. Vigor, Lochroe and Gay Fox had been up with the pace for much of the way, but now they began to tire, as did Bob Tailed 'Un, who had run strongly from the start but simply could not tolerate the pace as the tempo increased inside the final mile.

One horse that seemed to have plenty of work to do with a mile to run was the Gold Cup winner Linwell. He had considerable ground to make up on the leaders but Scudamore steadily crept him into contention and, with three fences to jump, the horse was on the heels of the leaders.

As Newlands Prince began to retreat after a brave run, it was the youngster Mandarin that now leapt into the lead. Mandarin had been near the front for most of the way, and now he had his challengers in trouble as he threw down his bid for glory. Only The Callant, Hall Weir, Linwell and the staying-on French-bred horse Bremontier had any hope of clawing him back.

The horse that appeared most likely to challenge Mandarin was Hall Weir but, going very well at the time, the latter over-jumped the second last and crumpled to the ground in agonising fashion. Although it was difficult to judge a potential outcome, Hall Weir's jockey Peter Pickford was adamant the horse would have won.

Now it was Linwell's turn to rally and, giving an enormous 16lbs to Mandarin, the Gold Cup winner came to challenge for the lead at the final fence. Linwell received tremendous encouragement from the crowd as he headed for the finishing line and, for a moment, the first running of the Hennessy looked destined to have the top weight's name carved upon it. But Gerry Madden roused Mandarin for one final effort and the young horse responded admirably, fighting back and ultimately overthrowing Linwell halfway up the run-in before holding on to record a three-length win. Linwell had given his all in defeat but, as it turned out, this defeat would prove no disgrace at all as, in time, Mandarin would become a magnificent champion. Bremontier edged out The Callant for third, with Vigor the last of thirteen to complete the course.

The Hennessy was the first big win of Madden's career, one that, up to this point, had seen him partnering mostly novices or suspect jumpers. Fulke Walwyn was praised considerably for sticking with the jockey when the trainer could easily have opted for Champion Jockey Fred Winter for Mandarin, as Winter – who had won the Grand National earlier in the year on Sundew – was without a ride in the race after his intended mount, the grey Glorious Twelfth, was withdrawn the day before.

1957 HENNESSY GOLD CUP RESULT

FATE	HORSE	AGE/WEIGHT	JOCKEY
1st	MANDARIN	6.11.0	P.G. MADDEN
2nd	LINWELL	9.12.2	M. SCUDAMORE
3rd	BREMONTIER	10.10.13	A. ROSSIO
4th	The Callant	9.11.12	M. Batchelor
5th	Dilston	9.10.6	T. Brookshaw
6th	Bob Tailed 'Un	8.10.8	J.A. Bullock
7th	Newlands Prince	7.10.4	Mr R. McCreery
8th	The Ovens	7.10.6	T. Molony
9th	Lochroe	9.11.12	A.R. Freeman
10th	Tea Fiend	8.10.0	S. Mellor
11th	Much Obliged	9.11.9	H.J. East
12th	Ron's Nephew	10.10.11	B. Pitman
13th	Vigor	9.11.7	W. Rees
Fell	Lough Ennel	9.11.4	T. Mabbutt
Fell	Springsilver	7.10.10	W.J. Brennan
Fell	Hall Weir	7.10.9	P. Pickford
Fell	Gay Fox	11.10.1	V. Speck
Pulled Up	Gay Donald	11.11.6	A. Grantham
Pulled Up	Ross Lake	10.10.0	R.E. Jenkins

Weight is in stone & pounds

16 November 1957
Going – Good
Winner – £5,272
Time – 6 mins 32.8 secs
19 Ran
Winner trained by Fulke Walwyn at Lambourn, Berkshire
Winner bred by M.K. Hennessy
Winner owned by Mme K. Hennessy
Mandarin, bay gelding by Deux Pour Cent – Manada

Betting – 4/1 The Callant, 7/1 Lochroe, 8/1 Linwell & Mandarin, 10/1 Much Obliged & The Ovens, 100/8 Bremontier & Hall Weir, 100/7 Newlands Prince & Springsilver, 20/1 Lough Ennel, 25/1 Bob Tailed 'Un, Dilston, Gay Donald, Gay Fox, Ron's Nephew, Ross Lake, Tea Fiend & Vigor.

As for Mandarin, it was hard to imagine a more appropriate winner of the very first Hennessy. The horse went on to enjoy an incredible career, one fuelled by big-race wins, and five years later the horse would return to the race, seeking further Hennessy glory.

TAXIDERMIST

From the very first Hennessy to the present day, two factors seem to have attached themselves to the race. The first – and the 1958 running displayed this in its most magnificent form – is the Hennessy's uncanny knack for producing ultra-tight, nail-biting finishes, while the second is a common trend that the race is normally won by a young, improving horse, quite often a second-season chaser. The 1958 race, when the result was settled, laid the groundwork for these distinctive traits.

The overwhelming favourite in 1958 was the previous year's hero, Mandarin. Stronger physically than the year before and visibly packed with muscle before the race, Mandarin had raced just once before the Hennessy in the current season, when second over an insufficient two miles at Newbury. Mandarin, having won the race in 1957 and finished runner-up for the second consecutive season in the Whitbread at Sandown shortly afterwards, deservedly carried top weight, with 12st his allotted burden.

The Whitbread at the end of the previous season was to be the key race in determining the possible outcome of the 1958 Hennessy. As well as Mandarin, the winner of the Whitbread, Taxidermist, and the third-placed horse Kerstin were in the line-up. Like Mandarin, Taxidermist was trained by the Lambourn maestro Fulke Walwyn and was an up-and-coming six-year-old with a high level of talent, as his Whitbread victory showed. Kerstin, a tough, brown mare, had won the Cheltenham Gold Cup in March and seemed certain to give a strong account of herself, despite her hefty weight allocation of 11st 9lbs. Already in the current season Kerstin had finished second in a pair of three-mile handicap chases at Ayr and Kelso, and lay behind only Mandarin – a horse that had beaten her twice before – in the betting, starting at 5/1.

Among the other interesting contenders in the 1958 field were Caesar's Helm, Valiant Spark and Just Awake. The seven-year-old Caesar's Helm

Taxidermist and Mr John Lawrence.

was a giant of a horse owned by Mr Jim Joel. The bay had enjoyed a promising campaign the season before, when his results had included a narrow defeat in the Great Yorkshire Chase at Doncaster and a fine win in the Mildmay of Flete Chase at the Cheltenham Festival. In a field where eleven of the thirteen runners were aged eight or under, nine-year-old Valiant Spark was a virtual veteran. An exuberant and eye-catching jumper, Valiant Spark had been runner-up in the National Hunt Handicap Chase at the Cheltenham Festival but, on his latest appearance in the Grand Sefton Trial Chase at Hurst Park three weeks prior to the Hennessy, the horse had fallen when travelling strongly. The talented second-season chaser Just Awake, from the yard of Peter Cazalet, was another that had fallen on his only start of the season, at Cheltenham. However, Just Awake had been one of the finest novice chasers of the season before, claiming the Broadway Chase at the Cheltenham Festival as one of his victories, and the horse fully warranted a place in the line-up.

With the going extremely soft and with two furlongs further to run than the 1957 race, the 1958 Hennessy required stamina and guts from a potential victor and, as the field broke away, it was Valiant Spark that set the gallop to Haytedder, El Griego II and Kerstin. Early on, the Fred Winter-ridden Gaillac was the back-marker.

The 50/1 shot El Griego II took up the running at the sixth fence from Valiant Spark, Kerstin, Mandarin – who was making the odd jumping error – Haytedder and the huge Caesar's Helm, and there was little change in the running order until Valiant Spark took control again at the twelfth.

One horse that appeared out of sorts was Taxidermist, ridden by Mr John Lawrence. Taxidermist was a horse that appreciated good ground and, at the water jump on the first circuit, the horse was running with such disdain that Lawrence considered pulling him up. But Taxidermist soldiered on and, with a mile to go, the race began to heat up tremendously. The second water jump, five fences from home, was to be a key point in the contest. It was there that the leader Valiant Spark fell and interfered with Mandarin who, despite having made numerous minor errors in his round, was still in contention at the time of the incident.

Now it was the Gold Cup winner Kerstin that held the lead, and the mare went on from Lady Brave, the rapidly improving Gaillac (who had been brought steadily through the field by Winter), Mandarin and Caesar's Helm, the latter being another that was challenging with increasing intent from fence to fence.

Two fences out and, with Lady Brave having fallen, the race seemed destined for whichever horse's stamina would stretch the furthest, as Kerstin, Caesar's Helm and Gaillac locked together for the final fight to the line. Mandarin's huge weight burden had gotten the better of him, while Taxidermist was even further back and, taking the last, it was Kerstin that set sail for the winning post in a commanding position, chased by Caesar's Helm.

Taxidermist was ten lengths behind in fifth jumping the last, but the soft going was blatantly slowing down the horses in front of him, and the Whitbread winner was the one horse that was not stopping. Although Kerstin was tiring, she was holding Caesar's Helm, Gaillac and Mandarin, but Taxidermist – making up an enormous amount of late ground – was finishing with raw power and iron-hearted determination.

As Kerstin slowed again near the line, Taxidermist rocketed past the lumbering Caesar's Helm and the Gold Cup heroine to win the Hennessy by a short head. With the result too close to call at first glance, it was Kerstin that was initially led into the winner's enclosure, until an announcement confirmed that Taxidermist had indeed got up to win. Kerstin had given 8lbs to the winner and, like Linwell the year before, came away from the race with great credit. Caesar's Helm had confirmed his affection for Cheltenham by finishing a creditable third with Gaillac fourth and Mandarin fifth.

The dramatic winning burst of Taxidermist had given Walwyn two wins from two Hennessys, with both winners six-year-olds. It was against Walwyn's advice (because of the state of the ground) that owners Mrs Peter Hastings and Mrs Fulke Walwyn had elected to run Taxidermist yet, in the end, connections could afford to smile and reflect on the horse's brave, enthralling and (from his position at the final fence) unlikely Hennessy victory.

1958 HENNESSY GOLD CUP RESULT

FATE	HORSE	AGE/WEIGHT	JOCKEY
1st	TAXIDERMIST	6.11.1	MR J. LAWRENCE
2nd	KERSTIN	8.11.9	S. HAYHURST
3rd	CAESAR'S HELM	7.11.4	G. SLACK
4th	Gaillac	6.10.3	F. Winter
5th	Mandarin	7.12.0	P.G. Madden
6th	Ruddy Glow	9.10.0	A. Honeybone
7th	El Griego II	8.10.0	R. Akehurst
8th	Just Awake	6.10.5	A.R. Freeman
Fell	Lady Brave	8.10.4	P. Cowley
Fell	Valiant Spark	9.10.2	A. Oughton
Fell	Rose's Pact	7.10.1	T. Dearie
Pulled Up	Haytedder	8.10.0	S. Mellor
Pulled Up	Oscar Wilde	8.10.0	R.E. Jenkins

15 November 1958
Going – Soft
Winner – £5,302 10s
Time – 7 mins 29.2 secs
13 Ran
Winner trained by Fulke Walwyn at Lambourn, Berkshire
Winner bred by Knockaney Stud
Winner owned by Mrs P. Hastings
Taxidermist, bay gelding by Ujiji – Rage Bleu

Betting – 10/11 Mandarin, 5/1 Kerstin, 8/1 Oscar Wilde, 10/1 Taxidermist, 100/6 Just Awake & Lady Brave, 20/1 Gaillac & Valiant Spark, 25/1 Caesar's Helm, Haytedder & Rose's Pact, 50/1 El Griego II & Ruddy Glow.

KERSTIN

Having been denied victory by the narrowest of margins twelve months before, the nine-year-old mare Kerstin returned to Cheltenham in 1959 to try and go one place better. Having succumbed to the late burst of Taxidermist in the 1958 Hennessy, Kerstin had then been laid low with injury before running in the Grand National in March, where she was unfortunately knocked over at Becher's Brook second time round when in the process of running a fine race. The horse had run well behind the improving Ace Of Trumps at Wetherby in the current season and appeared primed for another serious crack at the Hennessy. Kerstin was trained in the North by Major Calverley Bewicke and there was no doubting the mare acted better at Cheltenham than any other course, as she had been runner-up to Linwell in the 1957 Gold Cup, won that race a year later, all but won the 1958 Hennessy and had also won a National Hunt Handicap Chase at the festival in her younger days.

Kerstin was joined as 4/1 market leader by a youngster considered the up-and-coming star of the chasing ranks. The six-year-old Pas Seul had been bitterly unlucky not to have won the Cheltenham Gold Cup in March as, with the race at his mercy, he had fallen at the final fence in the most agonising manner. That particular run had illustrated perfectly what Pas Seul was all about; blessed with the brilliance to become the best yet prone to calamitous errors. He had, nevertheless, drawn the gaze of the handicapper and was hence allotted top weight of 12st in the Hennessy, eclipsing the mark of Kerstin, despite not having run in the current season.

With twenty-six runners, the blossoming status of the Hennessy had attracted a huge field, and among those holding decent chances were Brunel II, Siracusa, Lochroe, Reprieved and Polar Flight. The mount of the excellent Tim Brookshaw, Brunel II had been third in April's Whitbread Gold Cup – a race that had proved a more-than-useful guide to the first two runnings of

the Hennessy – and had been sharpening his game with a number of recent runs in flat-race contests. Siracusa was one of four six-year-olds in the race (outsider Solray was the youngest in the field at just five) and the horse was aiming to emulate the race's first two winners, Mandarin and Taxidermist, by also winning at that age. Siracusa was a fine jumper, as was evident from taming the fearsome Aintree Grand National fences in early November when finishing second in the Grand Sefton Chase, while at the Cheltenham Festival earlier in the year (a meeting where the diminutive veteran Lochroe had finished third in the Gold Cup) the horse had won the Mildmay of Flete Chase, a race previously won by the 1958 Hennessy third Caesar's Helm. Another from the six-year-old class was the talented Reprieved, a horse that had won half-a-dozen races the season before, while the Frank Cundell-trained nine-year-old Polar Flight was another that adored Cheltenham, having finished second to Kerstin in the 1958 Gold Cup.

With the going perfect, the large field charged away at a strong pace, headed by the previous year's winning jockey Mr John Lawrence aboard the seven-year-old Quelle Affaire and joined in the leading bunch by Croizet, Dark Island and Kerstin. Although Quelle Affaire and Dark Island began to drop away somewhat after the seventh fence, the horse that continued to run a bold but surprising race was the 33/1 outsider Croizet. The horse was a novice, having been one of the top point-to-pointers in the North the previous season. The surprise came from the fact that, in his three novice

Quelle Affaire leads Dark Island over the second fence in 1959.

chases prior to the Hennessy, Croizet had given no inkling of a major showing in the big race, yet now he was running the race of his life.

But, as well as Croizet had run, Kerstin was a horse of class and courage, and her jockey Stan Hayhurst sent the mare up to join the leader with a mile to run. It was not long before Kerstin – in spite of shouldering a big weight in a fast-paced race – shrugged off Croizet and came clear of the pack and, leaving the likes of Pas Seul, Lochroe, Siracusa and the useful Fred Winter-ridden novice Marcilly trailing in her wake, the mare set sail for home, rounding the long bend towards the third last.

In behind, Brunel II had emerged as the main danger to Kerstin, overhauling the gallant Croizet three out. It was there that Pas Seul, having made up considerable ground, took a nasty fall when beginning to get into the race. His fall may well have been significant for, as in the previous year's race, Kerstin began to get very tired in the latter stages, with Hayhurst working overtime to keep the mare up to her task. Brunel II was well noted as a strong finisher and, by the final fence, had closed right up on Kerstin and seemed ready to deny the mare Hennessy glory.

From the final fence to the winning line, the picture changed continuously. From being merely a neck ahead touching down on the flat, Kerstin found extra reserves and spurted clear, only to tire again halfway up the run-in, hanging left in the process. It was now that Hayhurst was forced to pull the horse aggressively to her right and, as he did so, the jockey lost both his irons.

Such an episode would have seriously dented the winning chance of many lesser horses but, although both Brunel II and the rallying Croizet frantically chased the mare in the closing stages, neither could match her class or courage. Having been straightened out skilfully by Hayhurst, Kerstin crucially found another gear, and visibly picked up again to dash home a five-length winner. Brunel II held off the admirable effort of Croizet by a neck for second, with outsiders Carrasco and Haytedder next followed by the staying-on Polar Flight.

Tremendous applause greeted Kerstin on her return to the winner's enclosure, with many understanding her brave performance had made up for the heartbreaking loss in 1958. Winning owner Mr G.H. Moore had purchased Kerstin from Mr Jim Powell of Nenagh, County Tipperary, along with the mare's two brothers, Bridge Of Honour and Vindicated, who won eight and ten races respectively, and sister Lady Nenagh, twice a winner. A truly prolific family, but there was no doubting that the newest Hennessy winner, Kerstin, was the jewel in the crown.

1959 HENNESSY GOLD CUP RESULT

FATE	HORSE	AGE/WEIGHT	JOCKEY
1st	KERSTIN	9.11.10	S. HAYHURST
2nd	BRUNEL II	9.11.4	T. BROOKSHAW
3rd	CROIZET	7.10.2	P.G. MADDEN
4th	Carrasco	7.10.3	R. Curson
5th	Haytedder	9.10.2	J. Dowling
6th	Polar Flight	9.11.9	M. Scudamore
7th	Beau Chevalet	6.10.2	R. Akehurst
8th	Dark Island	10.10.2	F. Whittle
9th	Quelle Affaire	7.10.2	Mr J. Lawrence
10th	Lochroe	11.11.12	A.R. Freeman
11th	Trinculo	8.10.7	V. Speck
12th	Marcilly	9.10.6	F. Winter
13th	Siracusa	6.10.3	B. Wilkinson
14th	Clover Bud	9.10.3	J. Lehane
15th	Devon Customer	7.10.2	D. Gale
16th	Seas End	7.10.2	O. McNally
Fell	Pas Seul	6.12.0	W. Rees
Fell	Turmoil	9.10.9	A. Oughton
Fell	San Lorenzo	8.10.4	G. Scott
Fell	Solray	5.10.2	G. Hindley
Fell	Aureus	9.10.2	Mr P. Slade
Pulled Up	Baby Don	9.10.12	H. Beasley
Pulled Up	Limonali	8.10.7	D. Nicholson
Pulled Up	Clanyon	11.10.4	G. Underwood
Pulled Up	Reprieved	6.10.2	P. Major
Pulled Up	Amoureux II	8.10.2	P. Cowley

14 November 1959
Going – Good
Winner – £5,074 +2s 6d
Time – 7 mins 4.6 secs
26 Ran
Winner trained by Major C. Bewicke at Alnwick, Northumberland
Winner bred by Mr C. Burke
Winner owned by Mr G.H. Moore
Kerstin, brown mare by Honor's Choice – Miss Kilcash

Betting – 4/1 Kerstin & Pas Seul, 8/1 Brunel II, 10/1 Polar Flight & Siracusa, 100/8 Clanyon, 100/7 Dark Island, Limonali, Lochroe & Marcilly, 20/1 Quelle Affaire & Reprieved, 25/1 Beau Chevalet, Carrasco, Clover Bud & Turmoil, 33/1 Amoureux II, Aureus, Baby Don, Croizet, Devon Customer, Haytedder, San Lorenzo, Seas End, Solray & Trinculo.

KNUCKLECRACKER

There had been two significant changes made by the time of the fourth Hennessy Gold Cup in 1960. The first, and most important, was the change of venue. The switch from Cheltenham to Newbury gave the Berkshire course a legitimate 'big chase' handicap and the flat, even track offered competitors a far different challenge than the undulating circuit at Cheltenham. The second alteration was moving the race back a week to avoid a clash with the well-established November Handicap, a move that would offer the still-fledgling Hennessy far greater exposure and coverage.

Favourite for the 1960 race was the Irish raider Zonda, winner of the Irish Grand National at Fairyhouse in 1959. Partnered by the excellent Pat Taaffe (who was extremely confident the horse would win), Zonda carried top weight of 12st and had strong form to his name. A nine-year-old bay, the horse had finished third behind former Hennessy runners Pas Seul and Lochroe in the Cheltenham Gold Cup in March and later finished third in the Irish Grand National while, on his most recent start in the current season, Zonda had easily disposed of former Gold Cup winner Roddy Owen in a race at Leopardstown a week before the Hennessy.

If Zonda was the class horse in the twenty-strong field of 1960, then the undoubted form horse was the seven-year-old Knucklecracker. Trained and ridden by Bicester-based Derek Ancil, Knucklecracker was unbeaten in three chases over three miles in the current season, with his wins coming at Cheltenham, Folkestone and Stratford. In his most recent victory, at Cheltenham, Knucklecracker had defeated the highly rated Frenchman's Cove, a subsequent Sandown winner and a future leading contender for both the Gold Cup and Grand National. The one concern regarding Knucklecracker was whether he would truly stay the Hennessy distance of three miles two furlongs, a trip made slightly more taxing due to the soft ground present following all-day rain on the Friday and even more rain through half of Friday night.

Commanding plenty of interest in the betting market were a trio of talented performers, Oxo, Winning Coin and Plummer's Plain. It was a huge bonus for the race to have in its field the Grand National winner of 1959, Oxo, ridden, as at Aintree, by Michael Scudamore. Oxo was a very popular horse that had many followers at Newbury. His most recent performance had seen him return to Aintree a few weeks before the Hennessy, where he finished third in the Grand Sefton Chase with a big weight on soft ground. That race was the first time Oxo had appeared on a racecourse since finishing third behind Mandarin in the 1959 King George VI Chase. Dave Dick's mount, the eight-year-old Winning Coin, had finished the season with four straight wins and had carried that form over to the current season when winning a three-mile chase at Wincanton most recently in fine style, while the seven-year-old Plummer's Plain brought the 1960 Whitbread Gold Cup form into the Hennessy, the horse having won the Sandown race in April.

The rain that had begun on Friday reared its head again at the start of the race, dousing the huge crowd that had turned up to watch the first Newbury Hennessy. Not surprisingly, it was the horses at the lower end of the handicap that set out to make their light weights tell in the testing conditions. Rock's Cross, one of two horses trained by Neville Crump (1959 faller San Lorenzo was the other), was the early leader, and was ridden by Gerry Scott, a man that had won the Grand National earlier in the year aboard Merryman II. Chasing Rock's Cross was a group consisting of K.E., Tea Fiend, Ankerdine, Coleen Star, Prince Seppal, Plummer's Plain and Scottish Flight II, with the higher-weighted trio of Zonda, Oxo and Knucklecracker further back. There were groans of disapproval as the much-fancied Winning Coin fell at the second fence, but the remainder continued in a race that seemed sure to test stamina to the limit.

By the start of the second circuit and with the race picture gradually beginning to change, it was the Whitbread winner Plummer's Plain that made a bold move to wrest the lead from Rock's Cross. However, for the quietly fancied San Lorenzo, the race ended abruptly with a fall at the same fence that had claimed Winning Coin on the first circuit.

Plummer's Plain moved swiftly clear of the pack, carving open a twelve-length lead from his nearest pursuer Ankerdine and, as it transpired, it was a move that was carried out with such force that the majority of the field were left in desperate trouble, with many tiring rapidly. Only

The 1960 winner Knucklecracker.

Knucklecracker and Zonda remained in contention, the pair merely a few lengths adrift of second-placed Ankerdine.

As cavalier and thrusting as his attack had been, Plummer's Plain's imminent decline was equally as notable. There was to be no Hennessy victory to add to his Whitbread success, a fact evident when the horse tired alarmingly three-quarters of a mile from home, his challenge petering out meekly. Although Ankerdine took over briefly, he was soon passed by Zonda and Knucklecracker at the cross fence, with the Irish horse holding a narrow advantage. But, at the fourth last, the vastly progressive Knucklecracker took command of the race, seizing a lead that he was never to relinquish as he continued his rise up the chasing ladder.

Stripping the top weight of his lead, Knucklecracker gradually drew clear over the remaining fences, with Ancil affording a glance over his shoulder to check for dangers and, by the last, the combination had opened up a gap of fifteen lengths to the beleaguered Zonda. The Irish raider was so exhausted that he clouted the last and was very fortunate to stay on his feet. Knucklecracker, though, was not stopping and, looking extremely fresh, the horse finished the race in fine style to run out an easy and most convincing winner. Zonda – understandably, given his big weight – trawled in a very tired horse, but received much credit for finishing second, while much further back Fearless Cavalier – a horse that had never won a chase – edged out Scottish Flight II for third place.

Plummer's Plain eventually finished sixth of the thirteen that completed, yet Oxo had never been travelling well and was always behind, eventually pulling up with half a mile to run.

Knucklecracker had been the most comfortable and impressive winner of the four Hennessys staged, hunting round the first circuit before unleashing a clinical challenge on the second. The horse had been difficult to train, for his tall, angular frame had proved somewhat brittle, and Derek Ancil had suffered his share of problems keeping the horse sound. One of the more interesting features of the horse's rise to prominence came courtesy of his diet where by, as a supplement to his regular food intake, Knucklecracker was given a daily quart of stout.

Knucklecracker was owned by Major L.S. Marler, who had purchased the horse for 2,000 guineas at the Ascot Sales, winning two races with him the previous season and now four more in the current campaign. It was with great delight that the Major accepted the winning trophy from Madame Maurice Hennessy, while Ancil received two trophies for his achievements as both winning trainer and jockey.

1960 HENNESSY GOLD CUP RESULT

FATE	HORSE	AGE/WEIGHT	JOCKEY
1st	KNUCKLECRACKER	7.11.1	D. ANCIL
2nd	ZONDA	9.12.0	P. TAAFFE
3rd	FEARLESS CAVALIER	9.10.4	J.R. GUEST
4th	Scottish Flight Ii	8.10.6	W. Rees
5th	Clover Bud	10.10.11	D. Nicholson
6th	Plummer's Plain	7.10.8	R.R. Harrison
7th	Ankerdine	9.10.4	P. Cowley
8th	Carrasco	8.10.5	F. Winter
9th	Rock's Cross	8.10.12	G. Scott
10th	Prince Seppal	7.10.5	P.G. Madden
11th	The Bell	9.10.13	J. Lehane
12th	K.E.	7.10.9	F. Whittle
13th	Soltown	8.10.4	C.F. McCormack
Fell	Winning Coin	8.11.5	D.V. Dick
Fell	San Lorenzo	9.10.9	H.J. East
Pulled Up	Oxo	9.11.3	M. Scudamore
Pulled Up	Limonali	9.10.4	P. Pickford
Pulled Up	Tea Fiend	11.10.4	S. Mellor
Pulled Up	Coleen Star	6.10.4	G. Slack
Pulled Up	Oakleigh Way	8.10.4	J. Fitzgerald

26 November 1960
Going – Soft
Winner – £5,218 10s
Time – 6 mins 59.2 secs
20 Ran
Winner trained by Derek Ancil at Middleton Stoney House, nr Bicester, Oxon
Winner bred by Captain R. Petre
Winner owned by Major L.S. Marler
Knucklecracker, bay gelding by Caudillo – Allegorie II

Betting – 4/1 Zonda, 5/1 Oxo, 7/1 Winning Coin, 8/1 Plummer's Plain, 10/1 Clover Bud, 100/7 Knucklecracker & Tea Fiend, 100/6 Carrasco, Rock's Cross, San Lorenzo, Scottish Flight II & The Bell, 20/1 K.E., 25/1 Ankerdine, Coleen Star, Limonali & Prince Seppal, 33/1 Fearless Cavalier, Oakleigh Way & Soltown.

1961

MANDARIN

The excellent chaser Pas Seul, winner of the 1960 Cheltenham Gold Cup and unlucky not to have also won that race in both 1959 and 1961, was all set to carry top weight in the 1961 Hennessy Gold Cup. But when trainer Bob Turnell withdrew his horse at the eleventh hour, after deeming the ground to be slightly too fast for his charge, the handicap was condensed, greatly benefiting those at the top end of the weights, including Olympia, Mandarin, Knucklecracker and Blessington Esquire.

Vying for favouritism on the day were the 1960 Irish Grand National winner Olympia and Nicolaus Silver. The Irish mare Olympia – a seven-year-old trained by Tom Dreaper – was the horse left to shoulder top weight, carrying 11st 10lbs. Having won the Munster National at Limerick the month before, Olympia fitted the fledgling Hennessy profile of a likely winner, being a young, progressive horse in good form prior to the race. It was to be the mare, partnered at Newbury by Pat Taaffe, that began the race as 3/1 favourite. The attractive grey horse Nicolaus Silver had won the Grand National at Aintree earlier in the year, and carried an enticing 10st 5lbs in the Hennessy. The horse had also finished close to Pas Seul in the Whitbread in April before returning to Aintree on his latest start of the current season to win the Grand Sefton Chase. The nine-year-old was trained by Fred Rimell and the horse's chance beforehand seemed outstanding.

Knucklecracker's progress since his eye-catching win twelve months before had been anything but smooth. The fragile horse had a history of breaking blood vessels and the problem had surfaced once more on his latest start at Newbury, where he was immediately pulled up. However, Derek Ancil regained the horse's fitness in time to defend his title, although Knucklecracker had slightly more weight to carry on this occasion. The

Grand National winner Nicolaus Silver was much fancied for the 1961 Hennessy.

ground was far quicker than in 1960 and, as a result, Knucklecracker started at 20/1, again ridden by his trainer.

Well supported in the betting market were Blessington Esquire, Springbok and Mandarin. As a six-year-old, the chestnut Blessington

Esquire was inexperienced but talented. The horse, ridden at Newbury by David Nicholson, had won the Mackeson Novices' Chase at Cheltenham in impressive style the week before the Hennessy, yet he was a horse that had never raced in a field of such class before. Springbok was another youngster on the rise. The horse had finished third behind Pas Seul in the Whitbread in April, and the Neville Crump-trained challenger had been primed for the Hennessy following a three-mile chase win at Kelso earlier in the season. In comparison to Blessington Esquire and Springbok, Mandarin was one of the veterans in the field of twenty-two. Joined in the line-up by his stablemate and fellow former winner, the apparently declining Taxidermist, Mandarin had blossomed into one of the chasers of the century since his 1957 Hennessy triumph, mixing talent and toughness in equal measure. Mandarin had twice won the King George VI Chase, was a heartbreaking second three times in the Whitbread Gold Cup and had been third in the Cheltenham Gold Cup. Additionally during that period, the horse had broken down and been fired, while he had also broken a bone in his stifle when finishing third in another King George. A second Hennessy win would mark another glorious achievement for the horse as well as confirming Fulke Walwyn to be the master of all trainers.

It was Fearless Cavalier, third in 1960, that was the early leader from Polar Flight, Hindhead, Domstar, Springbok and Seeker, while the favourite Olympia was kept tucked away towards the rear of the field by Taaffe.

Over the initial fences, the Grand National winner Nicolaus Silver fenced as though he was still at Aintree, jumping far too extravagantly, giving the obstacles plenty of air and losing a good deal of ground, while Dandy Tim sent his jockey flying after making an horrendous blunder at the second. Unfortunate for another reason was the incident that befell the previous year's hero Knucklecracker. The brittle chaser broke a blood vessel for the second consecutive race, and Ancil was forced to pull him up.

One of the features of the race was the fluent, accurate jumping of former winner Mandarin. The popular chaser was travelling and jumping with the zest of his younger days, belittling the thought that he may not be quite the force of old because of a series of injuries and, with a mile to run, the horse took the lead, forcing his way confidently past Polar Flight and Springbok, the pair that had been showing the way on the second circuit.

As the field jumped the fences down the back straight for the final time, the leading group consisted of Mandarin, Springbok, Blessington Esquire, Fearless Cavalier, John O'Groats, Superfine and Hindhead, as Polar Flight

began to tire badly. However, the fortunes of two horses were about to take totally contrasting twists. Having been hunted round casually by Taaffe early on, Olympia charged up from the back to join the leaders and, jumping the cross fence five out, the favourite appeared to be cruising as they turned for home. For Blessington Esquire though, the race was to reach a sad conclusion. The youngster had jumped very well and still held every chance when he broke down – regrettably quite badly – and was pulled up sharply with three-quarters of a mile to run.

Arriving at the first fence in the home straight, the fourth last, the two horses at the top of the handicap, Olympia and Mandarin, were locked in battle with the remainder struggling to stay in contention. Olympia jumped the fence upsides Mandarin, and another young, progressive winner of the race seemed likely to emerge. But, a fence later, it was clear that the speed in which Olympia had been driven from the back to join the leaders had taken its toll on the mare and, although just headed at the

David Nicholson contested many Hennessys as both a jockey and trainer.

third last, Mandarin was as tough a horse as could be found in training. Fighting back ferociously, he soon wiped out Olympia's slight advantage.

Putting in an enormous jump at the final fence, the crowd erupted as Mandarin shot away up the run-in. Churning towards the line under jockey Willie Robinson, Mandarin opened up a decisive lead and Olympia was beaten. At the finish, Mandarin had won by a length and a half from John O'Groats, a 25/1 shot that had stayed on powerfully. The runner-up was beginning a sequence that would see him compete in the next four Hennessys. Weary but gallant, Olympia was also passed before the line by the fast-finishing Taxidermist, and the favourite had to settle for fourth.

By common consensus, Mandarin was the most iron-hearted, genuine and consistent chaser in the land, and his second Hennessy victory merely underlined that status. The sheer fact that his two Hennessy wins had spanned five seasons was testament to his class and durability. It was indeed a marvellous performance from a marvellous horse, while much credit went to Walwyn for coaxing Mandarin through a series of injuries, allowing the horse to return to the racecourse to finish third behind Saffron Tartan and Pas Seul in March's Gold Cup, and now claim his second Hennessy title.

While jockey Robinson celebrated his first Hennessy success, a thought was spared for the unlucky Fred Winter, the man who would have partnered Mandarin had it not been for a fall at Sandown the previous week in which the jockey broke his collarbone.

As Madame Hennessy received her trophy from HM Queen Elizabeth, the owner revealed she had one remaining dream for her grand chaser; a win in the 1962 Cheltenham Gold Cup. Come March 1962 and, aged eleven, Mandarin finally realised that dream for her owner, gloriously capturing chasing's Blue Riband. He never ran in the Grand National, but he bowed out from racing in a most fitting way, highlighting his status as one of the all-time greats by winning the Grand Steeplechase de Paris in magnificent style before heading into a richly deserved retirement.

1961 HENNESSY GOLD CUP RESULT

FATE	HORSE	AGE/WEIGHT	JOCKEY
1st	MANDARIN	10.11.5	G.W. ROBINSON
2nd	JOHN O'GROATS	7.10.1	MR D. SCOTT
3rd	TAXIDERMIST	9.10.8	MR J. LAWRENCE
4th	OLYMPIA	7.11.10	P. TAAFFE
5th	Springbok	7.10.1	P. Buckley
6th	Superfine	8.10.4	Sir Wm. Pigott-Brown
7th	Mac Joy	9.10.9	M. Scudamore
8th	Hindhead	10.10.1	P. Jones
9th	Kilmore	11.10.4	J. Gifford
10th	Seeker	6.10.1	Mr A. Biddlecombe
11th	Reprieved	8.10.1	C. Moore
12th	O'Malley Point	10.10.10	J. Fitzgerald
13th	Nicolaus Silver	9.10.5	H. Beasley
14th	Fearless Cavalier	10.10.1	J.R. Guest
15th	Polar Flight	11.10.2	P. Pickford
16th	King's Nickel	7.10.1	T.W. Biddlecombe
Pulled Up	Knucklecracker	8.11.3	D. Ancil
Pulled Up	Blessington Esquire	6.11.2	D. Nicholson
Pulled Up	Clover Bud	11.10.1	Mr A. Oliver
Pulled Up	Domstar	8.10.1	J. Curran
Pulled Up	Go Forward	7.10.1	R.J. Hamey
Unseated Rider	Dandy Tim	8.10.1	B. Wilkinson

25 November 1961
Going – Good
Winner – £5,230 17s 6d
Time – 6 mins 32.4 secs
22 Ran
Winner trained by Fulke Walwyn at Lambourn, Berkshire
Winner bred by M.K. Hennessy
Winner owned by Mme K. Hennessy
Mandarin, bay gelding by Deux Pour Cent – Manada

Betting – 3/1 Olympia, 9/2 Nicolaus Silver, 7/1 Mandarin, 8/1 Springbok, 10/1 Mac Joy, 100/9 Blessington Esquire, 20/1 Knucklecracker, 22/1 Hindhead & O'Malley Point, 25/1 John O'Groats, Superfine & Taxidermist, 33/1 Clover Bud, Dandy Tim, Kilmore, Reprieved & Seeker, 50/1 Fearless Cavalier & Polar Flight, 66/1 Domstar, Go Forward & King's Nickel.

1962

SPRINGBOK

The sixth Hennessy Gold Cup in 1962 appeared to be, on paper, the most open edition yet. The mammoth field of twenty-seven has never been bettered numerically and almost certainly will not be now that the maximum field has been set, in more recent times, at twenty-five. The race featured a previous Hennessy victor in Knucklecracker as well as three horses that had previously finished runner-up in John O'Groats, Zonda and Brunel II. Also in the line-up were a future Grand National winner and runner-up in Team Spirit and Carrickbeg, a Becher Chase winner in Mr Jones and a plethora of the era's most talented staying chasers, including Rough Tweed, Cocky Consort and Springbok, as well as one of the smarter novices from the previous season in the grey, Sea Horse.

Despite an abundance of highly recognisable names in an ultra-competitive field, it was one of the least exposed runners that began the race as favourite. Trained by Mr S.T. Hewitt, Pride Of Ivanhoe was a strapping seven-year-old and had been extremely well backed in the days leading up to the race. The horse had won his last two races, both three-mile handicap chases, at Cheltenham and Wetherby respectively, yet his starting price of 13/2 reflected just how open the race was, considering the previous longest price of a Hennessy favourite had been 4/1.

The long-time ante-post favourite had been the talented Cocky Consort, a nine-year-old shouldering top weight of 12st, largely on the back of a fine performance in March's Cheltenham Gold Cup when he had finished third behind Mandarin and Fortria, winner of both the Mackeson and the Irish Grand National. Cocky Consort had then contested the Whitbread at Sandown in April, where he was running a beautiful race in the lead until falling three fences out. A stablemate of Mr Jones, Cocky Consort was well fancied, although there was a slight concern over his ability to handle the ground, which was very soft.

Since his win in the 1960 Hennessy, the form of Knucklecracker had dipped well below his best efforts. The horse had suffered regularly from broken blood vessels – including in the previous year's race – and the recurring problem had badly hampered his progress. However, in the current season, his trainer Derek Ancil had managed to bring the horse back close to his former powers, and Knucklecracker had pleasingly recorded four early season victories, each with the utmost simplicity. In one of his wins, at Ludlow, Knucklecracker beat the talented Rough Tweed, and that horse then franked the form by winning the valuable Ansells Brewery Chase at Worcester.

As well as the classy Rough Tweed, Yorkshire trainer Neville Crump was represented by the tough stayer Springbok. Fifth behind Mandarin in

Pride Of Ivanhoe and jockey Mr P. Hewitt started as favourites for the 1962 race.

Rough Tweed would finish as runner-up in 1962.

the 1961 Hennessy on good ground, the softer conditions in 1962 were expected to be much to Springbok's liking. Partnered on this occasion by Gerry Scott, Springbok was one of the most consistent chasers in training. The bay eight-year-old had finished third in April's Whitbread before beginning the current campaign with a three-mile chase win at Hexham followed by a narrow defeat to Cocky Consort at Doncaster. His general consistency as a chaser together with his noted appreciation of conditions saw Springbok start the 15/2 second favourite.

Anticipation levels were sky high as the twenty-seven began their journey towards the first fence in what promised to be one of the most exciting and entertaining Hennessys in the race's brief history, with the early leaders being Wingless, Coleen Star, Generous Star, Gold Wire, Caesar's Helm and Knucklecracker. The 1958 third Caesar's Helm was the first notable casualty, the big horse coming down at the ninth fence and, passing the stands for the first time, it was the top weight Cocky Consort that proudly led the pack, hotly pursued by Wingless, Threepwood, Eton Prince, Springbok, Opening Bars and Knucklecracker.

One of Springbok's traits was a knack of coming from off the pace to mount a challenge in his races – such as when passing eight horses in the last half-mile to finish third in the April's Whitbread. However, on this occasion, Scott had the horse positioned prominently from halfway and, when Threepwood and Generous Star both fell at the final fence in the back straight (six out), the horse was left in front.

The leading group was now Springbok, Wingless, Knucklecracker and Cocky Consort, although the lattermost had been badly hampered by the fallers at the sixth last, having been in front jumping the water – where Gold Wire came down. The interference seemed to knock the stuffing out of Cocky Consort and, thereafter, he was never a danger.

Having marched into the home straight, Springbok surged past Wingless and Knucklecracker as they jumped four out and, approaching the third last, he was joined by his stablemate Rough Tweed, a horse steadily brought into the race under David Nicholson.

Over the remaining fences, the race developed in to a desperate battle between the stablemates, as first one then the other looked likely to emerge victorious. Springbok had edged ahead on the run to the second last but, jumping the fence, Rough Tweed had again drawn upsides, seemingly travelling the better. Rough Tweed sprinted away from two out like a cheetah, apparently destined to add his name to the list of Hennessy winners. But, tenacious and with an abundance of stamina, Springbok fought back, Scott – with a broken right hand in plaster – driving the horse up to Rough Tweed's quarters, and was down by a mere half-length at the last.

Normally such an efficient jumper, Springbok made an horrendous mistake at the final fence, the horse decelerating to a virtual standstill before sluggishly making his way up the run-in. In contrast, Rough Tweed jumped the fence impeccably, was again quickly away, and neatly carved open a three-length lead as the pair headed for the line.

It was now that Springbok's superior stamina came into play. With less weight than his rival and on tiring ground, Springbok was able to mercilessly grind down Rough Tweed and, in dramatic fashion, cut his stablemate down once and for all in the dying strides, getting up to win by a head. It was a cruel way for Rough Tweed to be beaten, but he simply could not match Springbok's reserves of stamina on ground that favoured the winner. It had been a dogfight, and the winner was as tough as he was determined. Behind the front two, Knucklecracker had stayed on resolutely for third place, six lengths adrift, while Carrickbeg and Brown Diamond overtook the tiring Wingless to claim fourth and fifth respectively. Of the remainder, Cocky Consort was perhaps unlucky, travelling very well until the incident six out, eventually fading to finish twelfth, while the favourite, Pride Of Ivanhoe, was most disappointing, never factoring into the race and finishing eleventh.

The most elated man at Newbury was trainer Neville Crump, who saddled both Springbok and Rough Tweed, and he reserved special praise for Scott, stating that the brave jockey richly deserved such a victory after a succession of mind-numbing injuries. Scott had won the Grand National aboard Merryman II in 1960 but the jockey had broken his leg on two occasions since. Scott had then broken his hand when Merryman II had fallen at Kelso in late October and subsequently aggravated the injury in a fall at Newcastle a week before the Hennessy.

Springbok was bred by Major Vernon Miller (formerly of the 8th Hussars) out of a tough-staying mare called Empire Song, a horse that had finished fourth in a Becher Chase at Aintree. Unusually for a big-chase winner, Springbok was sired by an Epsom Derby winner in April The Fifth, while the newest Hennessy winner was owned by Colonel Lord Joicey, who had purchased the horse from Miller.

1962 HENNESSY GOLD CUP RESULT

FATE	HORSE	AGE/WEIGHT	JOCKEY
1st	SPRINGBOK	8.10.8	G. SCOTT
2nd	ROUGH TWEED	8.11.2	D. NICHOLSON
3rd	KNUCKLECRACKER	9.11.6	S. MELLOR
4th	CARRICKBEG	6.10.6	P. SUPPLE
5th	Brown Diamond	7.10.6	F. Shortt
6th	Wingless	7.10.3	A. Biddlecombe
7th	Opening Bars	8.10.3	F. Winter
8th	John O'Groats	8.10.0	J.R. Guest
9th	Zonda	11.11.13	Mr A. Cameron
10th	Team Spirit	10.10.7	G.W. Robinson
11th	Pride Of Ivanhoe	7.11.6	Mr P. Hewitt
12th	Cocky Consort	9.12.0	C. Stobbs
13th	Mr Jones	7.10.9	P. Buckley
14th	Fen Street	9.10.8	M. Scudamore
15th	Eton Prince	9.10.8	T. Brookshaw
16th	Chavara	9.10.3	P. Cowley
17th	Woodbrown	8.10.3	K. Boulton
18th	Trim Ruina	8.10.3	P. Pickford
19th	Sea Horse	8.11.0	T.W. Biddlecombe
Fell	Stenquill	7.11.3	J.A. Bullock
Fell	Gold Wire	10.10.9	Mr J. Ciechanowski
Fell	Threepwood	9.10.3	S. Hayhurst
Fell	Caesar's Helm	11.10.3	D. Mould
Fell	Generous Star	7.10.3	J. Gifford
Pulled Up	Brunel II	12.10.6	W. Rees
Pulled Up	Turmoil	12.10.3	Mr J. Brackenbury
Pulled Up	Coleen Star	8.10.3	P. Harvey

24 November 1962
Going – Soft
Winner – £5,272 2s 6d
Time – 6 mins 45.2 secs
27 Ran
Winner trained by Neville Crump at Middleham, Yorkshire
Winner bred by Major J.C. Vernon Miller
Winner owned by Lord Joicey
Springbok, bay gelding by April The Fifth – Empire Song

Betting – 13/2 Pride Of Ivanhoe, 15/2 Springbok, 9/1 Carrickbeg, 10/1 Knucklecracker, 100/7 Cocky Consort & Opening Bars, 100/6 John O'Groats & Rough Tweed, 18/1 Mr Jones, 20/1 Wingless, 25/1 Brown Diamond, Caesar's Helm & Fen Street, 33/1 Eton Prince, Sea Horse, Stenquill, Team Spirit & Threepwood, 40/1 Generous Star, Woodbrown & Zonda, 50/1 Brunel II, Chavara, Coleen Star, Gold Wire, Trim Ruina & Turmoil.

1963

MILL HOUSE

The 1963/64 season of National Hunt racing was perhaps the most significant and identifiable in the sport's history. Undoubtedly there had been great staying chasers before this period: the brilliant Golden Miller, a five-time Cheltenham Gold Cup winner and once a Grand National winner in a glorious spell in the 1930s; the triple Gold Cup winner Cottage Rake in the 1950s and, more recently, the tough, versatile and ultra-consistent Mandarin. However, what made the imminent campaign so mesmerising was the presence of two horses that took the sport to new levels, so much so that, in the case of one of them, it was a level high enough to earn the title of 'greatest racehorse of all time'.

Mill House was the reigning Cheltenham Gold Cup winner, having captured the title emphatically in March. The horse was a giant; a powerful-striding bay with a thumping, relentless galloping style that earned him the simplistic but imperious nickname of 'The Big Horse'. Only a six-year-old, Mill House was already considered a great champion, one that inspired awe and amazement whenever he took to the racecourse. Trained by Fulke Walwyn, Mill House was considered a worthy replacement for the trainer's great warrior Mandarin, and was thought to have even more class than the dual Hennessy winner. Mill House had won his final three chases of the previous season, including the Gold Cup, and would be making his seasonal debut in the Hennessy. He would also be carrying top weight of 12st, though that seemed irrelevant considering Mill House's mountainous structure. As it was, Mill House was hotly favoured to take the seventh running of the race, earning a starting price of 15/8.

Though very well respected at the time, the second of the two horses was trained in Ireland by Tom Dreaper and was no match for Mill House in terms of looks or body frame. The horse, another six-year-old, was called Arkle, a bay horse owned by Anne, Duchess of Westminster. Arkle's reputation had been quietly blossoming in his homeland since the previous season, when he had won seven consecutive races as a novice, including the Broadway Chase at the Cheltenham Festival. The horse jumped with the spring and accuracy of a deer, yet the most striking feature of Arkle and the way he raced was his ability to patiently 'stalk' opponents, before delivering exquisite speed to pull clear at the end of races, usually crushing his opponents by extremely large margins. Ridden by Pat Taaffe, there was concern that the soft ground present at Newbury in 1963 would blunt Arkle's finishing speed, whereas Mill House had a proven liking for such going, having powered through identical conditions to win the Mandarin Chase at Newbury the season before.

The 1963 Hennessy was to be the first time that Mill House and Arkle met on a racecourse. Though most believed Mill House to be the superior horse, countless raiding Irishman refused to accept that Arkle, this apparent new wonder-horse, could be beaten. The clash generated much hype in the preceding days, and it was easy to forget that there were other talented individuals engaged in the contest.

As well as the previous year's hero Springbok, the race featured Hamanet, Duke Of York and Pappageno's Cottage. Hamanet was an improving eight-year-old trained by Ryan Price and ridden by Josh Gifford. The horse had won five of six races in the current season and, although he had not beaten animals of outstanding quality, both trainer and jockey were confident of a bold showing from the horse. Fred Winter's mount, Duke Of York, had finished third to Mill House in the Gold Cup, but less exposed and a potential dangerous rival for the big two was Pappageno's Cottage, the mount of Tim Brookshaw, and a horse that had won the Scottish Grand National at the end of the previous season by twenty lengths.

All stands and enclosures were packed to the limit as the eagerly awaited battle began. Right from the outset, Mill House stamped his authority on proceedings, attacking each fence with a colossal appetite, soaring the obstacles as if they were twigs. He was joined by the outsider Solimyth, who attempted to match the giant's stride and gallop; an attempt that sadly failed after an initial brave effort. The first casualty was Pappageno's Cottage, who frustratingly fell at the first open ditch, but for the remainder of the race the only other horse of the ten that did not complete was the disappointing Duke Of York, who was pulled up by Winter.

The further they went, the more dominant Mill House became, devouring his fences with a series of enormous leaps as well as showing

Mill House (right) got the better of Arkle in 1963, but it would be the Irish horse that enjoyed the best of their intense rivalry.

clever attributes when he approached the odd fence on a short stride. For all of Mill House's dominance, the Irish challenger Arkle remained in live contention throughout. Approaching the third last, there must have been some concern in the minds of Mill House followers for, although second-placed Happy Spring was clearly held, Arkle appeared to have more to offer still. Could the Irish horse seriously rattle the cage of the mighty Mill House? The question was left in limbo following the third last, the last open ditch, when (only a length and a half behind Mill House) Arkle slipped on landing, denting his momentum and costing the horse any winning chance. The 1962 winner Springbok also clouted a fence in the home straight, weakening rapidly to eventually finish seventh.

The timing of the mistake was crucial – it was Arkle's only blunder – and it is impossible to say whether he would have beaten Mill House,

who performed at his finest on the day, despite not being 100 per cent fit, according to jockey Willie Robinson. All that can be said is that Arkle was travelling very well at the time and, with the benefit of peeking into the future, the contrasting fortunes of the two horses suggest the result may well have been different.

As it was, Mill House flew the second last and ended up winning in majestic style, giving 2st and an eight-length beating to Happy Spring. Coming home nonchalantly, Arkle took third. His colours had been lowered, but the appetites had been whetted for his next meeting with Mill House, which, as it transpired, would be in the Cheltenham Gold Cup of 1964.

For now, Mill House remained the golden horse of racing. His win elevated him to a status comparable with some of the best chasers of the century. He was rated the finest since Golden Miller, and the win gave

Fulke Walwyn his fourth Hennessy success following the victories of Mandarin (twice) and Taxidermist.

Indeed, much of the credit for Mill House's performance fell on the shoulders of Walwyn. In the past, the great trainer had worked wonders in getting injured and battled-scarred chasers such as Plummer's Plain and Mandarin back to the racecourse to win big races, and he had also won another Cheltenham Gold Cup previously with another six-year-old, Mont Tremblant. Here he had produced Mill House to win the Hennessy on his first run of the season and successfully charted the big horse's path to greatness.

1963 HENNESSY GOLD CUP RESULT

FATE	HORSE	AGE/WEIGHT	JOCKEY
1st	MILL HOUSE	6.12.0	G.W. ROBINSON
2nd	HAPPY SPRING	7.10.0	R. VIBERT
3rd	ARKLE	6.11.9	P. TAAFFE
4th	John O'Groats	9.10.0	P. Kelleway
5th	King's Nephew	6.10.6	S. Mellor
6th	Hamanet	8.10.0	J. Gifford
7th	Springbok	9.10.1	P. Buckley
8th	Solimyth	7.10.0	W. Rees
Fell	Pappageno's Cottage	8.10.3	T. Brookshaw
Pulled Up	Duke Of York	8.10.10	F. Winter

30 November 1963
Going – Soft
Winner – £5,020 10s
Time – 7 mins 1.8 secs
10 Ran
Winner trained by Fulke Walwyn at Lambourn, Berkshire
Winner bred by Mrs B.M. Lawlor
Winner owned by Mr W.H. Gollings
Mill House, bay gelding by King Hal – Nas Na Riogh

Betting – 15/8 Mill House, 5/2 Arkle, 8/1 Duke Of York, 9/1 Springbok, 100/9 Happy Spring, 100/7 Hamanet & King's Nephew, 100/6 Pappageno's Cottage, 50/1 John O'Groats & Solimyth.

ARKLE

After the 1963 Hennessy, in which Mill House had been so impressive, there were few outside of Ireland that believed Arkle would turn the tables come Cheltenham. In hindsight, the Hennessy may have been a mere blip on the road to Arkle's total domination of the chasing world that would last for the next three years. What Arkle did at Cheltenham in the Gold Cup not only served notice that it was he, not Mill House, that was the true powerhouse of the two, but the win (many believed) crushed Mill House's spirit, effectively destroying the soul of his great rival.

The racing world was similarly stunned by the authority of Arkle's win at Cheltenham. Mill House had been considered such a bomb-proof juggernaut that the result left many searching for words of explanation, including Fulke Walwyn. The third meeting between the two horses came in the 1964 Hennessy and was widely regarded as a rematch following Cheltenham, though the manner in which their horse had been demoralised in the Gold Cup must have meant the Mill House team entered the Newbury race with a fair degree of trepidation; half eager for another crack at Arkle yet half worried their prizefighter may suffer another beating.

As the current Gold Cup champion, Arkle was allotted top weight of 12st 7lbs, 3lbs more than Mill House. Despite defeat at Newbury the year before, Arkle had remained unbeaten since, winning his only start of the current campaign in a two-and-a-half-mile chase at Gowran Pak. With Pat Taaffe on board again, Arkle began the race 5/4 favourite.

Once more, Mill House would be making his seasonal bow in the Newbury race. The horse had a fond affection for the track, being a multiple winner at the Berkshire course. Whether or not Mill House's spirit had been broken by his defeat in the Gold Cup could only truly be judged by taking on Arkle once more, yet the big horse had run a fine race in

the end-of-season Whitbread Gold Cup in April, giving an incredible 3st to an up-and-coming horse in Dormant and finishing a gallant second. In a major boost for his army of followers, glowing reports made their way from Lambourn days before the contest, enthusing that Mill House had schooled brilliantly at Windsor racecourse to conclude his preparation, and this news helped to shrink Mill House's starting price to 13/8.

Faced with the daunting prospect of squaring up to the two most recent Cheltenham Gold Cup winners, many trainers bypassed the Hennessy with their horses and, as a result, the field of nine was the smallest yet since the race began. With two horses in the field that had previously finished runner-up in the Hennessy (John O'Groats and Happy Spring), the most interesting of the outsiders was a horse trained by Peter Cazalet called The Rip. Owned by Her Majesty The Queen Mother, the nine-year-old bay had been highly rated two seasons before but had lost his way somewhat. The Rip was a big horse, with his only run of the season being a promising second at Sandown.

Arkle was a most convincing winner in 1964.

As the race got under way, the first surprise was that it was Arkle and not Mill House that burst out into the lead. Normally Mill House liked to set the pace of his races, with Arkle usually appreciative of being held up, yet the first circuit of the 1964 Hennessy turned into a jumping exhibition from the big two. Pat Taaffe and Arkle had ensured an electric pace and, for the first lap, the most recent Gold Cup hero and Mill House jumped side by side, each attacking their fences with zest. Very quickly, the remainder were under intense pressure from the gallop.

By the start of the second circuit the two had pulled well clear, with Mill House able to match Arkle's enthusiasm and exuberance. However, halfway down the back straight, Arkle increased the tempo further, speeding between fences like some mad hare and, all of a sudden, Mill House was struggling. Seven fences out, Arkle had gone two lengths ahead and, despite a clumsy error a fence later that briefly let Mill House back in, the Irish horse swept onwards in unforgiving fashion.

Rounding the turn for home and three lengths adrift, Mill House was clearly beaten; crushed and deflated as at Cheltenham, unable to match Arkle's ability to quicken away when it mattered. Another Irish raider, Ferry Boat, came out of the pack to briefly challenge early in the home straight but, with a five-length advantage at the second-last fence, Arkle's supremacy and class were overwhelming and, in the manner of a truly outstanding horse, he accelerated away again, jumping the last fence in glorious isolation before breezing home by ten lengths. Ferry Boat finished next, but poor Mill House had had the inner will ripped from him, and it was slightly sad to see him trudge home in fourth, passed by The Rip on the run to the line.

Arkle's win demolished any doubts as to which horse was the undisputed number-one chaser. The horse, despite one blunder, had been immaculate; swift, calculated and cutthroat, draining the fight from Mill House long before the finish.

There would be a barrage of glory days ahead for Arkle, yet, just one week after his Hennessy victory, he demonstrated that, even in defeat, he was awesome. With top-class horses Flying Wild and Buona Notte on 10st 6lbs and 10st 12lbs respectively, Arkle shouldered a colossal 12st 10lbs in the valuable Massey-Ferguson Gold Cup at Cheltenham and still got within two lengths of victory. The horse of a lifetime had truly emerged.

Jockey Pat Taaffe.

1964 HENNESSY GOLD CUP RESULT

FATE	HORSE	AGE/WEIGHT	JOCKEY
1st	ARKLE	7.12.7	P. TAAFFE
2nd	FERRY BOAT	7.10.0	T.M. JONES
3rd	THE RIP	9.10.0	W. REES
4th	Mill House	7.12.4	G.W. Robinson
5th	Pappageno's Cottage	9.10.4	A. Biddlecombe
6th	Happy Spring	8.10.0	S. Davenport
7th	Hoodwinked	9.10.5	P. Buckley
Pulled Up	John O'Groats	10.10.6	D. Nicholson
Pulled Up	Vultrix	6.10.0	S. Mellor

5 December 1964
Going – Good
Winner – £5,516 2s 6d
Time – 6 mins 35.6 secs
9 Ran
Winner trained by Tom Dreaper at Kilsallaghan, County Dublin, Ireland
Winner bred by Mrs M.K. Baker
Winner owned by Anne, Duchess of Westminster
Arkle, bay gelding by Archive – Bright Cherry

Betting – 5/4 Arkle, 13/8 Mill House, 8/1 The Rip, 20/1 Pappageno's Cottage, 25/1 Happy Spring & John O'Groats, 33/1 Ferry Boat, Hoodwinked & Vultrix.

ARKLE

A common occurrence during Arkle's period of utter domination in the 1960s was the extremely small number of runners that faced him every time he raced. So authoritative had his performances become that opponents rarely seemed prepared to take him on in force. Indeed, in his three Cheltenham Gold Cup-winning races of 1964, 1965 and 1966, Arkle faced a meagre total of ten horses in all.

Having crushed his old rival Mill House once more, this time by twenty lengths in the Gold Cup in March, just seven rivals took on the great horse at Newbury in the new campaign, as Arkle sought his second consecutive Hennessy Gold Cup triumph. Arkle had beaten one of his Hennessy opponents, Brasher, by five lengths in April's Whitbread (the champion giving an extraordinary amount of weight away), and the horse had begun the current campaign with another hefty defeat of Mill House – as well as another top-grade chaser, the chestnut Rondetto – in a three-mile chase at Sandown in early November. At the time of the 1965 Hennessy, Arkle was at the absolute peak of his powers, and anything less than victory for the mighty horse – despite a colossal weight allocation of 12st 7lbs – would have been a huge shock. Confidence in Arkle was sky high, and his starting price of 1/6 resoundingly reflected the fact.

Of the other seven, only John O'Groats had run in the race before, but the most interesting challengers, most likely to cause a surprise appeared to be Freddie, Brasher and Wayward Queen. Second favourite on the day was the robust Scottish raider Freddie from the stable of Reg Tweedie. Freddie had run a fine race to be second to Jay Trump in the 1965 Grand National, and there was no doubting stamina was the horse's forte. Freddie had finished fourth on both his starts during the current season; at Wetherby and Carlisle, and in the Hennessy he was partnered by Pat McCarron. Brasher was another tough stayer, one that had won a Scottish Grand National, while the seven-year-old Wayward Queen – trained by Frank Cundell and ridden by John Cook – came into the race on the back of a recent three-mile chase win at Windsor.

This particular running of the Hennessy would prove to be the most conclusive of all time. Right from the outset, Arkle set about making the race his own, and he was joined by his Whitbread victim Brasher. Throughout much of the contest, the pair duelled for the lead, a spectacle that seemed certain to result in only one outcome – a victory for Arkle. The two built up such a lead that, by the fifth-last fence, they were twenty-five lengths clear of Freddie and the rest.

Brasher, ridden by Jimmy Fitzgerald, had certainly helped rouse Arkle's competitive spirit but, even in receipt of a staggering 35lbs, he had no answer once the pair entered the home straight for the final time, as Arkle cruised further and further clear, his class gloriously evident. Despite Pat Taaffe giving the great champion a few slaps to freshen him up at the last,

Considered the finest steeplechaser of all time, Arkle again won the Hennessy with ease in 1965.

Arkle came home unchallenged and unbothered with the minimum of fuss, recording an incredibly easy fifteen-length victory. Freddie's stamina and perseverance were enough to earn him second place, catching the tired but game Brasher on the run-in.

Arkle joined Mandarin as a dual Hennessy winner and, after the race, many were calling for the horse (proven emphatically in every other major chase) to be allowed to compete in the 1966 Grand National. The National was a race that asked every possible question of a staying chaser; jumping ability, stamina, courage and class. There seemed no reason why Arkle would be less inclined to adapt to the daunting but unique fences at Aintree than any other winner of that great race, although he would undoubtedly have had to shoulder the maximum weight burden over four and a half miles – a distance he had never tried. But it was never to be; Arkle's owner, Anne, Duchess of Westminster, had vowed never to risk Arkle in the National, fearing her beloved horse would befall some harmful incident. Instead, the great horse was again steered towards Cheltenham in a bid to record a hat-trick of Gold Cup wins.

1965 HENNESSY GOLD CUP RESULT

FATE	HORSE	AGE/WEIGHT	JOCKEY
1st	ARKLE	8.12.7	P. TAAFFE
2nd	FREDDIE	8.10.3	P. McCARRON
3rd	BRASHER	9.10.0	J. FITZGERALD
4th	Wayward Queen	7.10.6	J. Cook
Fell	Happy Arthur	8.10.1	G. Milburn
Pulled Up	Game Purston	7.10.0	P. Cowley
Pulled Up	John O'Groats	11.10.0	P. Kelleway
Pulled Up	Norther	8.10.0	T. Norman

27 November 1965
Going – Good
Winner – £7,099 5s
Time – 6 mins 49 secs
8 Ran
Winner trained by Tom Dreaper at Kilsallaghan, County Dublin, Ireland
Winner bred by Mrs M.K. Baker
Winner owned by Anne, Duchess of Westminster
Arkle, bay gelding by Archive – Bright Cherry

Betting – 1/6 Arkle, 9/1 Freddie, 20/1 Wayward Queen, 25/1 Brasher, Happy Arthur & John O'Groats, 50/1 Norther, 100/1 Game Purston.

1966

STALBRIDGE COLONIST

The 1966 Hennessy Gold Cup, with what appeared to be a most disappointing turnout of just six runners, actually transpired into one of the most interesting and informative editions of all time. With the now three-time Cheltenham Gold Cup winner Arkle in the field, the line-up was, as usual in his presence, on the small side. However, when the final careers of the six horses are analysed, two could boast winning the Cheltenham Gold Cup, another was twice placed in the same race and another was twice runner-up in the Grand National. In addition, the 1966 Hennessy was a thrilling race, with a decisive sting in its tail.

Arkle, unsurprisingly, was a red-hot fancy to win his third Hennessy. The season before had probably been his finest as the horse won all five of his races, including the Hennessy, the King George VI at Kempton and, of course, his third Gold Cup at Cheltenham. Unlike the two previous seasons, Arkle had been denied a preparatory run. He had been due to make his seasonal debut at Sandown in early November, but was forced to withdraw with a cut leg. Even so, the horse had reportedly been working extremely well at Tom Dreaper's yard and, despite being asked to give an enormous 35lbs in weight to the likes of the promising chestnut What A Myth, Arkle was backed as his status commanded, starting the race 4/6 favourite.

Second favourite at 7/2 was a serious challenger in the form of What A Myth. Trained by Ryan Price and ridden by Paul Kelleway, What A Myth was a soft-ground-loving nine-year-old with stamina to burn. The horse had enjoyed a marvellous campaign the season before; indeed, his only defeat in his last eight races had come at Aintree in the Grand National when, running a fine race, he came down at the second Becher's Brook. The horse certainly had a touch of class, especially when conditions were soft underfoot and, despite Newbury being bereft of that ground come Hennessy day, he was

The grey Stalbridge Colonist shocked Arkle by winning in 1966.

very nicely weighted considering What A Myth was himself usually more familiar with giving weight away to others rather than receiving it.

Freddie, again runner-up in the Grand National, was once more in the Hennessy line-up and was joined in the field by the useful Kellsboro' Wood and the seven-year-olds Master Mascus and Stalbridge Colonist. Trained by David Thom and ridden by Jeff King, Master Mascus was an improving chaser that had won two of his four starts during the season. However, Master Mascus had recently injured a leg when beaten by Freddie in a race at Sandown in early November, so his fitness for a race such as the Hennessy was questionable. Outsider of the six runners was the little grey horse Stalbridge Colonist. Listed at 25/1, it was true that the horse came into the race in shocking form, having run a couple of poor races in France before trailing home a remote fifth in a two-mile chase at Ascot the week before the Hennessy. His performance at Ascot was so discouraging that it left the impression that all may not have been well with the horse, one that had enjoyed a memorable novice season, winning a staggering eleven times from fourteen starts. In addition, the grey had been stranded in France over the summer because of the 'swamp-fever' ban, meaning horses in that country could not travel to England. In hindsight, there were perhaps excuses for the horse's poor Ascot run. Even so, Stalbridge Colonist was virtually ignored in

What A Myth and jockey Paul Kelleway finished third.

the betting market, partly because he had never won a chase beyond two and a half miles, and the horse trained in Buckinghamshire by Ken Cundell appeared a most unlikely winner of the 1966 Hennessy.

Arkle had looked tremendous in the paddock before the race and carried with him the awe of a supreme champion. His authority transcended into the race itself for, despite Freddie leading at the first fence, Arkle soared over the second to assume command. For much of the first circuit, it appeared Arkle was well on course to match his splendid performance of the year before, as he took each fence with grace and style, drawing unanimous applause from the Newbury crowd. As he led the field past the stands for the first time, anything other than a convincing Arkle win seemed out of the question.

As well as Arkle, the other five horses were jumping well, confirming the initial thoughts that, although disappointing numerically, the field was

a quality one and, heading down the back straight for the final time, it was Arkle that led by two lengths from Freddie, Kellsboro' Wood, Stalbridge Colonist and Master Mascus, with What A Myth bringing up the rear yet far from out of contention.

With a mile to run, Freddie – who had been made to work hard for his win at Sandown earlier in the month – began to struggle, and it was clear that, as soon as they turned for home with the tempo increased, the dual Grand National runner-up was beaten.

Early in the home straight, Arkle looked in total control, travelling imperiously and jumping with his usual panache, comfortable holding his nearest challenger Kellsboro' Wood. Master Mascus too was beginning to weaken but, hovering like hawks directly behind were the lightly weighted duo of Stalbridge Colonist and What A Myth. It was clear by the second last that Stalbridge Colonist was mounting a serious challenge, sticking to Arkle with steely determination. Cruising into second place with jockey Stan Mellor sitting motionless in the saddle, the little grey horse came to join Arkle at the final fence and, although the champion held a narrow lead, he put in an uncharacteristically awkward jump, whereas the grey flew the fence and was into his stride swiftly.

With just 10st on the back of Stalbridge Colonist compared to the 12st 7lbs carried by Arkle, the grey's challenge was delivered with serious intent, with the crowd almost stunned to see Arkle threatened in such a way. But, of course, Arkle was a horse like no other and, despite the enormous weight concession, he fought back bravely, snapping angrily at the heels of Stalbridge Colonist as the winning line loomed. It was an almighty battle, enlightening the entire run from the last fence to the finishing post before a mesmerised crowd but, on this occasion, the huge gulf in weight was too much for even Arkle to overcome, although he came ever so close to winning; defeated by just half a length in possibly his most courageous performance ever. What A Myth too had stayed on well, finishing a further length-and-a-half away in third with Kellsboro' Wood fourth.

The victory of Stalbridge Colonist came as a huge surprise given the horse's most recent efforts, and there were many among the large Newbury crowd somewhat disgusted with the result, partly due to the fact that connections of the winner chose to wait until after the race to offer various excuses for the horse's previous run at Ascot. Nevertheless, Stalbridge Colonist turned into one of the finest, toughest and most consistent chasers of the 1960s. He ran in three Cheltenham Gold Cups and was twice unlucky not to win, going down by three-quarters of a length to Woodland Venture in the 1967 race and finishing a close third behind Fort Leney a year later. The third time he contested Cheltenham's Blue Riband event, Stalbridge Colonist – owned by former Plymouth Argyle Football Club chairman Ron Blindell – fell in a soft-ground race won by none other than What A Myth.

As for the great Arkle, his shock defeat was his first for twenty-three months and only his third defeat in twenty-six chases. Sadly, the most wonderful horse the sport has ever witnessed was soon to run his last race. After the Hennessy, he won well at Ascot before a date at Kempton in the King George. In that race, he cracked a pedal bone in his hoof and the injury was so severe that it led to his retirement. Arkle was a truly magnificent horse and, when looking back through the years, the fact that his name twice appears on the Hennessy Roll of Honour lends great credit, substance and class to the history of one of the sport's finest races.

1966 HENNESSY GOLD CUP RESULT

FATE	HORSE	AGE/WEIGHT	JOCKEY
1st	STALBRIDGE COLONIST	7.10.0	S. MELLOR
2nd	ARKLE	9.12.7	P. TAAFFE
3rd	WHAT A MYTH	9.10.2	P. KELLEWAY
4th	Kellsboro' Wood	6.10.0	J. Haine
5th	Master Mascus	7.10.0	J. King
6th	Freddie	9.10.7	P. McCarron

26 November 1966
Going – Good
Winner – £5,713 10s
Time – 6 mins 48.6 secs
6 Ran
Winner trained by Ken Cundell at Compton, Buckinghamshire
Winner bred by H.W. Dufosee
Winner owned by Mr R. Blindell
Stalbridge Colonist, grey gelding by Colonist II – Eesofud

Betting – 4/6 Arkle, 7/2 What A Myth, 13/2 Freddie, 10/1 Master Mascus, 22/1 Kellsboro' Wood, 25/1 Stalbridge Colonist.

RONDETTO

The three previous Hennessy Gold Cups, all featuring the mighty Arkle, had small fields numerically. Even though the field for the 1967 race was nothing out of the ordinary size-wise, its rise in number to thirteen was, nevertheless, a pleasant change. There may have been no Arkle or Mill House, but the 1967 field was not short on quality. Far from it; the top two in the handicap, the 1966 hero Stalbridge Colonist and the third horse What A Myth, had both gone close to winning the Cheltenham Gold Cup in March, finishing second and third respectively to Woodland Venture. In addition, the field was graced with a decent mix of experienced and talented chasers, as well as some young, improving individuals, a mix that pointed to a highly competitive renewal.

With 11st 5lbs to carry on this occasion, What A Myth was the 5/1 favourite. The chestnut had begun the season in fine form, winning both his races at Plumpton and Huntingdon, albeit facing moderate opposition. Trainer Ryan Price was extremely confident that What A Myth could win the Hennessy, as the horse had been sparkling on the gallops at home and, once more, the horse was partnered by his regular jockey Paul Kelleway.

Although What A Myth was favourite, it was very tight at the top of the betting market. Next, on 11/2, came the previous year's winner, Stalbridge Colonist. The horse had given his all at Cheltenham in the Gold Cup, only going down by half a length to Woodland Venture. The grey's good form had continued into the current campaign, and his most recent outing had produced a three-mile chase defeat of Rondetto at Sandown in early November. However, his climb towards the upper echelon of the chasing ladder had not come without the inevitable rise in the handicap. Compared with the 10st he had carried to victory twelve months previously, Stalbridge Colonist now shouldered top weight of 11st 7lbs, a severe burden for a small horse.

As well as the out-of-form 1966 Grand National winner Anglo and the 1967 Grand National runner-up Honey End, other interesting challengers for the 1967 Hennessy included Rondetto, Bassnet, Three No Trumps and Woodlawn. Rondetto, a most consistent eleven-year-old chestnut, had been one of many unlucky horses in a bizarre Grand National earlier in the year. Rondetto had been in the lead and seemingly travelling strongest of all when a freak pile-up occurred at the twenty-third fence, ruining the chances of every horse in the race bar the immortalised winner, Foinavon. Rondetto, trained by Bob Turnell and ridden by Jeff King, arrived at Newbury in super form, having run well in three chases already in the current season. David Nicholson's mount, the eight-year-old Bassnet, had warmed up for the Hennessy with an all-the-way win on the course in early November, while the improving Three No Trumps – a Peter Cazalet-trained eight-year-old with speed and stamina – was well backed for the race having run a promising trial in Ascot's Black and White Gold Cup, despite unfortunately falling half-a-mile from home having travelled strongly throughout. Trained by Fulke Walwyn, Woodlawn too was an improving chaser, the eight-year-old having won over three miles at Cheltenham in November.

Similar to many of the ten previous Hennessys, the 1967 edition was destined for a thrilling conclusion. On good ground, the early pace was strong, largely down to the efforts of Ice Revue, Flosuebarb and Larbawn. The race was strongly run throughout, with the focal point arriving early on the second circuit, at the second fence after the water jump. Disputing the lead with Ice Revue at the time, Larbawn crashed out of contention, badly hampering Stalbridge Colonist – who had been travelling imperiously just behind the leaders. Brushing the top of the fence, the grey was forced to swerve violently on the landing side to avoid the fallen Larbawn, losing valuable ground and momentum as he did so.

From there, the race really picked up in earnest and, jumping the last in the back straight, Ice Revue continued to lead from a trio of keenly poised rivals in Regal Wine, Bassnet and the favourite, What A Myth. The lattermost had been eased beautifully into the race by Kelleway, having been towards the rear on the first circuit. By this stage, the race had already lost Tibidabo after the horse had unseated John Cook, while Anglo had disappointed again, ultimately pulled up by Eddie Harty. Woodlawn too had ruined his chance by blundering badly at the water, and was in a hopeless position with a mile to run.

It was Bassnet that eventually overthrew the game Ice Revue, and it was rough justice that the long-time leader came down at the third-last

Larbawn and jockey Macer Gifford.

The popular chestnut Rondetto became the first horse aged eleven to win the Hennessy.

fence having been passed by Bassnet a fence earlier. Flying the second last four lengths to the good, a win for Bassnet looked probable although, in behind, Regal Wine, What A Myth and now Rondetto were staying on mercilessly. More incredibly, Stalbridge Colonist had also fought his way into the reckoning and was now only a few lengths behind the leaders at the final fence.

Jumping the last, Bassnet tired alarmingly, his stamina being sapped from within, and those in behind were hunting him like dogs. Ruthlessly, What A Myth was the first to engulf the leader, with Rondetto and Regal Wine quick to follow suit, and a three-way battle to the line ensued. As the veteran Rondetto – in receipt of 18lbs from What A Myth – edged ahead of the favourite, a fourth challenger invaded the party as, finishing like a train, Stalbridge Colonist screamed past Regal Wine and then What A Myth, finally

setting his sights on Rondetto. However, this was to be the veteran chestnut's day and, asked by King for one final effort, Rondetto held on for victory by a head from the fast-finishing grey. Stalbridge Colonist failed in the bravest of fashions to concede 20lbs to Rondetto, yet the horse would have had a wonderful chance of a second consecutive victory if not for the drama and the interference on the second circuit, so powerfully had he finished the race. It had been the most dramatic and mesmerising finish to a Hennessy yet. As well as the front two, What A Myth was at the quarters of the leaders at the line in finishing third, with Regal Wine a neck back in fourth; it simply could not have been any closer. Having led at the last, Bassnet had no answer to the powerful finish of the front four, and eventually settled for fifth.

It was a most popular Hennessy result, for Rondetto was a greatly adored veteran chaser, winner of seventeen races between 1961 and

Jeff King, one of the strongest jockeys of his era.

1967 HENNESSY GOLD CUP RESULT

FATE	HORSE	AGE/WEIGHT	JOCKEY
1st	RONDETTO	11.10.1	J. KING
2nd	STALBRIDGE COLONIST	8.11.7	S. MELLOR
3rd	WHAT A MYTH	10.11.5	P. KELLEWAY
4th	Regal Wine	9.10.0	Mr A. Kemp
5th	Bassnet	8.10.7	D. Nicholson
6th	Woodlawn	8.10.7	G.W. Robinson
7th	Honey End	10.10.0	J. Gifford
Fell	Ice Revue	8.10.4	W. Shoemark
Fell	Larbawn	8.10.4	M.C. Gifford
Fell	Flosuebarb	7.10.0	J. Guest
Pulled Up	Three No Trumps	8.10.8	D. Mould
Pulled Up	Anglo	9.10.3	E.P. Harty
Unseated Rider	Tibidabo	7.11.0	J. Cook

25 November 1967
Going – Good
Winner – £5,941
Time – 6 mins 42.8 secs
13 Ran
Winner trained by Bob Turnell at Ogbourne Maisey Lodge, nr Marlborough,
   Wiltshire
Winner bred by Mrs Julia Bourke
Winner owned by Mr A. Mitchell
Rondetto, chestnut gelding by Caporetto – Roundandround

Betting – 5/1 What A Myth, 11/2 Stalbridge Colonist & Woodlawn, 6/1 Bassnet,
13/2 Three No Trumps, 8/1 Honey End, 100/8 Ice Revue & Rondetto, 100/6
Larbawn, 20/1 Tibidabo, 25/1 Regal Wine, 40/1 Anglo & Flosuebarb.

1966. Owned by eighty-seven-year-old Mr Alec Mitchell, Rondetto had missed much of the previous season having suffered from damaged ribs and a broken bone behind his knee. Much credit went to Turnell for aiding in the horse's recovery and preparation to win such a race, as Rondetto played his part in shaping the early history of the Hennessy Gold Cup.

1968

MAN OF THE WEST

The two most recent winners of the Hennessy Gold Cup, Stalbridge Colonist and Rondetto, featured among the field for the 1968 race. Stalbridge Colonist had again run a fine race in the Cheltenham Gold Cup in March, beaten by only a neck and a length by Fort Leney and The Laird. The grey had begun the current season by again succumbing to The Laird at Ascot the week before the Hennessy, and the horse now tried to join Mandarin and Arkle as dual winners of the race. Just a month away from turning thirteen, Rondetto was still going strong. He too was looking for another Hennessy victory, and the chestnut had warmed up impressively for the big race with a win on the course earlier in the month.

Making his first appearance in the Hennessy was the 1967 Cheltenham Gold Cup winner Woodland Venture. The horse, trained by Fred Rimell, had not raced because of injury for a full eighteen months, before making a pleasing comeback in early November, finishing third to Larbawn at Cheltenham. While Woodland Venture remained a solid jumper, it remained to be seen whether a race such as the Hennessy would come too soon in the horse's comeback from injury.

The older element aside, the 1968 Hennessy revolved largely around the younger generation of chasers, and a batch of improving horses ready to dismantle the old guard. Despite the fact that one of these youngsters, the six-year-old Titus Oates (rated Gold Cup-quality by his trainer Gordon Richards), was taken out of the line-up on the day because of heavy ground, Fearless Fred, Arcturus and Specify were all genuine prospects for the 1968 Hennessy. Fearless Fred was another horse trained by Rimell and was the elected mount of Terry Biddlecombe. Having been rated the top hunter-chaser in Ireland the season before, the six-year-old bay Fearless Fred had made a fine start to his career at Rimell's yard, winning on his

debut at Ascot before unveiling his potential with a fine recent win in the Badger Brewery Chase at Wincanton. Favourite on the day, largely due to his proven stamina and the fact the ground had turned into a bog, was Arcturus. A seven-year-old bay trained by Neville Crump, Arcturus had won the previous season's Scottish Grand National and, in the current season, defeated Titus Oates in the Emblem Chase at Wetherby. Specify, a six-year-old partnered by Bob Davies, was unproven at the Hennessy trip. Despite never attempting the distance of the Newbury race, trainer Denis Rayson was very confident the horse would run well after Specify had been beaten by only a short head in the Mackeson Gold Cup at Cheltenham in early November.

Also among the group of young chasers was a horse called Man Of The West, a bay seven-year-old trained by Fulke Walwyn. The difference between Man Of The West and the likes of Fearless Fred, Arcturus and Specify was that Man Of The West's recent form was poor and he had missed the entire previous season with ligament problems. This was not to say that Man Of The West was without talent. As a novice, Walwyn had won three chases with him and the horse's future had appeared bright. However, following his year off with injury, Man Of The West

Fulke Walwyn trained his fifth Hennessy winner in 1968.

The well-backed Fearless Fred with jockey Terry Biddlecombe.

had disappointed in the current campaign, delivering mediocre runs at Cheltenham and Nottingham, as well as unseating Willie Robinson at Ascot, and these performances ensured that the horse started as one of the outsiders in the field of eleven.

With the ground almost unraceable, it was clear the 1968 Hennessy would develop into a thorough test of stamina and, directly from the start, it was Fearless Fred and Man Of The West that set about dictating proceedings. For the entire first circuit, the leading pair took each other on, jumping like antelopes and churning admirably through the ground as those behind struggled to remain in close contention. Nearest the front two were Arcturus, Specify and Stalbridge Colonist, although the lattermost made a mistake at the water jump, costing him valuable ground.

By the start of the second circuit, Fearless Fred and Man Of The West really had their opponents in trouble as they continued the strong gallop,

leaving the majority toiling in the heavy ground. John Cook's mount Aurelius refused at the twelfth while, at the same fence, Woodland Venture blundered away any remote winning chance and the former Gold Cup winner was eventually pulled up with five fences to jump.

Five fences from home the battle began heating up immensely. Fearless Fred poached a slight lead and at first it appeared likely that his superior recent form would tell. But with 8lbs less to carry, Man Of The West was soon on terms again as the two turned for home. Man Of The West had clearly shaken off the rust that had hampered his first three races since his long layoff and, although the two remained together at the third last, it was he that was travelling the stronger as the race reached its conclusion. Man Of The West hit the second last slightly but, by now, Fearless Fred could give no more and he was passed by the staying-on Arcturus between two out and the last. Having jumped the last well, Man Of The West tired somewhat on the run-in, and the favourite Arcturus began to eat into his lead. However, with determination and a pleasing resilience, Man Of The West maintained his effort under Robinson, holding the similarly tiring Arcturus by four lengths with Fearless Fred twenty lengths away in third. Next home were Stalbridge Colonist and Rondetto, while Specify – whose finest moment would come when winning the Grand National in 1971 – fell on the second circuit.

It was a heart-warming win for a horse that had suffered badly with tendon and ligament injuries. As such, rich credit rightly went to trainer Fulke Walwyn who, together with the help and expertise of his stable staff and vets, had nursed Man Of The West back to full fitness to give owner Mr Donovan Drewery a wonderful success.

It was Walwyn's fifth Hennessy victory since the race began in 1957 yet, had it not been for the absence of his more established stable stars Mill House and Dormant, Man Of The West may not have run at all. The winner was sired by Manicou, a horse that was owned by HRH The Queen Mother, and it was she who presented the trophy to the winning connections of the 1968 Hennessy Gold Cup.

1968 HENNESSY GOLD CUP RESULT

FATE	HORSE	AGE/WEIGHT	JOCKEY
1st	MAN OF THE WEST	7.10.0	G.W. ROBINSON
2nd	ARCTURUS	7.10.10	P. BUCKLEY
3rd	FEARLESS FRED	6.10.8	T.W. BIDDLECOMBE
4th	Stalbridge Colonist	9.12.4	S. Mellor
5th	Rondetto	12.10.12	J. King
6th	Regal Wine	10.11.0	Mr A. Kemp
7th	San Angelo	8.10.11	G. Lee
Fell	Specify	6.10.0	B.R. Davies
Pulled Up	Woodland Venture	8.12.4	E.P. Harty
Pulled Up	Bassnet	9.11.1	Mr R. Davies
Refused	Aurelius	10.10.7	J. Cook

30 November 1968
Going – Heavy
Winner – £7,400
Time – 7 mins 24.8 secs
11 Ran
Winner trained by Fulke Walwyn at Lambourn, Berkshire
Winner bred by S.W. Bridge
Winner owned by Mr D. Drewery
Man Of The West, bay gelding by Manicou – Our Ideal

Betting – 7/2 Arcturus, 9/2 Fearless Fred, 6/1 Woodland Venture, 8/1 Rondetto & Stalbridge Colonist, 9/1 Specify, 100/8 Aurelius, 100/6 Bassnet, 20/1 Man Of The West & San Angelo, 25/1 Regal Wine.

SPANISH STEPS

The fifteen horses that lined up for the firm-ground Hennessy Gold Cup of 1969 gave the race an immensely competitive edge. With five of the runners priced at 15/2 or shorter, there were plenty of in-form animals in the field, most of which were newcomers to the race, with only Larbawn and Kellsboro' Wood having run in the race before.

It was one of the two old hands, Larbawn (a faller in the year Rondetto won) that began the race as favourite. The oldest horse in the field and one with a big weight of 12st 3lbs, it was at the end of the previous season when Larbawn had really begun to demonstrate his full ability. Larbawn had concluded the previous season with three consecutive wins, including the Whitbread Gold Cup at Sandown. A bay gelding by that most excellent sire of staying chasers, Vulgan, the key to Larbawn's performances was the presence of good, quick ground – such as was present at Newbury in 1969. Larbawn, partnered in the Hennessy by Macer Gifford, had started the current season well, running a bold race while conceding a lot of weight when coming second at Cheltenham two weeks before the Hennessy.

There was no doubting that the outstanding novice of the season before had been the brilliant Spanish Steps. A six-year-old trained, owned and bred by the wheelchair-stricken Edward Courage, Spanish Steps had developed into a classy stayer as a novice, recording a number of major victories, including the Totalisator Champion Novice Chase at the Cheltenham Festival, as well as finishing third behind Larbawn and Titus Oates in the Whitbread. Spanish Steps had raced just once before the Hennessy, finishing second to the prolific Moonduster at Newbury.

Commanding a great deal of attention in the betting market were a trio of Hennessy newcomers in Playlord, Lord Jim and Winsome Win.

With 12st 5lbs to shoulder, the Gordon Richards-trained Playlord was top weight. Like Spanish Steps and Larbawn, Playlord was another that had enjoyed a wonderful season in the previous campaign, winning four races including the valuable Great Yorkshire Chase and the Scottish Grand National. The latest horse trying to add to Fulke Walwyn's Hennessy collection was the brown gelding Lord Jim, a consistent stayer that had finished third on his only start of the season at Ascot. Comparable more in terms of ability to Man Of The West rather than some of Walwyn's higher-profile Hennessy winners such as Mandarin and Mill House, Lord Jim was a genuine chaser that rarely ran a bad race, and the horse had finished third behind Spanish Steps at the Cheltenham Festival in March. The form horse of the current season was definitely the mare Winsome Win, a winner of all four of her races preceding the Hennessy. Although her wins had come in moderate company, Winsome Win was extremely well weighted in the Hennessy with just 10st to carry, whereas her weights for future races were far greater.

Spanish Steps, ridden by John Cook, was a fine winner of the Hennessy.

Don't Weaken (10) and Lord Jim (13) in action during the 1969 race.

It was the favourite Larbawn that began the race in front and, on the firm ground he relished, set about providing a strong, aggressive gallop. By the sixth fence, he led from Cottager, Miss Hunter, Teryrose, Kellsboro' Wood and Lady Mynd.

In total contrast to the previous year's race, where Man Of The West and Fearless Fred had dominated the race virtually from the moment the tape went up, this particular renewal saw a whole host of horses mount serious challenges. With six fences to jump it was Larbawn that led, with both Lady Mynd and Cottager breathing down his neck, with the improving Spanish Steps in fourth followed by a large pack consisting of Playlord, The Inventor, Lord Jim, Limeburner, Permit and Don't Weaken.

It was at the cross fence where the real drama of the race unfolded. With Larbawn in the lead and going strongly, Lady Mynd was just a length down on the inside, while Cottager was the same distance behind on Larbawn's outside. Totally independently, both Lady Mynd and Cottager fell, with Lady Mynd rolling to her left and Cottager to his right. The

incredible fact was that Spanish Steps had jumped the fence directly behind these two, meaning that if either of the pair had rolled the other way, Spanish Steps would surely have been brought down. That fate befell both Playlord and Limeburner, who were put out of the race in the most unfortunate of circumstances.

Playlord had been travelling well when he was brought down, yet neither he nor any other in the race had been going as strongly as the fortunate Spanish Steps and, having received his share of luck, the horse switched into a higher gear and closed right up to Larbawn by the first fence in the home straight, the fourth last. By the next, Spanish Steps was just in front and from there on in there was only going to be one winner. Drawing further and further clear in the closing stages, Spanish Steps was able to ease home at his will under John Cook, with Larbawn very tired some way back and none of the others able to mount any kind of late challenge. Crossing the line a fifteen-length winner, the six-year-old Spanish Steps equated into a fine winner of the race, giving an impression great things may be around the corner for him. Larbawn had indeed got very tired towards the end, but was able to hold off Lord Jim and take second with Winsome Win fourth.

On the fast ground, Spanish Steps' winning time had taken two seconds off the course and distance record set by Mandarin when he had won his second Hennessy in 1961. The thumping gallop had unsurprisingly resulted in a number of fallers, and Cottager's jockey Joe Guest was taken to Reading hospital for precautionary X-rays.

It had been the biggest win of jockey John Cook's career to date, although he would later win the Grand National aboard Specify in 1971, while Mr Courage, who received the trophy from members of the Hennessy family, had bred Spanish Steps from his fine staying mare Tiberetta, herself placed in three Grand Nationals.

Spanish Steps had progressed again from his novice campaign, completely reversing the Whitbread Gold Cup form by trouncing Larbawn. Although his destiny did not include success in the Cheltenham Gold Cup (which quickly became the target following his Hennessy win), he was placed in that race in 1970, finished fourth in both the 1973 and 1974 Grand Nationals and third in the same race in 1975. In the history of the Hennessy Gold Cup, Spanish Steps remains not only one of the most impressive winners of the race but also one of the finest horses to have graced the event.

Wheelchair-bound trainer Edward Courage shares a joke with the Queen Mother.

1969 HENNESSY GOLD CUP RESULT

FATE	HORSE	AGE/WEIGHT	JOCKEY
1st	SPANISH STEPS	6.11.8	J. COOK
2nd	LARBAWN	10.12.3	M.C. GIFFORD
3rd	LORD JIM	8.10.0	G.W. ROBINSON
4th	Winsome Win	7.10.0	Roy Edwards
5th	Kellsboro' Wood	9.10.5	A. Turnell
6th	Miss Hunter	8.10.0	Mr J. Fowler
7th	Permit	6.10.4	P. Buckley
8th	Hove	8.10.8	J. Gifford
9th	Don't Weaken	8.10.0	D. Mould
10th	The Inventor	8.10.0	B.R. Davies
Fell	Cottager	9.10.0	J.R. Guest
Fell	Lady Mynd	7.10.0	D. Cartwright
Fell	Teryrose	7.10.0	G. Thorner
Brought Down	Playlord	8.12.5	R. Barry
Brought Down	Limeburner	8.10.0	J. Haine

29 November 1969
Going – Firm
Winner – £6,090 10s
Time – 6 mins 30.6 secs
15 Ran
Winner trained by Edward Courage at Banbury, Oxon
Winner bred by Mr E.R. Courage
Winner trained by Mr E.R. Courage
Spanish Steps, bay gelding by Flush Royal – Tiberetta

Betting – 4/1 Larbawn, 7/1 Lord Jim, Playlord & Spanish Steps, 15/2 Winsome Win, 10/1 Permit, 100/7 The Inventor, 100/6 Lady Mynd, 20/1 Hove, 25/1 Cottager & Don't Weaken, 33/1 Kellsboro' Wood, Limeburner, Miss Hunter & Teryrose.

BORDER MASK

The 1969 Hennessy winner Spanish Steps returned to Newbury in 1970 to defend his crown. Following his win the year before, Spanish Steps was made favourite for the Cheltenham Gold Cup, with wins in the Benson & Hedges Gold Cup at Sandown and the Gainsborough Chase merely strengthening his prospects for that race. However, Spanish Steps was never really travelling with serious intent at Cheltenham, eventually finishing third behind L'Escargot and French Tan and, when he ran a bitterly disappointing race in the subsequent Whitbread Gold Cup, the suspicion that the horse may have gone 'over the top' by Cheltenham was fully justified. After a summer holiday, Spanish Steps returned for the new season fresh and in good form, winning his first start of the campaign at Doncaster. At just seven years of age, many believed there was plenty of improvement to come from Spanish Steps, and he was well fancied to emulate Mandarin and Arkle by winning the Hennessy twice. However, having carried 11st 8lbs to victory in 1969, Spanish Steps was now asked to shoulder a colossal 12st 7lbs as he prepared to defend his crown.

Favourite for the race was Gay Trip, a bay eight-year-old trained by Fred Rimell. Gay Trip – a recognised two-and-a-half mile horse – had won the Grand National earlier in the year, so the perception was that the Hennessy trip would not pose a problem. The horse had run well in the recent Mackeson Gold Cup at Cheltenham, being among the leaders until slipping on landing two fences from home. With Roy Edwards aboard, Gay Trip began the race as the 5/1 market leader.

One of the most intriguing Hennessy candidates in 1970 was the injury-plagued Border Mask. Trained by Peter Cazalet and ridden by David Mould, Border Mask had been in superb winning form the previous season and was being hotly touted for the Grand National until breaking

down with suspensory trouble following a fall in the Mildmay Memorial Chase at Sandown in January. A strong, athletic eight-year-old bay, Border Mask had been nursed back to health by the team at Cazalet's Kent-based yard and returned to start the season with a win at Sandown three weeks before the Hennessy, impressing greatly in doing so.

As usual, the Hennessy had a highly competitive edge to it, with Huperade, Freddie Boy, Lord Jim and The Spaniard all boasting decent chances. The six-year-old Huperade was a challenger from Arthur Stephenson's Northern yard, and was perhaps the least exposed runner in the field. Huperade was a fast-improving individual and had run four times so far during the season, winning his last three. Freddie Boy was another talented but injury-riddled horse. Trained by Fred Winter and ridden by Richard Pitman, Freddie Boy had been rated as Gold Cup-class before being fired two seasons previously. The horse had made it back to the racecourse and had won his first start of the season, although his huge

The Grand National winner Gay Trip goes to post for the 1970 Hennessy under Roy Edwards.

Border Mask makes a bad mistake at the second last fence when leading Lord Jim.

weight of 12st 4lbs seemed rather harsh. The 1969 third Lord Jim had gone on later to win the Mandarin Chase at Newbury, yet was considered a touch slow to win a race like the Hennessy, while The Spaniard, a Scottish Grand National winner, was a talented horse but a somewhat erratic jumper.

It was a Hennessy of much incident, and it was the newest Grand National winner in Gay Trip that proceeded to take the field along at a good, strong gallop, followed by the chancy-jumping horse The Spaniard. It was at the seventh fence when the drama began to unfold. The six-year-old outsider Foxtor was a faller at the fence and, as the horse was clambering to his feet, he cannoned into the following Spanish Steps, an impact that was severe enough to send John Cook flying from the previous year's winner. Gay Trip continued to hack along in front, enjoying the flat track at

Newbury as he had done at Aintree in April, and his closest pursuers taking the water jump were Bay Tarquin, Freddie Boy and Lord Jim.

It was to be Lord Jim that made the next decisive move. Starting out for a second circuit, the Stan Mellor-ridden horse challenged Gay Trip for supremacy and subsequently took control of the race. In behind these two, recovered invalids Freddie Boy and Border Mask were both travelling nicely as well.

Just as Mellor had sent Lord Jim forward to strip Gay Trip of the lead, Mould similarly began his challenge aboard Border Mask, thrusting the horse into contention at the cross fence. Turning for home, Border Mask and Lord Jim were neck-and-neck, hotly chased by Freddie Boy. But when Border Mask nosed ahead at the third last, the writing appeared to be on the wall. Border Mask had jumped magnificently the entire way, belittling his recent serious injury. He was clearly a horse whose level of class was potentially sky high and, approaching two out, a potential destruction of the remainder looked likely. At the second last however, Border Mask made such a terrible mistake that he looked sure to hit the deck. As Mould urged his mount for a long stride, Border Mask responded by getting too close to the fence and crashing right through it. The crowd gasped at the severity of the blunder, fearing the horse had ruined his chance. It was of tremendous credit to both horse and rider that Border Mask was able to stay on his feet, and that he lost no ground was remarkable.

His one mishap behind him, Border Mask safely negotiated the final fence before easing home for an excellent ten-length win to crown his comeback from injury. Lord Jim, a more-than-useful stayer, had lacked the speed to stay with the winner over the final fences, yet took an honourable second ahead of Freddie Boy, Huperade, Gay Trip and The Laird. As one former sidelined warrior achieved his moment of glory, the sadness of the race stemmed from the injury incurred by the brave Freddie Boy. The horse had been hampered by the riderless Spanish Steps during the race and had returned home very sore. Later, it was revealed by Pitman that the horse was still travelling very well when he broke down on his near foreleg going to the second last, and the fact that the horse finished at all demonstrated his courage. It was to be Freddie Boy's last race as he was retired soon after.

The closing fences and the soft, tiring ground had contributed to a number of late casualties. Bay Tarquin had fallen four from home, the reckless fencing of The Spaniard had continued throughout the race and he eventually fell three out, while the 20/1 shot Beau Bob was the last to capsize two fences from the finish. However, Border Mask had survived his blunder to carve his name onto the Hennessy Roll of Honour. Cazalet had rated Border Mask a serious Grand National candidate the season before, having purchased the horse in the North a couple of seasons previously after a pair of point-to-point wins. Now Cazalet, owner Mrs Monica Arnold and all associated with the horse could rejoice in Border Mask's recovery from injury to become the Hennessy Gold Cup winner of 1970.

1970 HENNESSY GOLD CUP RESULT

FATE	HORSE	AGE/WEIGHT	JOCKEY
1st	BORDER MASK	8.11.1	D. MOULD
2nd	LORD JIM	9.10.7	S. MELLOR
3rd	FREDDIE BOY	9.12.4	R. PITMAN
4th	Huperade	6.10.5	T.S. Murphy
5th	Gay Trip	8.11.13	Roy Edwards
6th	The Laird	9.11.12	J. King
Fell	The Spaniard	8.11.1	B. Brogan
Fell	Bay Tarquin	7.10.8	P. Broderick
Fell	Beau Bob	7.10.0	R. Dennard
Fell	Foxtor	6.10.0	B.R. Davies
Pulled Up	Irish Moss	8.10.2	M.C. Gifford
Brought Down	Spanish Steps	7.12.7	J. Cook

28 November 1970
Going – Soft
Winner – £5,725 10s
Time – 6 mins 50.4 secs
12 Ran
Winner trained by Peter Cazalet at Tonbridge, Kent
Winner bred by H. McConnell
Winner owned by Mrs A.S. Arnold
Border Mask, bay gelding by Border Chief – Almzakin

Betting – 5/1 Gay Trip, 13/2 The Spaniard, 7/1 Border Mask & Spanish Steps, 8/1 Huperade, 9/1 Freddie Boy, 11/1 The Laird, 12/1 Lord Jim, 16/1 Bay Tarquin & Foxtor, 20/1 Beau Bob & Irish Moss.

1971

BIGHORN

A fine collection of talented chasers gathered at Newbury for the 1971 Hennessy Cognac Gold Cup, the word 'Cognac' having been inserted into the race's title in recognition of the region in South-West France where the sponsor's brandy was made.

Much of the excitement for the fifteenth running of the race focused on the presence in the field of the dual Cheltenham Gold Cup winner, the Irish-trained chestnut L'Escargot. At 33/1, the horse had become the longest-priced winner of the Gold Cup in 1970 when out-battling French Tan, and had followed that up with a far easier victory in March 1971. L'Escargot, normally a safe, reliable jumper, had fallen on his seasonal debut at Fairyhouse, yet it was the fact that the horse would be carrying 12st 7lbs that led to L'Escargot beginning the race merely joint-fifth in the betting. Trained by Dan Moore and ridden by Tommy Carberry, L'Escargot started the race at 10/1.

Joint favourites for the race were the 1969 winner Spanish Steps and the exciting grey stayer Grey Sombrero. As usual Spanish Steps had a hefty weight to carry, but the seven-year-old Grey Sombrero had been very kindly treated, getting into the race with a lightweight 10st 1lb. Trained by David Gandolfo, Grey Sombrero was a front-running, bold-jumping horse with stamina to burn, and had won the previous season's Midlands Grand National, as well as winning both his races in the current season.

Foxtor, a faller in the 1970 Hennessy but a winner of three races in the current campaign, as well as previous fancies Lord Jim and The Spaniard, lent fine strength in depth to the race, while three newcomers similarly offered punters some enticing betting options. The three horses were Saggart's Choice, Young Ash Leaf and Bighorn. Saggart's Choice, seeking to become the first Northern-trained horse to win since Springbok in 1962,

was trained by his former owner Tony Kemp, and was a fast-improving bay stayer. The horse had good form over the Hennessy distance and had scored easy wins at Ayr and Haydock already during the season. The seven-year-old mare Young Ash Leaf – another Northern-trained horse – had been ante-post favourite for the race for some time. Although frequently clumsy at her fences, Young Ash Leaf had shown herself worthy of consideration for such a race by beating the established Titus Oates over three-and-a-quarter miles at Doncaster three weeks before the Hennessy. With the possible exception of Grey Sombrero, the least-exposed runner in the field was the seven-year-old Bighorn, a brown gelding firmly on the rise. Bighorn had finished the previous season strongly and had looked distinctly like a horse ahead of the handicapper when winning the Ansells Brewery Chase at Worcester very comfortably on his most recent start.

Although Saggart's Choice was the leader as the thirteen-strong field flew over the first fence, it was Grey Sombrero, in his customary style, that soon took up the running. As Grey Sombrero set about developing a lead, the next wave of runners included Tamalin, Lord Jim and Proud Tarquin. However,

Dual Cheltenham Gold Cup winner L'Escargot jumps a fence during the 1971 Hennessy.

Grey Sombrero started joint favourite in 1971.

the reigning Gold Cup hero L'Escargot made a hash of the fourth fence and his round became unusually littered with jumping errors from there on in.

As the pattern of the race emerged, the running order remained virtually unchanged as the second circuit began. Royal Toss, a nine-year-old skilfully ridden by Eddie Harty, came through to join the leading bunch while Tantalum was one that slowly lost ground. There was a shock at the fourteenth fence when Spanish Steps, as reliable and consistent a jumper as could be found, crashed out of contention, a fall in which his jockey Johnny Haine broke an arm.

But a whole host of horses remained in contention coming out of the back straight for the final time, with Saggart's Choice snatching the lead

back from Grey Sombrero, followed closely by Lord Jim, Royal Toss, Proud Tarquin, the retaliating Tantalum and the rapidly improving Bighorn. As the field surged into the home straight, jockey David Cartwright pulled Bighorn wide of the main group to make his challenge. Little could Cartwright have known that such a manoeuvre could well have won him the race.

At the fourth last, Grey Sombrero fell with Royal Toss unluckily falling over him. Proud Tarquin and Lord Jim were also hampered so badly that their chances of winning were vanquished. When the exhausted Foxtor came down a fence later, Bighorn only had Saggart's Choice ahead of him. The younger, more powerful and determined Bighorn took control of the race at the second last, nudging ahead of Saggart's Choice and, although he got a touch close to the last, Bighorn ran home powerfully and ultimately won the race very handsomely. Young Ash Leaf, typically, had made errors during the race, but her resilience had kept her in touch, and she finished six lengths away in second having passed Saggart's Choice in the closing stages. The Spaniard, Proud Tarquin, L'Escargot and Tantalum also completed, but it was Royal Toss that was the unlucky loser, as he had been travelling extremely well when he came to grief.

Bighorn, the third consecutive Hennessy winner returned at 7/1, was trained in Warwick by Charles Vernon Miller, and the victory was by far the trainer's biggest career success, the horse having been thoughtfully ridden by Cartwright. The trainer's father, Major Christopher Vernon Miller, formerly one of England's finest polo players, had bred Bighorn, just as he had the 1962 hero Springbok.

Bighorn's win continued a Hennessy tradition where the victor was a young, improving chaser and, as with the likes of Spanish Steps and Border Mask, a winner whose potential seemed unlimited.

1971 HENNESSY COGNAC GOLD CUP RESULT

FATE	HORSE	AGE/WEIGHT	JOCKEY
1st	BIGHORN	7.10.11	D. CARTWRIGHT
2nd	YOUNG ASH LEAF	7.11.2	P. ENNIS
3rd	SAGGART'S CHOICE	8.10.2	T. STACK
4th	The Spaniard	9.10.13	T.W. Biddlecombe
5th	Proud Tarquin	8.11.7	P. McCloughlin
6th	L'Escargot	8.12.7	T. Carberry
7th	Tantalum	7.11.4	D. Nicholson
Fell	Spanish Steps	8.12.3	J. Haine
Fell	Foxtor	7.10.7	B.R. Davies
Fell	Grey Sombrero	7.10.1	C. Candy
Pulled Up	Lord Jim	10.10.5	S. Mellor
Pulled Up	Lucky Edgar	6.10.0	R. Pitman
Brought Down	Royal Toss	9.11.0	E.P. Harty

27 November 1971
Going – Good
Winner – £6,131 75p
Time – 6 mins 37 secs
13 Ran
Winner trained by Charles Vernon Miller at Shipston-on-Stour, Warwickshire
Winner bred by Major J. Miller
Winner owned by Major J. Miller and Mr A. Kingsley
Bighorn, brown gelding by Tyrone – Ibex

Betting – 6/1 Grey Sombrero & Spanish Steps, 7/1 Bighorn & Young Ash Leaf, 10/1 L'Escargot & Lord Jim, 11/1 Foxtor, 12/1 Proud Tarquin & The Spaniard, 13/1 Tantalum, 14/1 Saggart's Choice, 16/1 Royal Toss, 20/1 Lucky Edgar.

Bighorn leads Saggart's Choice en route to winning the 1971 Hennessy.

CHARLIE POTHEEN

The magnificent career of Arkle in the mid-1960s cemented that horse's place firmly as the greatest chaser of all time. It was therefore inevitable that, in the years that followed, there would be countless contenders labelled 'the new Arkle', particularly if the horse hailed from an Irish stable.

The first horse to be given this unfortunate tag was indeed an Irish horse, the much-hyped Sea Brief. If comparisons between the great Arkle and Sea Brief were deeply unfair, the two horses were nevertheless owned by the same person, Anne, Duchess of Westminster. Sea Brief was trained by Jim Dreaper and, hype notwithstanding, was indeed an exciting chaser of some promise, having won four out of five novice chases the season before. His one defeat as novice, however, had come at a crucial time, in the important Totalisator Champion Chase for Novices at the Cheltenham Festival. On that occasion, Sea Brief had been a red-hot favourite but ran well below par and finished fourth. Sea Brief had begun the new season strongly, the six-year-old winning his only start at Punchestown where he was in receipt of 20lbs from L'Escargot. Dreaper seriously fancied Sea Brief in the Hennessy, and the Irish would not hear of defeat for the horse. As such, Sea Brief began the race the 2/1 favourite.

Next in the betting came another fast-improving six-year-old in the shape of Moonlight Escapade. A bay, Moonlight Escapade was a stablemate of the previous year's hero Bighorn and, like that horse, Moonlight Escapade was to be ridden in the Hennessy by David Cartwright. Like Sea Brief, Moonlight Escapade had been prolific the previous season, winning five races, mostly novice events. The current campaign had seen the horse go from strength to strength, winning all three of his races before the Newbury showdown. It had been his most recent performance – in the Ansells Brewery Chase at Worcester – that had seriously rocketed Moonlight Escapade into Hennessy contention. The horse had been mightily impressive at Worcester, giving weight away to some experienced chasers and beating them with some ease.

Moonlight Escapade's win at Worcester, together with the definite potential of the David Mould-partnered Jomon, meant the first three in the betting were six-year-olds, and there were other youngsters such as Ballysagert and Charlie Potheen that were also ready to make their mark. Ballysagert, trained in the North by Arthur Stephenson, carried top weight of 11st 8lbs. The horse had been second to Clever Scot in the Totalisator Novice Chase at the Cheltenham Festival, where he had finished ahead of both Charlie Potheen and Sea Brief, yet the bay's form in the current season had been mediocre, and he was without a win from four runs. Charlie Potheen, a big brute of a horse and an ex-point-to-pointer, was making his seasonal debut at Newbury. The brown gelding was notoriously aggressive during his races and was one of three challengers from the yard of Fulke Walwyn, the others being Prairie Dog and The Pooka. Taking the ride on Charlie Potheen was Richard Pitman, deputising at the last minute for the injured Barry Brogan.

The early leader in the race was the Jeff King-ridden Roman Holiday, but it was not long before Charlie Potheen had forced and barged his way to the head of affairs. Pitman had tried to settle Charlie Potheen in behind Roman Holiday, but his mount had proved far too headstrong, and so Pitman simply allowed the horse to make his own running.

Charlie Potheen was quick to open up a substantial lead, with Roman Holiday and Sea Brief his closest pursuers. Early on, Sea Brief looked every inch the class act he was being made out to be, fencing with fluency and accuracy. At the water jump, an enormous leap by Charlie Potheen drew rich applause from the watching masses and, as the second circuit began with all thirteen runners still standing, it was still the powerfully built horse that led, tracked by Roman Holiday, Sea Brief, Tantalum, Esban, Prairie Dog and Ballysagert.

Bereft of casualties the first circuit may have been, but the second was to feature a pair of significant ones. At the thirteenth fence, the first ditch in the back straight, Moonlight Escapade came down having hit the fence extremely hard. Worse was to come three fences later when the David Nicholson-ridden Tantalum fell with such severe force that the horse broke his back and had to be destroyed.

On good ground, the pace generated by Charlie Potheen had been strong and, having given his mount a short breather, Pitman sent the leader

Sea Brief was the big hope of Ireland in 1972.

Charlie Potheen goes to post for the
1972 Hennessy.

charging onwards once more as they rounded the turn into the home straight. Charlie Potheen was now travelling imperiously and, although his old adversary Ballysagert moved past Roman Holiday into second, the leader never looked seriously threatened. Despite hanging to the left over the remaining fences, the horse stayed on powerfully and stormed home an eight-length winner. Roman Holiday managed to force his way back past Ballysagert on the run-in to snatch second, and the jockey of the runner-up, Jeff King, was quick to express his displeasure at the way Charlie Potheen had been allowed to bully his way past his horse during the race. Sea Brief's bubble had been well and truly burst and, although a very good jumper, the Irish horse was exposed for lacking top-class speed.

The amazing fact regarding Charlie Potheen's robust Hennessy win was that it was an incredible sixth win in the race for Walwyn. The trainer had made it his own, enjoying prolific success in the relatively new race. Walwyn had purchased Charlie Potheen on behalf of Mrs Joy Heath for 4,000 guineas after the horse had failed to reach the reserve price at the Ascot Sales eighteen months before.

Pitman was having his first ride on Charlie Potheen in the Hennessy, and the jockey was informed on the morning of the race that the horse could be a somewhat tricky ride and to let him do his own thing should Charlie Potheen pull too hard during the race, which was what ultimately transpired. The horse was indeed a difficult ride, but had nevertheless

1972 HENNESSY COGNAC GOLD CUP RESULT

FATE	HORSE	AGE/WEIGHT	JOCKEY
1st	CHARLIE POTHEEN	7.11.4	R. PITMAN
2nd	ROMAN HOLIDAY	8.10.8	J. KING
3rd	BALLYSAGERT	7.11.8	J. ENRIGHT
4th	Prairie Dog	8.10.10	A. Branford
5th	Rouge Autumn	8.10.4	K.B. White
6th	Sea Brief	6.11.7	V. O'Brien
7th	The Pooka	10.10.0	J. Nolan
8th	Highland Seal	9.10.6	R. Atkins
9th	Esban	8.10.7	J. Bourke
10th	Notification	7.10.13	W. Smith
Fell	Tantalum	8.11.4	D. Nicholson
Fell	Moonlight Escapade	6.10.11	D. Cartwright
Pulled Up	Jomon	6.11.3	D. Mould

25 November 1972
Going – Good
Winner – £5,975 75p
Time – 6 mins 32.6 secs
13 Ran
Winner trained by Fulke Walwyn at Lambourn, Berkshire
Winner bred by J.T.D. Musson
Winner owned by Mrs B. Heath
Charlie Potheen, brown gelding by Spiritus – Irish Biddy

Betting – 2/1 Sea Brief, 13/2 Moonlight Escapade, 7/1 Jomon, 8/1 Ballysagert, 10/1 Charlie Potheen & Tantalum, 11/1 Roman Holiday, 20/1 Rouge Autumn, 25/1 Esban, 33/1 Highland Seal, Notification, Prairie Dog & The Pooka.

Richard Pitman partnered Charlie Potheen to Hennessy glory.

proved a fine Hennessy winner and would go on to run with honour in the Cheltenham Gold Cup. Charlie Potheen had now won four career chases, all at Newbury, with his latest success proving to be his finest hour.

RED CANDLE

Charlie Potheen had progressed even further after winning the 1972 Hennessy Cognac Gold Cup. After his Newbury victory, the giant horse won Doncaster's Great Yorkshire Chase before running a race of high quality to be third to The Dikler and Pendil in the Cheltenham Gold Cup – The Dikler being a horse very much in the Charlie Potheen mould, an ox of an animal, headstrong and massive. Charlie Potheen had then displayed real class when carrying 12st in the Whitbread Gold Cup, shouldering his big weight magnificently, leading all the way and winning the Sandown race. Naturally, those four performances ensured stern attention from the handicapper for his future engagements and, for the 1973 Hennessy, the horse carried top weight of 12st 4lbs. He was favourite too, even though his only run of the current season had resulted in a fall three fences from home when taking on the brilliant Australian-bred chaser Crisp at Newbury in October. Taking the mount on Charlie Potheen on this occasion was Ron Barry, looking to give trainer Fulke Walwyn an incredible seventh Hennessy success.

A pair of former winners returned to compete in the race, having missed the 1972 renewal. Now ten years of age and ridden by Philip Blacker, Spanish Steps was running in his fourth Hennessy. Spanish Steps had finished second to Charlie Potheen in the previous season's Great Yorkshire Chase, but had failed to make an impression in the Cheltenham Gold Cup. But, popular as ever, the horse began the race as one of the favourites amid reports of excellent workouts at home. The 1971 Hennessy winner Bighorn had not enjoyed the best fortune since his finest hour two years previously, and his preparation for the 1973 race had been haunted by injury concerns. However, the horse had won his only start of the season at Nottingham and had his winning partner of two years before, David Cartwright, in the saddle.

Eight-year-old Red Rum had won one of the most memorable Grand Nationals of all time earlier in the year. At Aintree, Red Rum – as well as the rest of the field – had surrendered to Crisp an enormous lead as that horse boldly attempted to make all in the race. However, as Crisp tired, Red Rum kept on resolutely to snatch the race at the death and begin his love affair with that particular race. Red Rum was trained near Aintree by Donald 'Ginger' McCain, and the horse had been in terrific recent form, winning three of five races as he attempted to become the first Grand National winner to also win the Hennessy.

The six-year-old Nereo, an easy recent winner at Worcester, the improving Tony Dickinson-trained Anthony Watt (ridden by Dickinson's son Michael), and the brown gelding Cuckolder, also trained and ridden by a father and son team, Bob and Andy Turnell, each held sound claims in their first Hennessy raids. But it was another newcomer, Red Candle, that was significantly backed on the day. Recognised as a two-and-a-half-mile

Red Candle and Red Rum (noseband), pictured here at Cheltenham, fought out a tremendous battle for the 1973 Hennessy.

Red Candle won the Hennessy under jockey Jim Fox.

horse, the good-to-firm ground had raised hopes the horse would stay the longer trip. The gelding's recent form was poor, but he was a horse that had won a Mackeson Gold Cup in his time and he was certainly no forlorn hope.

Charlie Potheen provided the first piece of drama in the race when he whipped around at the start and, as the runners were sent on their way, he had lost some twelve lengths. Although this was a significant deficit, by the third fence Charlie Potheen had bulled his way aggressively to the front to take control from Roman Holiday, Spanish Steps and Anthony Watt, though the energy exercised in doing so may well have deprived the 1972 hero of some much-needed fuel come the business end of the race.

At the third ditch, the outsider Great Haven fell and, in doing so, David Cartwright was smacked from the saddle on Bighorn, ending the horse's

interest in the race. There were to be no more casualties in the race, but what lay in store was a further chapter in a long line of fantastic Hennessy finishes.

Charlie Potheen was still in front as the field prepared to swing into the home straight for the final time. But the horse had not been able to dominate like he had the year before, and he had Roman Holiday, Spanish Steps and Cuckolder breathing down his neck, with both Red Rum and Red Candle poised craftily just behind. Approaching the fourth last and, with Spanish Steps beginning to fade, it soon became apparent that Charlie Potheen would not be joining the likes of Mandarin and Arkle as a dual Hennessy winner, and it was Red Rum that took over at the fence.

Red Candle had crept steadily into contention and, at the next fence, jockey Jim Fox sent his mount forward to challenge Red Rum. It was now that the Grand National winner made his sole error, blundering at the obstacle and giving the advantage to Red Candle. Seizing his opportunity, Red Candle stole a one-length lead at the final fence. Even though he had made an error at the third last, Red Rum was, as one would expect from a Grand National winner, an excellent jumper and, flying the last, the horse got right back into the fight, quickly drawing level with Red Candle on the flat and setting up one of the most titanic finishes in Hennessy history.

Halfway up the run-in, Red Rum was able to surge ahead, taking a half-length lead and, with merely a hundred yards to run, jockey Brian Fletcher appeared to have the race won. But with a stone less on his back, Red Candle displayed fierce tenacity and, with Fox driving him out powerfully, the horse was able to overthrow the gallant Red Rum with twenty yards to run for a narrow win. Further back, Anthony Watt finished like a train to edge Cuckolder for third.

Red Rum had run a fantastic race given the weight differential. He may not have won the Hennessy but his name would, in time, become perhaps the most famous in the sport, winning a total of three Grand Nationals (as well as twice finishing second in the same race) and a Scottish Grand National.

He may have been something of a surprise Hennessy winner, but Red Candle had battled all the way to the line to earn victory for the very small stable of Ricky Vallance, based in Devizes, Wiltshire, where David Elsworth was at the time an assistant trainer. Elsworth would enjoy many big-race winners in his own right in the future courtesy of splendid horses such as Desert Orchid and Rhyme 'N' Reason. Red Candle was owned by Mrs Cathleen O'Shea and had been purchased as a three-year-old from breeder Joseph Reid and sent into training with Owen Brennan near Nottingham. After a period of illness, Red Candle was frequently switched from stable to stable. He spent time at Charlie Hall's yard before moving to the Stockbridge stable of Vernon Cross. For a short time, the horse was leased out and sent to Mick O'Toole's in Ireland before Mrs O'Shea took him back fifteen months before his Hennessy victory, placing the horse with Vallance, where he would enjoy the most successful period of his racing career.

1973 HENNESSY COGNAC GOLD CUP RESULT

FATE	HORSE	AGE/WEIGHT	JOCKEY
1st	RED CANDLE	9.10.4	J. FOX
2nd	RED RUM	8.11.4	B. FLETCHER
3rd	ANTHONY WATT	7.11.0	M. DICKINSON
4th	Cuckolder	8.10.1	A. Turnell
5th	Nereo	7.10.0	V. Soane
6th	Spanish Steps	10.11.10	P. Blacker
7th	Prairie Dog	9.10.2	A. Branford
8th	Roman Holiday	9.10.7	J. King
9th	Charlie Potheen	8.12.4	R. Barry
Fell	Great Haven	8.10.0	J. Glover
Brought Down	Bighorn	9.11.0	D. Cartwright

24 November 1973
Going – Good to Firm
Winner – £7,435
Time – 6 mins 37.6 secs
11 Ran
Winner trained by Ricky Vallance at Bishops Cannings, Devizes, Wiltshire
Winner bred by J.G. Reid
Winner owned by Mrs Catherine O'Shea
Red Candle, bay gelding by Autumn Gold – Rose Gallica

Betting – 9/2 Charlie Potheen, 6/1 Anthony Watt, Nereo & Spanish Steps, 15/2 Cuckolder, 8/1 Red Rum, 9/1 Bighorn, 12/1 Red Candle, 14/1 Prairie Dog, 18/1 Roman Holiday, 25/1 Great Haven.

1974

ROYAL MARSHAL II

and was a horse that liked to dictate proceedings in his races, although whether the horse could employ such tactics successfully with conditions so heavy remained to be seen. Like Kilvulgan, Royal Marshal II was a confirmed mudlark and a horse with considerable stamina, unsurprising since he was a half-brother to the 1972 Grand National winner Well To Do. Like Well To Do, Royal Marshal II was trained by Tim Forster and was a horse whose jumping had improved tremendously over the previous twelve months. As a novice, Royal Marshal II had won two of seven races and also finished third behind a future Cheltenham Gold Cup winner

Two factors were seen as essential for any potential winner of the 1974 Hennessy Cognac Gold Cup – a light weight and a genuine love of testing conditions. The going for the 1974 race was officially heavy after torrential rain had left the course thoroughly saturated. The conditions were expected to be detrimental to those at the higher end of the handicap, with assured stamina a necessity to complete the course. The conditions resulted in a wide-open betting market although, with a few obvious class horses aside, it was an unusually weak-looking Hennessy.

Top weight was the winner of the 1973 Cheltenham Gold Cup, the Fulke Walwyn-trained giant The Dikler, quite simply an enormous beast of an animal. The Dikler was a bay horse with a big white face and, like Walwyn's 1972 hero Charlie Potheen, could be aggressive and headstrong for those that rode him. The horse had possibly not received the praise he deserved for winning the Gold Cup, as the hot favourite Pendil was thought, by common consensus, to have thrown the race away between the final fence and the line, perhaps blinding the fact that The Dikler was in his own right a most talented horse, one that remained consistent at the highest level for a considerable amount of time. The Dikler was tough and courageous, as well as being a fine jumper, and the horse was partnered in the Hennessy by Alan Branford.

Among those prominent in the betting in 1974 were Kilvulgan, Glanford Brigg and Royal Marshal II. The highly rated seven-year-old Kilvulgan was a horse that had suffered from injury problems the previous season, yet he was a talented horse that greatly appreciated the mud, and chiefly for this reason the horse started favourite. Kilvulgan was owned by Mr Jim Joel, was trained by Bob Turnell and ridden by his son Andy. An eight-year-old bay, Glanford Brigg had been a prolific winner the season before

A giant of a horse, The Dikler jumps a fence during the 1974 race.

The favourite Kilvulgan clears a fence.

and fellow mudlark Ten Up in the Sun Alliance Chase at the Cheltenham Festival, a race in which Glanford Brigg had finished second. Graham Thorner took the mount on Royal Marshal II, the brown gelding starting at 11/2.

Many of the horses came into the race in winning form, including the Fred Rimell-trained duo Rough House and Iceman, the grey Tee-Cee-Bee, Money Market and Kilvulgan's stablemate, Cuckolder. It was a credit to Newbury that the race was able to go ahead at all, such a battering had the course taken from the weather. In the event, one of the fences on the

far side was omitted but, as the thirteen runners lined-up, there was great anticipation for the spectacle that lay in wait.

The grey horse Tee-Cee-Bee threw his chance away immediately, whipping round at the start and unseating Bob Davies as the runners were sent on their way. Of the twelve that remained, it was Rough House that led over the first two fences, but Glanford Brigg took over his customary position at the head of affairs by the third fence and soon began jumping with glorious zest, carving open a clear advantage. Glanford Brigg had clearly set out to test the stamina of his rivals to the limit, and with many of the field blatantly

Royal Marshal II hits the front,
chased by the grey Iceman.

struggling in the conditions, the horse was still in front as he turned into the home straight. In behind Glanford Brigg, however, were a bunch of horses still in touch, including Iceman, The Dikler and Money Market. But the horse going best of all was Royal Marshal II and, despite a slight error at the fourth last, the horse was cruising, clearly enjoying conditions underfoot.

A fence later, Royal Marshal II jumped into the lead and, from there, the race was over as a contest. No other horse in the race possessed the drive or acceleration to get near the leader over the remaining fences and, ploughing through the ground like a tank, Royal Marshal II was able to cruise home an extremely comfortable winner by ten lengths, having turned the closing stages of the race into a procession. Iceman had always been in touch with the leaders and had run a fine race, but simply had no answer to the winner once Royal Marshal II had gone for home, while Moonlight Escapade had simply stayed on past tiring horses to take third. Money Market, Glanford Brigg and The Dikler were the only others to finish, the rest pulling up exhausted, including the hugely disappointing favourite Kilvulgan, who had been at the rear of the field throughout until pulling up on the second circuit.

Royal Marshal II had thoroughly relished his Hennessy experience of 1974, always jumping and travelling beautifully during the race, coming home gracefully as if the conditions had been made for him. His relentless galloping style and excessive stamina led many to believe the horse could become a second Grand National winner for his trainer, although Forster ruled out a bid for the next edition of the race in 1975 and, sadly, Royal Marshal II was destined never to partake in that particular event. He did, however, prove his class on numerous occasions thereafter, including when winning the King George VI Chase at Kempton later in his career.

Both Royal Marshal II and his half-brother Well To Do were bred by Mrs Lloyd Thomas, whose husband Hugh – killed in a fall in his fifties – had won the 1937 Grand National with Royal Mail. The late Mrs Heather Sumner had purchased both horses from Mrs Lloyd, with Royal Marshal II costing just £400. Sadly, Mrs Sumner had not survived to see Royal Marshal II win the Hennessy, but those that witnessed his performance saw one of the most convincing victories in the history of the race, where the winner out-jumped, out-galloped and out-stayed his helpless rivals.

1974 HENNESSY COGNAC GOLD CUP RESULT

FATE	HORSE	AGE/WEIGHT	JOCKEY
1st	ROYAL MARSHAL II	7.10.0	G. THORNER
2nd	ICEMAN	8.10.0	K.B. WHITE
3rd	MOONLIGHT ESCAPADE	8.10.0	D. CARTWRIGHT
4th	Money Market	7.10.0	J. King
5th	Glanford Brigg	8.10.12	S. Holland
6th	The Dikler	11.12.2	A. Branford
Pulled Up	Kilvulgan	7.11.2	A. Turnell
Pulled Up	Rough House	8.10.4	J. Burke
Pulled Up	Cuckolder	9.10.3	J. Haine
Pulled Up	Credibility	6.10.3	J. Francome
Pulled Up	Credo's Daughter	8.10.2	C. Goldsworthy
Pulled Up	Deblin's Green	11.10.0	N. Wakley
Left	Tee-Cee-Bee	8.10.4	B.R. Davies

23 November 1974
Going – Heavy
Winner – £7,542
Time – 6 mins 56.4 secs
13 Ran
Winner trained by Tim Forster at Letcombe Bassett, Berkshire
Winner bred by Mrs Lloyd Thomas
Winner owned by Mr J. Sumner
Royal Marshal II, brown gelding by Marshal Pil – Princess Puzzlement

Betting – 9/2 Kilvulgan, 5/1 Glanford Brigg, 11/2 Royal Marshal II, 8/1 Tee-Cee-Bee, 9/1 Cuckolder, 10/1 Credibility, 11/1 Iceman, Rough House & The Dikler, 14/1 Money Market, 16/1 Credo's Daughter & Moonlight Escapade, 33/1 Deblin's Green.

APRIL SEVENTH

Joint favourites for the 1975 Hennessy Cognac Gold Cup were a pair of horses that had been among the leading novice chasers from the previous season. Despite a two-year difference in age, both Tamalin and Fort Fox were in their first seasons out of novice company and it was, by and large, their form from the previous campaign that saw them sit atop what appeared a wide-open Hennessy betting market.

The older of the two was the talented eight-year-old brown gelding Tamalin, a Northern challenger from the yard of Gordon Richards. The horse had won five chases as a novice and, on his only start of the current campaign, had defeated the useful duo of Tregarron and San-Feliu at Carlisle, despite not being at optimum fitness. Jonjo O'Neill partnered Tamalin, and the horse was nicely weighted on 10st 12lbs, yet a possible detriment lay with the state of the ground, which was on the firm side of good.

Arkle had been the last Irish-trained horse to win the Hennessy ten years previously, but now there were high hopes that the six-year-old Fort Fox could end the drought. Like Tamalin, the chestnut Fort Fox had been a multiple winner during his novice season and, although he had yet to win from two races in the current campaign, the Ben Hannon-ridden youngster was well supported on the day after finishing runner-up to a future Cheltenham Gold Cup winner in Davy Lad at Punchestown on his most recent start.

Top weight was the dual Grand National winner Red Rum. After two wins at Aintree, as well as finishing second to the great L'Escargot in the same race earlier in the year, Red Rum had become the most popular horse in the country. Despite clearly being a far better horse at Aintree than anywhere else, Red Rum's form elsewhere had been, nevertheless, disappointing in recent times. In the current season, the horse had finished third to Meridian II at Carlisle, albeit giving a huge amount of weight away, and that run was followed by a mediocre fourth place behind Duffle Coat at Ayr and an unlucky third after slipping up behind Royal Frolic – the next Gold Cup winner – at Haydock. Red Rum's latest run had been a lethargic third behind fellow Hennessy contender Even Swell at Newcastle. It was after this latest run that trainer Ginger McCain decided to replace regular jockey Brian Fletcher with Ron Barry in an attempt to freshen the horse's way of thinking. Fletcher subsequently took the mount of the injury-plagued Iceman at Newbury, the runner-up from the previous year's race.

An indication of how open the 1975 Hennessy appeared came from the fact that the two longest-priced horses in the betting – Inycarra and Collingwood – came into the race in tremendous recent winning form, while the previous year's Whitbread Gold Cup winner April Seventh and the firm-ground loving Noble Neptune (trained by Fred Winter) were others with excellent chances.

Jonjo O'Neill goes to post aboard the 11/2 joint-favourite Tamalin.

Red Rum had won two Grand Nationals by the time of his second appearance in the
Hennessy.

Rough House (blue) jumps a fence during the Hennessy.

April Seventh and jockey Andy Turnell are led in victorious.

It was Collingwood, ridden by young Colin Hawkins, that took the field along at a strong pace, with Noble Neptune, Even Swell, Red Rum and Moonlight Escapade all eager to place themselves in the leading group, and right from the outset a fast-run race looked a certainty.

Noble Neptune was a nine-year-old chestnut that had been in sharp form in the early parts of the season, jumping better than at any stage of his career. Having won at Kempton and Sandown recently, Fred Winter had revealed his confidence in the horse's ability to run a major race in the Hennessy and, when the chestnut took up the running at the ninth fence, that confidence appeared well founded. Jumping with relish throughout the race, Noble Neptune bounced off the quick ground in the style of a horse thoroughly enjoying himself. Racing down the far side for the final

time, it was he that led, though pressing him tightly were Collingwood, Even Swell, Cuckolder, Red Rum and the improving Whitbread hero April Seventh.

Noble Neptune was considered to have fine stamina but, when he was swallowed up by Collingwood as the pack turned for home, he began to send out distress signals, and Credo's Daughter, Cuckolder, April Seventh and Red Rum all engaged in a fight for supremacy. Collingwood remained in front until the second last, where Andy Turnell asked his mount April Seventh to deliver his challenge. The two horses raced to the last together and it was April Seventh that touched down narrowly in front. Despite carrying a far heftier weight, April Seventh displayed the same finishing speed that had seen him triumph in the Whitbread and, although he had not raced since that day, he powered home to record a three-length win from the gallant Collingwood. Having trained the winner, Bob Turnell also had the pleasure of seeing his veteran Cuckolder come home in third place ahead of Noble Neptune, Credo's Daughter and Red Rum. The lattermost, according to McCain, had possibly lost some of the speed from his younger days through his monumental efforts at Aintree, and certainly he was stripped for pace at Newbury before staying on again in the closing stages. The ground had simply been too firm for Tamalin and he had trailed the field for much of the way before pulling up four out. Fort Fox too had been nearer the rear than the front when he made a bad blunder at the thirteenth, giving Hannon no chance of staying in the saddle. This would become a regular sight for followers of Fort Fox, as mistakes littered his career in the big chases, including when twice running in the Cheltenham Gold Cup.

A strong, bay gelding, April Seventh was a classy winner of the Hennessy. It was the second time Bob Turnell had trained the winner of the race, following Rondetto's victory in 1967, while for Andy Turnell the win would prove the highlight of his riding career before he made a successful switch to the training ranks.

1975 HENNESSY COGNAC GOLD CUP RESULT

FATE	HORSE	AGE/WEIGHT	JOCKEY
1st	APRIL SEVENTH	9.11.2	A. TURNELL
2nd	COLLINGWOOD	9.10.0	C. HAWKINS
3rd	CUCKOLDER	10.10.8	S.C. KNIGHT
4th =	Noble Neptune	9.10.9	V. Soane
4th =	Credo's Daughter	9.10.9	C. Goldsworthy
6th	Red Rum	10.11.9	R. Barry
7th	Moonlight Escapade	9.10.11	J. King
8th	Even Swell	8.10.0	G. Thorner
9th	Rough House	9.10.13	J. Burke
10th	Inycarra	8.10.0	C. Brown
11th	Iceman	9.10.8	B. Fletcher
Pulled Up	Tamalin	8.10.12	J.J. O'Neill
Unseated Rider	Fort Fox	6.11.2	B. Hannon

22 November 1975
Going – Good to Firm
Winner – £7,360
Time – 6 mins 31.6 secs
13 Ran
Winner trained by Bob Turnell at Ogbourne Maisey Lodge, nr Marlborough, Wiltshire
Winner bred by P.P. Sweeney
Winner owned by Mrs B. Meehan
April Seventh, bay gelding by Menelek – Loughlahan

Betting – 11/2 Fort Fox & Tamalin, 7/1 Noble Neptune, 8/1 Red Rum, 10/1 Rough House, 11/1 April Seventh & Credo's Daughter, 12/1 Iceman, 13/1 Cuckolder & Moonlight Escapade, 14/1 Even Swell, 16/1 Inycarra, 20/1 Collingwood.

1976

ZETA'S SON

The biggest field since 1962 lined up for the 1976 Hennessy Cognac Gold Cup, with twenty-one horses going to post. With the possible exception of the likes of Royal Marshal II and April Seventh, none of the runners could be considered of genuine Cheltenham Gold Cup class, in contrast to the Hennessy's early years which attracted plenty of chasing stars that graced the sport's Blue Riband event, such as Mandarin, Kerstin, Pas Seul, Mill House, Arkle and What A Myth. What the 1976 renewal did possess, however, was a batch of the most consistent staying chasers of the era and more than a few leading lights from the Grand Nationals of the mid-1970s, such as Rag Trade, Money Market, Churchtown Boy, Andy Pandy, Mickley Seabright and Lord Browndodd.

The two previous winners of the race, April Seventh and Royal Marshal II, were well supported on the day. April Seventh had 7lbs more to carry than in 1975, yet the horse had really impressed when winning at Wincanton on his seasonal reappearance, a performance good enough to earn him 17/2 favouritism for the Hennessy. Royal Marshal II had been dogged by injury problems since his fine win in 1974. Unlike April Seventh, the form of Royal Marshal II had been sketchy in the early stages of the current campaign, with his jumping proving erratic in two defeats at Wincanton, and it was accepted that he would have to improve greatly to make an impact at Newbury.

The seven-year-old bay Andy Pandy was one horse that was making a rapid ascent up the chasing ladder. One of three runners for Fred Rimell (the most recent Grand National winner Rag Trade and Mickley Seabright being the others), Andy Pandy was a fine, athletic jumper and was expected to enjoy the distance of the Hennessy, having won well over three-and-a-half miles at Warwick the weekend before Newbury.

As well as the top weight Tamalin and the fast-improving six-year-old Banlieu, each of Even Up, Ghost Writer and Zeta's Son held definite prospects in a wide-open Hennessy. Even Up was owned by 300 members of the *Daily Mirror* Punters Club and ran in the black-and-white colours of their president, Noel Whitcomb. Even Up was a tough stayer trained by Diane Oughton and had finished a close second to the subsequent Grand National winner Rag Trade in the Welsh Grand National in February. Ghost Writer was a nine-year-old chestnut seeking to give trainer Fulke Walwyn a seventh Hennessy success. Ghost Writer had actually been installed as ante-post favourite for the Hennessy having won at Ascot earlier in the season, but lingering doubts over his jumping ability led to him relinquishing that position come the day of the race. Zeta's Son, a classy brown horse trained at Wantage by Peter Bailey, had been unlucky not to have won the two-mile Arkle Chase at the Cheltenham Festival two seasons previously when he had slipped on landing after the final fence. As would be expected from a horse running in a race such as the Arkle, Zeta's Son possessed plenty of speed and, having run his only race of the season over two-and-a-half miles at Wincanton in early November, he shaped as the dark horse of the contest.

The eventual winner Zeta's Son goes to post under Ian Watkinson.

Well fancied beforehand, Ghost Writer (8) disappointed in the race itself.

Basking in glorious Newbury sunshine, the twenty-one runners charged off in pursuit of the richest ever Hennessy purse, and it was to be Le Robstan that set an electric pace together with Lord Browndodd and Money Market. Le Robstan was not jumping with any great fluency or rhythm, yet the horse continued to blaze a trail that had a number of the fancied runners struggling. The race had already lost Even Up, who had fallen at the fifth, when April Seventh made a bad blunder at the twelfth and was never a factor thereafter. Similarly, Ghost Writer – although travelling well enough on the first circuit – made a mess of the thirteenth and, despite receiving strong reminders from jockey Bill Smith, the horse struggled to make an impression from that point onwards. Andy Pandy and

Banlieu were also towards the rear as the race reached its closing stages in a fiercely run race.

In contrast to many of his market rivals, Royal Marshal II had performed well, rediscovering his past form and jumping with the sparkle that had seen him capture the Hennessy earlier in his career, and it was he that overthrew Le Robstan in the back straight, striking the front with a menacing grip on the race. Turning for home, Royal Marshal II opened up a decisive lead, tracked by the top-weight Tamalin, a horse that had been a major disappointment in the race twelve months before but one that clearly appreciated the more forgiving conditions on this occasion. In behind the front two, jockey Ian Watkinson had steadily brought Zeta's

Lord Browndodd jumps a fence.

Son through into a challenging position and, as the final cluster of fences were jumped in the home straight, the race lay between these three.

At the final fence, Zeta's Son attacked the leaders with serious intent. With Royal Marshal II beginning to weaken, and in receipt of 18lbs from Tamalin, the horse burst into the lead after the last, showing decisive speed as Watkinson sensed the opportunity to seize the race. Tamalin never gave up, but Zeta's Son had everything in his favour and, with his jockey timing the run perfectly, Zeta's Son held on willingly to win by a length and a half. Tamalin took second while Banlieu stayed on through beaten horses to snatch third place from Royal Marshal II, the lattermost going on to win the season's King George VI Chase.

The weekend proved a fantastic one for owner Michael Buckley, a London company director. First, his Zeta's Son had captured the richest ever Hennessy, then just seven hours later at Camden, South Carolina, USA, a horse he jointly owned – Grand Canyon – became the first ever British-trained winner of the Colonial Cup. Both Buckley and Bailey were in America at the time of Zeta's Son's victory, so the honour of collecting the trophy went to a business associate of Buckley's, Frank Watts.

That racing can throw forward more contrasting fortunes than any other sport was perfectly illustrated with the story of the 1976 Hennessy hero. Whether Zeta's Son would have proved up to Cheltenham Gold Cup class will never be known; certainly at just seven years of age he was open to further improvement. Instead, the horse was aimed at and ran in the 1977 Grand National, one of forty-two runners in one of the most competitive and memorable editions of that particular race, being the occasion when the great Red Rum, a former Hennessy runner-up, won the Aintree marathon for a record third time. Despite being one of just a handful of horses remaining in a fascinating race on the second circuit, Zeta's Son was well behind when jumping Valentines Brook, stumbling awkwardly after the fence and parting company with Watkinson. It later transpired the horse had broken a leg and sadly his life, all too brief, was lost.

1976 HENNESSY COGNAC GOLD CUP RESULT

FATE	HORSE	AGE/WEIGHT	JOCKEY
1st	ZETA'S SON	7.10.9	I. WATKINSON
2nd	TAMALIN	9.11.13	J.J. O'NEILL
3rd	BANLIEU	6.10.0	B.R. DAVIES
4th	ROYAL MARSHAL II	9.11.3	G. THORNER
5th	Tregarron	9.10.3	C. Tinkler
6th	Lord Browndodd	8.10.3	J. King
7th	Money Market	9.11.1	V. Soane
8th	Barmer	8.10.5	J. McNaught
9th	Mickley Seabright	8.10.4	Mr P. Brookshaw
10th	Capuchin	7.10.0	J. Barlow
11th	Andy Pandy	7.10.9	S. Moreshead
12th	April Seventh	10.11.9	A. Turnell
13th	Lean Forward	10.10.10	H.J. Evans
14th	Le Robstan	8.10.1	P. Haynes
15th	Top Priority	7.10.1	C. Read
16th	Carroll Street	9.10.0	R. Linley
17th	Super Do	9.10.0	B. McNally
18th	Ghost Writer	9.10.10	W. Smith
Fell	Even Up	9.11.2	R. Champion
Fell	Rag Trade	10.11.2	J. Burke
Fell	Churchtown Boy	9.10.1	John Williams

27 November 1976
Going – Good
Winner – £9,102
Time – 6 mins 45 secs
21 Ran
Winner trained by Peter Bailey at Wantage, Berkshire
Winner bred by J. McClintock
Winner owned by Mr M. Buckley
Zeta's Son, brown gelding by Orchardist – Southern Zeta

Betting – 17/2 April Seventh, 9/1 Ghost Writer, 10/1 Andy Pandy & Banlieu, 12/1 Even Up, Lord Browndodd, Royal Marshal II & Zeta's Son, 14/1 Le Robstan, 16/1 Mickley Seabright & Money Market, 18/1 Rag Trade, 20/1 Lean Forward, Tamalin & Tregarron, 25/1 Barmer & Top Priority, 40/1 Capuchin, 50/1 Churchtown Boy, 66/1 Carroll Street & Super Do.

1977

BACHELOR'S HALL

Top weight for the 1977 Hennessy Cognac Gold Cup was the classy Fort Devon, a horse attempting to give trainer Fulke Walwyn a seventh win in the race. Fort Devon was an imposing, bold-jumping eleven-year-old chestnut that had left England five years previously for a career in the United States, where he had won the prestigious Maryland Hunt Cup.

The horse had returned to England in November with the intention of a Cheltenham Gold Cup preparation. Come March 1977 at Cheltenham, Fort Devon ran a great race and still held every chance when capsizing four fences out, with the race eventually going to the Irish-trained Davy Lad. On his first start of the new season, Fort Devon had won at Newbury, and this performance, coupled with the presence of his favoured good ground, saw the horse installed as the 7/2 favourite for the Hennessy.

Tamalin was now competing in his third Hennessy, having flopped in 1975 before finishing second in 1976. As in 1975, the ground was not in the horse's favour, as Tamalin was definitely a horse that preferred softer conditions. Tamalin came into the race in terrific form, having won his seasonal debut at Carlisle in early November, then finishing second at Wetherby giving lots of weight away. Tamalin had been trained with the Hennessy very much in mind, the horse being a second Hennessy ride for the ultra-talented John Francome.

Bachelor's Hall was a horse attempting to become the first in history to win the two biggest early-season chases in the same season. Having been a gallant winner of the Mackeson Gold Cup at Cheltenham earlier in the campaign, the horse was now quietly fancied for Hennessy glory. Bachelor's Hall was an improving, well-weighted seven-year-old trained by Peter Cundell in Berkshire yet, if he was to win the Hennessy, the horse would have to prove he could perform over the distance, for all his previous runs had been over far shorter trips.

As well as Royal Marshal II and another inmate from Tim Forster's yard, Master Spy, a trio of horses with ties to the Grand National presented interesting alternatives to the market leaders. Prince Rock, the representative of the previous year's winning trainer/jockey combination of Peter Bailey and Ian Watkinson, had been a casualty in the famous 1977 Grand National won by Red Rum. Prince Rock was a sure-staying horse, albeit one with marginal speed, and he had won his most recent start at Chepstow. Churchtown Boy had gone agonisingly close to winning the Grand National earlier in the year, stalking Red Rum when the pair had pulled a long way clear of the remainder only to falter and fade at the death. With just 10st to carry, Churchtown Boy was one of the more interesting each-way possibilities. His finest chapter had yet to be written, but the Josh Gifford-trained Aldaniti would eventually become a most emotive Grand National winner, overcoming a catalogue of dreadful injuries while his jockey Bob Champion would defeat cancer en route to the pair winning at Aintree in 1981. As a youngster, the strapping chestnut

Eventual winner Bachelor's Hall parades under Martin O'Halloran.

Fort Devon leads Zongalero (noseband) and Royal Marshal II (green & yellow) during the race.

was a progressive horse, certainly with enough class to win a Hennessy, and Champion was also on board Aldaniti at Newbury.

As was his style, Fort Devon proceeded to dictate matters directly from the start, eagerly showing the way to Master Spy, Zongalero, Prince Rock and Double Negative. Aldaniti soon found himself ten lengths adrift of the others after two fences, having landed on the quarters of Churchtown Boy at the second fence, an incident that sent him down on his nose. Another towards the rear early on, although intentionally this time, was Bachelor's Hall. Realising the horse's stamina was unproven, jockey Martin O'Halloran had settled the horse at the back, hoping to preserve enough energy for the finish.

The pace that Fort Devon had set was not the strongest and, by the time the field had reached the back straight for the final time, and with the

outsider Graigue House the only departure during the contest, even the formerly detached Aldaniti had moved up close to the lead, with Master H and Tamalin also well in contention. Rounding the turn for home, the intensity picked up once more. From the bunch chasing Fort Devon, the likes of Zongalero, Royal Marshal II, Master Spy and Tamalin began to drop away to such an extent that, with three fences to jump, only three horses remained in the reckoning. The trio were Fort Devon, Aldaniti and Bachelor's Hall. Fort Devon still led, but Aldaniti had been challenging for supremacy with venom from the beginning of the home straight, while Bachelor's Hall quietly stalked the pair in behind.

It was a very hard race to call by the final fence, each horse seemingly holding an equal chance. Although there was merely a length separating the three, Fort Devon got too close to the fence and did not jump it cleanly. In contrast, Bachelor's Hall met the fence perfectly and shot away on the flat, accelerating swiftly past both Fort Devon and Aldaniti.

Even though Bachelor's Hall had stolen first march on him, Fort Devon was a warrior and responded in resilient fashion. Fighting back bravely, Fort Devon rallied as the line approached, yet the younger horse had stolen a decisive advantage and, showing impressive finishing speed, Bachelor's Hall held Fort Devon in a thrilling finale, winning the 1977 Hennessy by a neck. Three lengths back in third came Aldaniti, while the somewhat temperamental Banlieu – a horse that had been last at halfway – ran on past beaten horses at the end to take fourth, having finished third the year before.

Bachelor's Hall had won the race despite a 6lb penalty incurred for winning the Mackeson, and had become the first horse ever to complete the double in the same season. The Mackeson victory had given Cundell and O'Halloran the biggest wins of their respective careers; now the Hennessy triumph had eclipsed that within weeks. O'Halloran had started race riding as an apprentice for Doug Marks, registering a few victories on the flat. He then dropped away from the racing scene, returning to his native Ireland after working at a stud in France. Three years before his finest hour in the Hennessy, O'Halloran had recommenced his riding career, forming a successful working relationship with Cundell.

Bachelor's Hall – who was owned by Mr and Mrs Peter Harris – went from strength to strength after his Hennessy victory, marking him down as one of the finest winners of the race in the 1970s. The horse won the King George VI Chase and a Welsh Champion Chase before finishing a solid fourth to the excellent Midnight Court in the 1978 Cheltenham Gold Cup.

1977 HENNESSY COGNAC GOLD CUP RESULT

FATE	HORSE	AGE/WEIGHT	JOCKEY
1st	BACHELOR'S HALL	7.10.10	M. O'HALLORAN
2nd	FORT DEVON	11.11.10	W. SMITH
3rd	ALDANITI	7.10.0	R. CHAMPION
4th	Banlieu	7.10.5	B.R. Davies
5th	Zongalero	7.10.6	S. Smith-Eccles
6th	Tamalin	10.11.0	J. Francome
7th	Master H	8.11.4	Mr J. Weston
8th	Prince Rock	9.10.4	I. Watkinson
9th	Double Negative	7.10.1	C. Tinkler
10th	Master Spy	8.11.0	J. King
11th	Royal Marshal II	10.11.7	G. Thorner
12th	Brown Admiral	8.10.1	J. Burke
13th	Churchtown Boy	10.10.0	R. Hyett
Unseated Rider	Graigue House	9.10.5	E. Wright

26th November 1977
Going – Good
Winner – £8,972
Time – 6 mins 42.6 secs
14 Ran
Winner trained by Peter Cundell at Compton, Berkshire
Winner bred by Andrew Murphy
Winner owned by Mr and Mrs P. Harris
Bachelor's Hall, bay gelding by Dusky Boy – Fair Well

Betting – 7/2 Fort Devon, 11/2 Bachelor's Hall, 7/1 Tamalin, 11/1 Master Spy, 12/1 Banlieu, Prince Rock, Royal Marshal II & Zongalero, 13/1 Aldaniti, 15/1 Churchtown Boy, 16/1 Master H, 25/1 Brown Admiral & Double Negative, 33/1 Graigue House.

APPROACHING

The ground was firm for the 1978 Hennessy Cognac Gold Cup, and this served to seriously deplete the size of the field. Just nine horses were listed in the racecard on the day of the race, and one of those – the Whitbread Gold Cup winner Strombolus – was then withdrawn after trainer Peter Bailey decided the lightning-quick conditions would be unsuitable for his bay. As well as the disappointing size of the field, the quality was also sub-par, with only the 1978 Cheltenham Gold Cup third Master H and the Mildmay of Flete winner King Or Country carrying high-class form into the contest.

Master H, a nine-year-old chestnut gelding trained by Michael Oliver, was one of the most consistent chasers in the land. Having finished seventh behind Bachelor's Hall in the previous year's Hennessy, the horse had completed that season having won four chases, as well as finishing a highly respectable third behind Midnight Court and the fine Irish chaser Brown Lad in the Gold Cup at Cheltenham. The horse had made a winning seasonal reappearance at Chepstow in October before suffering a surprise defeat to stablemate Three Gems in a two-horse match at Nottingham. Most encouraging though were the glowing reports streaming from his trainer following a sequence of brilliant workouts and, with Reg Crank in the saddle, Master H found plenty of support come Hennessy day, starting at 9/2 in spite of carrying the significant burden of 12st top weight.

In truth, most of the 1978 Hennessy field were nothing more than average handicappers, yet both Approaching and King Or Country were seven-year-olds on the rise, the pair both possessing the potential for big-race success. Approaching was a chestnut gelding with a white face and wore a sheepskin noseband. The horse's trainer, Josh Gifford, had long targeted the Hennessy for Approaching and, with all four of the horse's

chase wins coming at Newbury, the race seemed an obvious one to gauge Approaching's quality. Approaching had won on the course seventeen days before the Hennessy, a win that led to the horse, ridden by Bob Champion, starting as 3/1 favourite.

Trained by David Barons, King Or Country had been imported from Ireland having won seven of his fourteen races the previous season, most importantly the Mildmay of Flete Chase at the Cheltenham Festival. The horse had recently run in the Mackeson Gold Cup at Cheltenham where, despite being struck into at the top of the hill, King Or Country had run admirably to take third place. Remembering Bachelor's Hall's conquest of both Mackeson

King Or Country parades before the 1978 race.

Approaching flies the last fence on his way to victory.

and Hennessy Gold Cups the season before, King Or Country was very well backed, starting the race as the 7/2 second favourite.

Right from the start the pace was exceptionally quick, with the nine-year-old Orillo showing the way. Orillo remained in front until the seventh fence, at which point the 25/1 shot William Penn took over, with Approaching nestled comfortably in behind. Approaching had settled into a beautiful rhythm under Champion, who had shed 7lbs in four days in an effort to ride at a reasonable weight in the big race. Some of Approaching's fencing was breathtaking and, by the fourteenth fence, he had pulled into the lead, taking each obstacle with precision and elegance.

At the fifth last, Approaching delivered a leap of such magnificence that he gained two lengths in the air and, rounding the turn for home, he comfortably led Master H, William Penn and the consistent veteran Red Earl. Towards the rear, as he had been for most of the way, was King Or

Country and, as those in the leading pack drove on towards the finish, the second favourite withered away tamely, ultimately coming home, most disappointingly, in last place.

Approaching was travelling with genuine class and, as Red Earl, William Penn and Orillo began to drift out of contention over the remaining fences, it was left to Master H to throw down the gauntlet to the leader. However, at the third last, the challenger pecked on landing and, with a huge weight differential, Master H struggled thereafter as Approaching ruthlessly seized his opportunity. Never stopping, Approaching cleared the final two fences gracefully and thundered home to a five-length victory with Master H second and William Penn third. The race gallop had been so fast on incredibly firm ground that Approaching's winning time clipped one-tenth of a second off Spanish Steps' race-record time, registered in the 1969 renewal.

Despite Champion having put up 4lbs overweight, Approaching had a huge advantage at the weights with Master H, yet the winner had jumped and travelled so well that there were simply no excuses for the beaten horses. Approaching had fully justified Gifford's decision to aim the youngster at the Hennessy, and it was clear that Approaching had improved significantly since a hobday operation carried out nine months previously. Gifford had purchased Approaching in Ireland four years before the 1978 Hennessy, and had patiently nurtured the horse through his early career. Approaching had now rewarded his trainer with a famous victory, firmly positioning the horse as one of the finest young chasers in the land. In the future, Approaching would run in many big races, featuring in two Cheltenham Gold Cups, and was good enough to take third place behind Master Smudge in the 1980 edition.

1978 HENNESSY COGNAC GOLD CUP RESULT

FATE	HORSE	AGE/WEIGHT	JOCKEY
1st	APPROACHING	7.10.2	R. CHAMPION
2nd	MASTER H	9.12.0	R. CRANK
3rd	WILLIAM PENN	7.10.0	C. CANDY
4th	Banlieu	8.10.3	B.R. Davies
5th	Orillo	9.10.0	R. Linley
6th	Parkhouse	9.10.5	C. Tinkler
7th	Red Earl	9.10.0	M. Murphy
8th	King Or Country	7.11.2	P. Leach

25 November 1978
Going – Firm
Winner – £9,056 50p
Time – 6 mins 30.7 secs
8 Ran
Winner trained by Josh Gifford at Findon, Sussex
Winner bred by N.Connors
Winner owned by Major D. Wigan
Approaching, chestnut gelding by Golden Vision – Farm Hill

Betting – 3/1 Approaching, 7/2 King Or Country, 9/2 Master H, 6/1 Orillo, 13/2 Banlieu, 15/2 Red Earl, 16/1 Parkhouse, 25/1 William Penn.

FIGHTING FIT

After the poor turnout and mediocre quality of the previous year's race, it was pleasing to see a large field filled with some terrific horses compete for the 1979 Hennessy Cognac Gold Cup, the good ground at Newbury attracting an intriguing and competitive collection of chasers.

Favourite for the 1979 race was the Fulke Walwyn-trained Gaffer, a horse that, as a novice chaser the previous season, had taken on the

best horses in the land in the Cheltenham Gold Cup. Hugely admired by his trainer, Gaffer was a tank-sized bay seven-year-old and was a super jumper blessed with rare athleticism. Gaffer had indeed been a fine novice, yet the problem with the horse was a tendency to collect niggling injuries. The horse had been well fancied at Cheltenham for the Gold Cup and unquestionably was capable of winning such a race, yet Gaffer pulled muscles in his back during the race and trailed in a poor fifth as the hardy Alverton ploughed to victory while the snow came down. Making his seasonal reappearance at Cheltenham, the horse recorded a low blood count after the race, throwing his Hennessy participation into doubt. However, following a superb workout just days before the big race, Gaffer was confirmed as a definite runner, even though he would have to shoulder joint-top weight of 11st 7lbs.

One of a septet of horses in the field aged seven, Straight Jocelyn was one of the most progressive young chasers in the land and could boast a fine record at Newbury, similar to the 1978 winner Approaching. With just half-a-dozen National Hunt appearances to his name, Straight Jocelyn had recorded four victories at Newbury – two hurdles races and a pair of chases. In addition, he had rounded out the previous season with a potential-packed, all-the-way success at Towcester to mark him down as one of the horses to watch for the 1979/80 campaign. Trained by Roddy Armytage, the bay had begun the current season by finishing second at Newbury in October, good enough to earn himself a quote of 11/2 and second place behind Gaffer in the betting market.

As well as the consistent challenger from Arthur Stephenson's Northern yard, The Fencer, and the Irish raider Mighty's Honour, three horses attracting public support were Zongalero, Master Smudge and Fighting Fit. Zongalero hailed from the in-form stable of Nicky Henderson and had proved a most reliable yardstick the season before. Zongalero had not won in the previous campaign but had finished second in such races as the Mackeson Gold Cup, the Massey-Ferguson Chase (both at Cheltenham) and, most notably, the Grand National at Aintree, where he played his part in a titanic struggle with the eventual winner Rubstic. The chestnut Master Smudge was a sure stayer, although soft ground suited him best. A fine jumper, Master Smudge had beaten a top-class field in the Sun Alliance Chase at Cheltenham in March and his finest hour would lie in wait at the next festival, where he would ultimately be crowned the Gold Cup winner on a disqualification. Much like Zongalero and Master Smudge, the Ken Oliver-trained Fighting Fit was a horse that appreciated a test of stamina yet, unlike those two, his

The favourite Gaffer lines up under Bill Smith.

Future Cheltenham Gold Cup winner Master Smudge finished fifth in the Hennessy under Richard Hoare.

jumping was, at times, rather suspect. The horse had been a prolific winner the season before, highlighted by winning the Scottish Grand National at Ayr with a magnificent finishing burst from the final fence. In the Hennessy, Fighting Fit was allotted a hefty weight, carrying 11st 7lbs, yet he too was a young horse of rich potential, and was well supported at 15/2.

At the start of the race, the field was reduced by one to fifteen as Jack Madness lived up to his name by unshipping his jockey and running loose, an incident that delayed the race by twenty-one minutes, with the horse eventually withdrawn once caught. It was to be the Irish horse Mighty's Honour, with Tommy Carberry on board, that led the field on their way with Master Smudge, Gaffer, Zongalero and Straight Jocelyn in

close attendance. Early on, the likes of County Clare, Ravir and Current Gold held positions towards the rear.

A huge groan could be heard from the Newbury crowd as the normally safe-jumping favourite Gaffer came down at the seventh, and there was further dismay when Straight Jocelyn capsized at the twelfth; the two market leaders hence rudely ejected from the contest. Fortunately, neither horse was hurt, although jockey Malcolm Bastard was lucky to escape serious injury following a spine-chilling fall from Rough And Tumble, a horse travelling well in third place when it fell at the thirteenth.

The horse had not been jumping with total conviction, yet Mighty's Honour doggedly held the lead for much of the race and still held

Fighting Fit jumps a fence with the hidden Zongalero.

command in the back straight for the final time but, in behind, Zongalero was beautifully positioned under Steve Smith-Eccles, while Royal Stuart, Master Smudge and the ever-improving Current Gold were creeping closer as well. Fighting Fit too had been patiently ridden, biding his time behind the leaders and, even though the horse had made a series of jumping mistakes (most notably at the thirteenth and fourteenth fences), he held every chance turning for home.

The impressive and resilient Zongalero out-jumped Mighty's Honour at the cross fence and swung into the home straight in pole position. Closely tracking the new leader were Philip Blacker's mount, the New Zealand-bred Royal Stuart and Fighting Fit. Master Smudge and Current Gold had

come into contention turning for home but, as Zongalero turned on the pressure once in the straight, the pair faded away. Zongalero and Royal Stuart engaged in a tremendous battle in the straight that lasted to the last fence yet, in behind, it was Fighting Fit that was poised to make a decisive move. As Zongalero shrugged off the challenge of Royal Stuart, Fighting Fit – having made significant headway from the fourth last – demonstrated the finishing power that had won him the Scottish Grand National the season before.

Driven home strongly by Richard Linley, Fighting Fit was able to wear down the gallant Zongalero on the run-in and won the Hennessy by a length and a half with Royal Stuart third, Current Gold fourth and Master

Smudge fifth. The brave Zongalero had finished second again in a major chase, yet he simply had no answer to the superior final burst of Fighting Fit.

Linley was having his first ride for the Oliver stable and had personally requested the mount after Jonjo O'Neill had turned it down to ride at Catterick. The way that Fighting Fit had travelled and stayed on resolutely suggested the Grand National could be the ultimate target. But Oliver, realising the horse was far from the greatest jumper, was quick to rule out Aintree given the unique size and difficulty of those particular fences.

Fighting Fit may not have been the most graceful of Hennessy winners, but he certainly possessed a dynamic engine, recording a fast time while impressively shouldering a hefty weight to become the twelfth winner of the race to carry over 11st to victory.

1979 HENNESSY COGNAC GOLD CUP RESULT

FATE	HORSE	AGE/WEIGHT	JOCKEY
1st	FIGHTING FIT	7.11.7	R. LINLEY
2nd	ZONGALERO	9.10.4	S. SMITH-ECCLES
3rd	ROYAL STUART	8.10.5	P. BLACKER
4th	Current Gold	8.10.3	R. Barry
5th	Master Smudge	7.11.3	R. Hoare
6th	Mighty's Honour	8.11.5	T. Carberry
7th	Tiepolino	7.10.5	M. O'Halloran
8th	Good Prospect	10.10.0	S. Moreshead
9th	The Fencer	7.10.4	R. Lamb
10th	Jimmy Miff	7.10.0	C. Kinane
Fell	Gaffer	7.11.7	W. Smith
Fell	Straight Jocelyn	7.10.12	H. Davies
Fell	Rough And Tumble	9.10.0	M. Bastard
Pulled Up	County Clare	10.10.0	M. Williams
Pulled Up	Ravir	6.10.0	B.R. Davies

24 November 1979
Going – Good
Winner – £11,065
Time – 6 mins 39.2 secs
15 Ran
Winner trained by Ken Oliver at Hawick, Scotland
Winner bred by Donal O'Brien
Winner owned by Mrs L. Carr
Fighting Fit, bay gelding by Harwell – Trimblestown Lady

Betting – 4/1 Gaffer, 11/2 Straight Jocelyn, 13/2 Zongalero, 15/2 Fighting Fit, 12/1 Current Gold, Master Smudge, Mighty's Honour, Tiepolino & The Fencer, 16/1 County Clare & Royal Stuart, 25/1 Good Prospect, Ravir & Rough And Tumble, 50/1 Jimmy Miff.

Hennessy winners Fighting Fit and jockey Richard Linley.

BRIGHT HIGHWAY

In 1977, Bachelor's Hall became the first horse in the same season to complete the big early season National Hunt double of the Mackeson Gold Cup at Cheltenham and the Hennessy Cognac Gold Cup. In 1980, another horse prepared to emulate the feat. The horse in question was an Irish raider called Bright Highway, and the horse was a more-than-worthy Hennessy

favourite despite being just six years of age. Trained in County Kildare by Michael O'Brien, the young bay had stayed on impressively to win the Mackeson, yet Bright Highway had never won a race over the distance of the Hennessy trip and his stamina remained in question. However, the general view was that Bright Highway was a horse very much in the ascendancy and that his stamina would not be an issue. As such, Bright Highway was made the rock-solid 2/1 favourite, despite being the youngest horse in the race, carrying a hefty 11st 6lbs and trying to become the first Irish-trained winner of the race since Arkle's second triumph in 1965.

Hennessy day in 1980 was greeted by grey skies and plenty of rain, casting a gloomy backdrop to one of jump racing's most exciting events of the season. One challenger that the rain was of great benefit to was Peter Scot, winner of the 1979 Welsh Grand National. Like many winners of the Chepstow marathon, Peter Scot was a horse that appreciated soft conditions and, although the official going read good to soft, the rain had certainly improved his chance of winning. Peter Scot was as sound a jumper as could be found in training, with just one fall in twenty-four runs over fences, while the horse trained by David Gandolfo had absolutely no worries regarding stamina. In the 1979 Welsh Grand National, Peter Scot had beaten useful former Hennessy performers Current Gold and Prince Rock, although it was after that Chepstow win that he suffered his only career fall when favourite for the Mildmay-Cazalet Chase at Sandown. Peter Scot had made a winning seasonal debut at Warwick just a week before the Hennessy and, with Paul Barton in the saddle, was expected to go very well at Newbury.

With former runner-up Zongalero the only horse in the field to have competed in the race before, it was one of the most intriguing Hennessys of recent seasons, and horses with strong claims included Father Delaney, Snow Flyer, Tarbank, Betton Gorse and Silent Valley. The top weight was Father Delaney, a bay gelding that had finished fourth behind Bright Highway in the Mackeson. Like Bright Highway, the Peter Easterby-trained Father Delaney had some stamina concerns, while another horse with plenty to prove was the Josh Gifford-trained bay Snow Flyer. Partnered by Richard Rowe, Snow Flyer had been a very talented horse in his younger days, yet injuries had seriously curtailed the horse's career, while a fall on his only run of the season at Newbury in early November was hardly the ideal preparation for a race such as the Hennessy. The chestnut Betton Gorse had been an erratic jumper in his youth, yet the horse had acquitted himself well in two starts during the current season, winning most recently at Sandown, while Tarbank's impressive early-season form (winning twice)

Bright Highway with jockey Gerry Newman.

Bright Highway had been fencing particularly well, exhibiting speed and precision at his obstacles and, as Delmoss started to lose touch, the favourite remained prominent, keeping the likes of Silent Valley and Tarbank for company. Snow Flyer too was going well and, despite having made a bad blunder at the second fence, he was soon involved with the leading group, in contrast to Peter Scot, the Welsh National winner kept off the pace by Barton. Father Delaney was somewhat further back while the normally keen and reliable Zongalero was really struggling, and it was no surprise when the horse was pulled up by Steve Smith-Eccles after the fourteenth.

At the start of the second circuit, Bright Highway jumped confidently to the head of affairs, seemingly determined to dictate matters for the rest of the way. The youngster was impressing tremendously against more seasoned competitors, and the natural pace he injected into the race on hitting the front seemed too much for many of his opponents to cope with. Silent Valley was his closest rival while, jumping the fences in the back straight, only Tarbank, Again The Same and the improving Peter Scot were able to remain in serious contention.

Five fences from home, Silent Valley delivered a mighty leap under Peter Scudamore that sent the horse into the slightest of leads and, rounding the turn for home, he and Bright Highway surged onwards to battle out the final stages. Tarbank was able to keep in touch with the leading duo but, when he capsized at the third last, the finish lay between Silent Valley and Bright Highway.

Clinging on desperately against a high-class opponent, Scudamore urged Silent Valley over the final fence and the partnership touched down narrowly in front. But Bright Highway was not only quick and ultra-talented, he was also a street-fighter. Clawing back Silent Valley's slender lead, jockey Gerry Newman and Bright Highway proved to be the stronger, grabbing the race at the death despite conceding plenty of weight to Silent Valley. Some way back in third came Peter Scot, who had found the pace too quick over the closing fences, with Again The Same fourth.

The stamina doubts that had been attached to Bright Highway before the race had been emphatically removed following the horse's courageous and deeply exciting victory over Silent Valley, as the Hennessy produced yet another fabulous finish. Ever since the first Hennessy in 1957 the race had produced a catalogue of enthralling finales, and the sight of Bright Highway discarding the concerns of inexperience, weight and stamina to overthrow a tough competitor in Silent Valley on the run to the line ranked alongside the finest of finishes the Newbury race had witnessed.

Peter Scudamore returns aboard the runner-up Silent Valley.

gave trainer Fulke Walwyn strong hope of a seventh Hennessy success. In its preceding years, the Hennessy had so often gone to a progressive young chaser and Silent Valley – a bay seven-year-old trained at the tiny Northumberland-based stable of Ian Jordon – was one that fell into that category. With stamina his forte, Silent Valley had finished runner-up in April's Scottish Grand National and had made all to win on his seasonal reappearance at Wetherby in October.

Despite persistent rain, anticipation levels were high as the twenty-fourth Hennessy began. The early leader was Delmoss, a notoriously hard-pulling sort who seemed to run the same way wherever he competed. Delmoss was a horse that always roared his way, almost obnoxiously, to the front, yet he very rarely lasted home in major staying chases.

It was somewhat surprising, however, to see Delmoss begin to fade as early as the ninth fence as the major players began to mount their challenges.

Wheelchair-bound trainer Michael O'Brien and jockey Gerry Newman enjoy Bright Highway's Hennessy win with the horse's owners (holding the trophy) and Madame Hennessy (right).

event at Cheltenham. He was certainly at least as good as the 1981 Gold Cup winner Little Owl, and was actually favourite for that race, as well as the 1982 Gold Cup (won by the excellent Michael Dickinson-trained Silver Buck) before injuries denied him the chance to take on the best. In 1983, Bright Highway was retired with persistent hock problems; however, in 1980, he was the king of Newbury, registering a performance beyond his years to win the prestigious Hennessy Cognac Gold Cup.

Trainer Michael O'Brien had been confined to a wheelchair ever since breaking his back in a fall six years previously, yet he derived great pleasure from the fact that it was he who had purchased Bright Highway as a two-year-old from his former boss Tosse Taaffe. O'Brien had then sold the horse on to American George Strawbridge, an owner that had various horses placed in several stables on this side of the Atlantic, and was an owner that regularly rode in point-to-point races at the time of Bright Highway's Hennessy win.

Jockey Gerry Newman was a rider who had not often ridden in England. However, when he had, the results had been phenomenal. As well as Bright Highway's victories in the Mackeson and Hennessy, he had also won a King George VI Chase aboard the 1974 Cheltenham Gold Cup winner Captain Christy.

That his 1980 Hennessy win remained the highlight of Bright Highway's career was a shame. The horse was probably the best young winner of the race since Spanish Steps in 1969, and seemed destined to challenge for many a Cheltenham Gold Cup in the early 1980s. Sadly, he was soon to suffer a terrible time with injury and never competed in the Blue Riband

1980 HENNESSY COGNAC GOLD CUP RESULT

FATE	HORSE	AGE/WEIGHT	JOCKEY
1st	BRIGHT HIGHWAY	6.11.6	G. NEWMAN
2nd	SILENT VALLEY	7.10.8	P. SCUDAMORE
3rd	PETER SCOT	9.11.0	P. BARTON
4th	Again The Same	7.11.9	P. Blacker
5th	Artistic Prince	9.10.0	R. Smart
6th	Snow Flyer	9.10.0	R. Rowe
7th	Father Delaney	8.11.10	A. Brown
8th	Scroggy	8.10.10	B. Reilly
9th	Betton Gorse	7.10.8	B.R. Davies
Fell	Tarbank	7.10.7	K. Mooney
Pulled Up	Zongalero	10.11.4	S. Smith-Eccles
Pulled Up	Mac Vidi	15.10.12	W. Smith
Pulled Up	Owenlus	10.10.0	P. Leach
Pulled Up	Delmoss	10.10.0	L. O'Donnell

22 November 1980
Going – Good to Soft
Winner – £11,110 50p
Time – 6 mins 49.4 secs
14 Ran
Winner trained by Michael O'Brien at Naas, County Kildare, Ireland
Winner bred by T. Taaffe
Winner owned by Mr G. Strawbridge
Bright Highway, bay gelding by Royal Highway – No Resemblance

Betting – 2/1 Bright Highway, 7/1 Father Delaney, 15/2 Tarbank, 8/1 Snow Flyer, 10/1 Betton Gorse, 11/1 Peter Scot, Silent Valley & Zongalero, 12/1 Again The Same, 20/1 Artistic Prince & Scroggy, 25/1 Mac Vidi, 50/1 Delmoss & Owenlus.

DIAMOND EDGE

By some considerable margin, Fulke Walwyn had been the leading trainer of Hennessy Cognac Gold Cup horses since the event began in 1957. He had won the very first running of the race with Mandarin and followed that up a year later by sending out Taxidermist to win. Further victories followed courtesy of Mandarin (again), Mill House and Man Of The West, while Charlie Potheen had provided Walwyn with his most recent success in 1972. Therefore, a quarter of all Hennessys had been won by Walwyn, with only Bob Turnell (Rondetto and April Seventh) having trained more than one winner among other trainers. Since Charlie Potheen's victory, many other horses had seemed capable of landing an incredible seventh victory for Walwyn, most notably The Dikler, Ghost Writer, Fort Devon, Gaffer and Tarbank, each being well fancied in their respective races. In an ultra-competitive 1981 Hennessy Cognac Gold Cup, Walwyn again had a serious challenger that held every chance of becoming the trainer's lucky number seven.

Despite shouldering top weight of 11st 10lbs, the bay ten-year-old Diamond Edge was favourite for the race, and deservedly so, given what he had achieved in his career prior to the Hennessy. A bold, dynamic jumper, Diamond Edge had won two Whitbread Gold Cups at Sandown, been favourite for the 1980 Cheltenham Gold Cup and finished fifth in the same race in 1981. The Hennessy was to be Diamond Edge's seasonal reappearance and marked the first time he ran at Newbury. Walwyn was confident of a big run from his charge, stating that Diamond Edge was working extremely well at home and always ran well when fresh. The race had long been the horse's early-season target and he was backed accordingly and, despite some seriously good rivals, Diamond Edge started the 9/2 favourite.

The previous year's race had been won by a brilliant youngster in Bright Highway and, while not quite in that class, perhaps the most progressive young horse in the 1981 race was the Northern raider Political Pop, sent down from the yard of Michael Dickinson. Horses from the North had not enjoyed a particularly successful time in past Hennessys, with only Kerstin in 1959 and Springbok in 1962 having won (Fighting Fit in 1979 was from a Scottish stable), yet Political Pop seemed ready to revive those fortunes. The bay seven-year-old had won six of seven chases the season before and, on his only start of the current campaign, had run encouragingly at Warwick, where he had only narrowly been beaten despite giving a lot of weight away. The fact that the Dickinson yard was back in top form following a bout of blood disorders only strengthened Political Pop's chance, and the well-weighted horse started the race as second favourite at 5/1.

As well as the 1980 Cheltenham Gold Cup winner Master Smudge, the 1978 Hennessy hero Approaching and the 1981 Grand National third Royal Mail, the nine-year-old Straight Jocelyn was an interesting

Diamond Edge (3) jumps the final fence ahead of Political Pop (left). In behind and partially hidden is Straight Jocelyn.

Winning jockey Bill Smith meets HRH The Queen Mother following his win on Diamond Edge.

candidate. Straight Jocelyn had been extremely well fancied for the 1979 Hennessy only to suffer a fall. Now, two years on, the horse came into the race with form equally as good and with a decent weight. Straight Jocelyn had won his last two races of the previous season, while he had also won both starts in the current season, at Lingfield and Chepstow, beating the next Cheltenham Gold Cup winner Silver Buck in the latter contest. These results saw Straight Jocelyn take third place in a fierce betting market where many horses came in for strong support, with only Sparkie's Choice and the grey Two Swallows largely unfancied.

It was the Gold Cup winner of 1980, Master Smudge, that was the early leader in the twenty-fifth running of the Hennessy, showing the way until the fourth fence where the exuberant Two Swallows took over, with Royal Mail, Captain John and Sugarally all in close attendance. Among those struggling to live with the early pace were Sparkie's Choice and the Gordon Richards-trained grey Man Alive.

Diamond Edge really warmed to his task. The favourite simply cruised round the first circuit, jumping brilliantly and displaying all the qualities of the classiest horse in the race. On the other hand, Political Pop was running a puzzling race, being well positioned early before losing his place and dropping back at the halfway stage. However, in a race of little incident, the second favourite battled his way back into contention on the second circuit and, remarkably, all fourteen runners retained some kind of chance jumping the last fence in the back straight, with the Chris Grant-ridden Sugarally just holding the advantage.

Rounding the turn for home and entering the straight, the favourite made his move, disconnecting from the large pack behind him and making his strike for glory. Jumping the fourth last in majestic style, Diamond Edge had five horses after him in hot pursuit, those being Lesley Ann, Captain John, Straight Jocelyn, the Richard Rowe-ridden Shady Deal and the improving Political Pop.

Approaching the third last, it appeared Diamond Edge would saunter to an easy victory, yet his only mistake of the race took place at that fence and he landed awkwardly over the obstacle, letting the others in for a second chance. The mistake saw Diamond Edge briefly headed for the lead by Shady Deal but, at the final fence, jockey Bill Smith got a tremendous jump out of the favourite, and he reclaimed the advantage setting off towards the finish line.

With both Shady Deal and Straight Jocelyn unable to quicken once on the flat and with the mare Lesley Ann a last-fence faller, it was left to

Political Pop to challenge Diamond Edge. But, try as he might, Political Pop could not wear down the favourite and after the race jockey Robert Earnshaw admitted that Diamond Edge had just been travelling too strongly to overhaul. At the line, Diamond Edge had won the Hennessy by half a length to Political Pop with a further six lengths back to Straight Jocelyn in third, followed next by Shady Deal and Captain John.

Fulke Walwyn was absolutely delighted with the performance of Diamond Edge (a very popular horse) and, bar one mistake, the winner had jumped with brilliance, displaying his class throughout. The now seven-time Hennessy-winning trainer had been so impressed with his charge that Walwyn confidently predicted that Diamond Edge would win the 1982 Cheltenham Gold Cup. Although the horse did not quite manage to achieve that feat (finishing fourth behind Silver Buck), Diamond Edge shone as one of the most popular Hennessy winners of the 1980s, thoroughly deserving his victory at Newbury in 1981. The incredible training achievement set by Walwyn will surely never be matched, let alone bettered as long as the Hennessy exists, and merely highlights Walwyn's skill as one of the finest trainers of his or any other era. To the present day, no other trainer has won the Hennessy more than three times.

1981 HENNESSY COGNAC GOLD CUP RESULT

FATE	HORSE	AGE/WEIGHT	JOCKEY
1st	DIAMOND EDGE	10.11.10	W. SMITH
2nd	POLITICAL POP	7.10.6	R. EARNSHAW
3rd	STRAIGHT JOCELYN	9.10.12	H. DAVIES
4th	Shady Deal	8.10.0	R. Rowe
5th	Captain John	7.11.5	P. Scudamore
6th	Approaching	10.10.11	B.R. Davies
7th	Master Smudge	9.10.10	S. Smith-Eccles
8th	Sparkie's Choice	8.10.9	C. Hawkins
9th	Royal Mail	11.10.8	S. Jobar
10th	Two Swallows	8.10.7	A. Webber
11th	Doddington Park	8.10.7	R. Linley
12th	Sugarally	8.10.8	C. Grant
13th	Man Alive	10.10.2	N. Doughty
Fell	Lesley Ann	7.11.5	C. Brown

28 November 1981
Going – Good to Soft
Winner – £14,239
Time – 6 mins 52.8 secs
14 Ran
Winner trained by Fulke Walwyn at Lambourn, Berkshire
Winner bred by S. Loughridge
Winner owned by Mr S. Loughridge
Diamond Edge, bay gelding by Honour Bound – Six Of Diamonds

Betting – 9/2 Diamond Edge, 5/1 Political Pop, 8/1 Straight Jocelyn, 9/1 Royal Mail & Shady Deal, 10/1 Approaching, 11/1 Doddington Park, 12/1 Captain John, Lesley Ann, Man Alive & Master Smudge, 14/1 Sugarally, 20/1 Sparkie's Choice, 33/1 Two Swallows.

BREGAWN

If Fulke Walwyn had dominated much of the National Hunt scene as a trainer since the 1950s, then the early 1980s belonged to Michael Dickinson. The former jockey had only been in charge at his Harewood stables in Yorkshire for two years yet, in that time, he had seen his reputation escalate to glittering heights. Dickinson could boast at his disposal such high-class performers as Badsworth Boy, Wayward Lad, Sabin Du Loir, Political Pop and the most recent Cheltenham Gold Cup winner Silver Buck.

In what would turn out to be a truly remarkable season for the Northern-based trainer, his two candidates for the 1982 Hennessy Cognac Gold Cup appeared the two most likely winners of the race. Representing Dickinson were the previous year's fifth Captain John and the most rapidly improving horse in training, Bregawn. The fiery chestnut Bregawn had once been labelled a careless jumper yet, towards the end of the previous season, the horse had started a consistent and eye-catching rise up the chasing ladder, winning the Great Yorkshire Chase at Doncaster before finishing second to Silver Buck in the Gold Cup. The current campaign had witnessed Bregawn continue that improvement, winning with ease on his two starts at Newton Abbot and Chepstow while, with an abundance of stamina, the horse was made 9/4 favourite for the Hennessy. Captain John too had previously suffered with jumping problems but, having moved to the Dickinson stable at the start of the season, he had shown signs of dramatic improvement with a fluent success at Kelso on his reappearance the week before the Hennessy. With both horses only eight years of age, there was every reason to believe Bregawn and Captain John had more improvement still to come.

Making his first appearance in the Hennessy was the high-class bay Night Nurse. Twice a winner of the Champion Hurdle at Cheltenham, Night Nurse had been switched to chasing and had taken to his new career with consummate ease, finishing second to Little Owl in the 1981 Cheltenham Gold Cup before starting as favourite for the same race in 1982. Night Nurse was a big horse, well made to carry the hefty 11st 12lbs he was asked to shoulder in the Hennessy. The horse was a good jumper, while his early-season form had been impressive, going down to the fast-improving Wayward Lad at Worcester before thrashing a fellow Hennessy contender in Scot Lane at Wolverhampton.

The soft ground present at Newbury in 1982 seemed tailor-made for two more-than-useful stayers, Lesley Ann and Corbiere. Lesley Ann, a mare trained by David Elsworth, was far from a safe jumper. The horse had won the Sun Alliance Chase at the 1981 Cheltenham Festival and she had taken part in many of the top staying chases since then. However, it was when those races reached their crucial stages that Lesley Ann proved vulnerable. She would have seriously threatened Diamond Edge in the previous year's Hennessy but for falling at the final fence, and was also in strong contention in the 1982 Gold Cup when she committed a race-costing blunder six fences out. At her best, Lesley Ann was a dangerous customer and, with ground conditions to suit, her stamina was expected to be a major asset. In contrast, the Jenny Pitman-trained Corbiere would prove to be one of the finest jumpers in the sport. At the time of the 1982 Hennessy, however, the chestnut had yet to fully distinguish himself as one of the top chasers in the land – that would all change by the season's end. Corbiere had missed nearly all of the previous season with injury and had been brought back patiently by Pitman, participating in a number of hurdle races before the Hennessy. At seven, Corbiere was the youngest horse in the race, and he shaped as the dark horse of the 1982 renewal.

For most of the opening two-and-a-quarter miles, the Jonjo O'Neill-ridden Night Nurse and the Ben De Haan-ridden Corbiere dictated proceedings, jumping boldly and trying to stretch the remainder of the field, closely monitored by Bregawn, Bold Argument and Earthstopper. But, five fences from home, the race was to change dramatically. Jockey Robert Earnshaw sent Captain John through to challenge for the lead and, jumping the fence with menace, the horse overtook Bregawn and Corbiere in mid-air and landed in the lead, just as Night Nurse began to weaken. In addition, Earthstopper came down at the same fence and, with Lesley Ann again ruining her round with sloppy jumping, it meant the three horses in contention coming into the home straight were Captain John, Bregawn and Corbiere, as both Sea Captain and Megan's Boy – though both staying on – failed to quicken from off the pace.

Bregawn goes to post in 1982 under jockey Graham Bradley.

Three of the best horses of the 1980s. Night Nurse (purple) jumps the water with
Corbiere (white face) to the right. Behind the two is eventual winner Bregawn (green).

Last fence in 1982 and Bregawn holds the
edge from his stablemate Captain John (6).

It was at the third last – the final ditch – where the Dickinson duo took control. With Corbiere unable to match the intensity of the leading two, Captain John and Bregawn flew the fence like hawks and pulled clear. The pair jumped two out together and, although the stablemates remained stride for stride at the last, it appeared that Graham Bradley had more in reserve aboard Bregawn. However, as Bradley asked his mount for a long stride at the last, Bregawn seemed to become distracted, blundering the obstacle and handing the lighter-weighted Captain John a three-length advantage on the flat.

Just as the favourite looked doomed, Bregawn displayed the resolve and determination that had aided his rise through the chasing ranks, a flame seemingly igniting inside the chestnut as he set about clawing back his stablemate's advantage. Bregawn was a horse with power, stamina and grit and, reorganised by Bradley, he attacked Captain John with venom. Surging past the leader, the favourite strode out to a convincing three-length win. Sea Captain had run on from a long way back to take third with Megan's Boy and Corbiere next. The lattermost had run a fine race and, later in the season, his excellent jumping and staying ability would see him land the Welsh Grand National followed by the Grand National itself, making Mrs Pitman the first woman to train a winner of the Aintree marathon.

His Hennessy victory had elevated Bregawn into the very highest class of the nation's staying chasers. His rise to the top had begun in the second half of the previous season and he was to reach his absolute peak at Cheltenham in March 1983, leading home four other Dickinson runners and winning the Gold Cup in relentless style, the runner-up being none other than Captain John. Bregawn was a horse that raced regularly, and his longevity saw him compete in two more Gold Cups at Cheltenham after his famous victory in 1983. However, it was not that long after that particular date with destiny that the horse started to develop a decidedly moody temperament, frequently disappointing in the top races.

But, for the best part of two seasons, there was no tougher chaser in the land, and the way he fought back tenaciously to win the 1982 Hennessy suggested a horse with a warrior-like mentality at his peak. Much of the credit for Bregawn's success rightly went to Dickinson, who became the first since Neville Crump (Springbok and Rough Tweed) to train the first two home in a Hennessy. Dickinson's reputation had blossomed dramatically within a short space of time, much like that of Bregawn's, and he was quickly establishing himself as one of the true maestros of his sphere. When top jockey Tommy Carmody had left the Yorkshire stable, Dickinson had refused to sign up a big-name replacement; instead entrusting a number of the yard's promising younger riders, and it was two of those – Bradley and Earnshaw – that fought out the finish to another memorable chapter in the history of the Hennessy Cognac Gold Cup.

1982 HENNESSY COGNAC GOLD CUP RESULT

FATE	HORSE	AGE/WEIGHT	JOCKEY
1st	BREGAWN	8.11.10	G. BRADLEY
2nd	CAPTAIN JOHN	8.11.0	R. EARNSHAW
3rd	SEA CAPTAIN	8.10.11	S. SMITH-ECCLES
4th	Megan's Boy	9.10.9	P. Scudamore
5th	Corbiere	7.10.6	B. De Haan
6th	Bold Argument	9.10.0	W. Newton
7th	Straight Jocelyn	10.10.13	A. Webber
8th	Scot Lane	9.11.1	C. Smith
Fell	Earthstopper	8.10.11	Mr G. Sloan
Pulled Up	Night Nurse	11.11.12	J.J. O'Neill
Pulled Up	Lesley Ann	8.11.0	R. Linley

27 November 1982
Going – Soft
Winner – £14,269 50p
Time – 6 mins 56.7 secs
11 Ran
Winner trained by Michael Dickinson at Harewood, Yorkshire
Winner bred by J. Fitzgerald
Winner owned by Mr J. Kennelly
Bregawn, chestnut gelding by Saint Denys – Miss Society

Betting – 9/4 Bregawn, 9/2 Captain John & Night Nurse, 9/1 Lesley Ann, 10/1 Megan's Boy, 11/1 Corbiere, 14/1 Sea Captain, 16/1 Earthstopper, Scot Lane & Straight Jocelyn, 50/1 Bold Argument.

Trainer Michael Dickinson and jockey Graham Bradley with the trophy.

1983

BROWN CHAMBERLIN

Favourite for the 1983 Hennessy Cognac Gold Cup was the talented Brown Chamberlin, hailing from the powerful Lambourn yard of trainer Fred Winter. The horse had seemed destined for a chasing career at the very highest level when taking the Sun Alliance Chase with ease as a novice in 1982. However, despite two early victories the following season, Brown Chamberlin inexplicably lost his way and his season petered out tamely, the low point arriving in the 1983 Cheltenham Gold Cup where he jumped miserably and was pulled up. It seemed that Brown Chamberlin was a horse that did not like to be rushed or bullied; neither did he appreciate a dogfight (completely the opposite to the 1982 hero Bregawn), sometimes sulking when this occurred. Some said the horse was delicate, yet he was a talented individual that needed coaxing to find his rhythm and desired tactics to suit his temperament, and was capable of brilliance when things went his way. After two wins to start the current season, the task of guiding the horse round Newbury was given to the exceptionally gifted John Francome and, having had success at the course before, Brown Chamberlin started the 7/2 favourite.

Among those that appeared most likely to challenge the favourite were Midnight Love, Gaye Chance, Everett and Silent Valley. Trained in Bishop Auckland by Denys Smith, Midnight Love was something of a character, but was also a horse with stamina on his side and one that had won on all types of ground, including the good-to-firm present at Newbury on Hennessy day. Purchased by Smith in Ireland, the trainer had sent out Midnight Love to win five handicap chases two seasons previously and, despite not winning the entire next season, the horse had rocketed back to his best form in the current campaign, winning at Catterick and Newcastle since the publication of the Hennessy weights, for which he was allotted a lenient

10st 11lbs. Gaye Chance was formerly a high-class hurdler, and the horse – trained by Mercy Rimell – was having his first run of the season in the Hennessy. Everett was the chief hope of Fulke Walwyn's yard and the horse had been a super staying hurdler before progressing into one of the previous season's top novice chasers, winning five of six completed starts. Owned by Killian Hennessy, the problem for Everett was a bad tendency to make jumping errors. Although Walwyn considered Everett a much-improved fencer, it remained to be seen whether the horse could withstand the fierce pressure of a race like the Hennessy. The strongest candidate for most emotive potential winner of the 1983 Hennessy was Silent Valley. The horse had finished second to Bright Highway in 1980 but had shortly after broken a bone in his leg. The horse had also suffered a variety of other injuries, and the fact that he was even fit enough to race in the Hennessy was an enormous credit to his trainer Ian Jordon. Despite his troubles, a three-mile chase win at Ayr the week before the big race sparked a major early morning gamble on Silent Valley, reducing his odds drastically to an eventual starting price of 7/1.

Brown Chamberlin and jockey John Francome.

Gaye Chance in the parade before finishing second in the race.

when knocking the third last, a mistake that seemed to rattle the horse, but Gaye Chance and Everett held their places behind Brown Chamberlin until the penultimate fence. Here however, the race was sealed. Having already made a number of minor errors, Everett's jumping woes surfaced once more as he hit the second last fence and crumpled to the ground, while Gaye Chance could not quicken sufficiently to stay with the leader.

With his rivals beaten, Brown Chamberlin came to the last fence with the race at his mercy and duly jumped the obstacle sweetly in the style of a horse that had thoroughly enjoyed the experience and had benefited from a fine ride from Francome. Running on strongly, Brown Chamberlin came home one of the easiest winners in Hennessy history, with ten lengths and twenty to spare over Gaye Chance and the gallant Silent Valley, with Midnight Love fourth. Whether or not Everett would have seriously threatened the winner will never be known, but Brown Chamberlin was a fine horse at his best, near Gold Cup-winning class, as evident by his second place behind the awesome machine that was Burrough Hill Lad in the 1984 Blue Riband event at Cheltenham.

It was a first Hennessy win for both Winter and Francome, and it was the jockey that received well-deserved praise for settling Brown Chamberlin

The Hennessy hero of 1978, Approaching – now a twelve-year-old – was the early leader in the race, proudly disputing affairs, closely followed by Royal Judgement, Brown Chamberlin and Gaye Chance, while mistakes at both the second and third fences saw outsider Integration quickly fall back from the main group, while fellow long shots Acarine and Fauloon were also under pressure sooner rather than later.

It was at the tenth fence when Francome unveiled his tactics on Brown Chamberlin. Sending his mount into the lead, the jockey quickly settled the favourite into a beautiful rhythm, the horse taking each fence in his stride in a poised, relaxed manner. This pattern continued throughout the second circuit and, one by one, horses began to struggle to match the favourite's march, including Midnight Love who belted the thirteenth to seriously dent his chances.

With Approaching and Royal Judgement both spent forces as Brown Chamberlin turned for home, and with Midnight Love failing to recover sufficiently from his mistake, it was left to Gaye Chance, Silent Valley and Everett to try and claw back the favourite. Silent Valley was still going well

Mercy Rimell, trainer of Gaye Chance.

into a perfect racing rhythm. In contrast to the majority of Hennessys that had preceded it, the 1983 renewal was won convincingly and with relative simplicity. The winner, however, was well up to standard, and thoroughly deserved his place on the illustrious Roll of Honour.

1983 HENNESSY COGNAC GOLD CUP RESULT

FATE	HORSE	AGE/WEIGHT	JOCKEY
1st	BROWN CHAMBERLIN	8.11.8	J. FRANCOME
2nd	GAYE CHANCE	8.11.0	S. MORESHEAD
3rd	SILENT VALLEY	10.10.1	P. SCUDAMORE
4th	Midnight Love	8.10.11	G. Bradley
5th	Approaching	12.10.5	P. Nicholls
6th	Royal Judgement	10.11.9	R. Rowe
Fell	Everett	8.11.4	S. Shilston
Pulled Up	Fauloon	8.10.10	W. Smith
Pulled Up	Acarine	7.10.4	H. Davies
Pulled Up	Hallo Dandy	9.10.3	N. Doughty
Pulled Up	Marnik	9.10.0	R. Earnshaw
Pulled Up	Integration	9.10.0	C. Brown

26 November 1983
Going – Good to Firm
Winner – £14,373
Time – 6 mins 35.8 secs
12 Ran
Winner trained by Fred Winter at Lambourn, Berkshire
Winner bred by Lt-Col. D.M. Baird
Winner owned by Mrs Basil Samuel
Brown Chamberlin, brown gelding by Space King – Jocelin

Betting – 7/2 Brown Chamberlin, 5/1 Everett & Midnight Love, 7/1 Marnik & Silent Valley, 11/1 Gaye Chance & Hallo Dandy, 14/1 Acarine, 20/1 Fauloon, 25/1 Approaching, Integration & Royal Judgement.

Fred Winter trained the winner in 1983.

1984

BURROUGH HILL LAD

The 1984 Hennessy Cognac Gold Cup marked the first time since 1971 that the reigning Cheltenham Gold Cup Champion ran in the race. Not since L'Escargot had the winner of chasing's Blue Riband featured in the Newbury event in the same year, yet now a horse widely considered the best staying chaser since Arkle was to take his chance in the race.

John Francome and Burrough Hill Lad are poised at the start of the 1984 Hennessy.

A near-black gelding with considerable range, power and athleticism, the awesome Burrough Hill Lad had thundered to victory at Cheltenham in March, beating a batch of the sport's premier chasers, including Wayward Lad and the previous year's Hennessy hero Brown Chamberlin. His Gold Cup success concluded a season where Burrough Hill Lad had progressed from being a promising young handicapper on a very low mark to one of the most dominant forces to grace the sport for many years, taking in a victory in the Welsh Grand National on his way to Gold Cup glory. Trained at Upper Lambourn by Jenny Pitman, the horse had been eased into the new season with a third place behind fellow Hennessy challenger, the Arthur Stephenson-trained Fortina's Express, but had quickly improved again to win at Wincanton next time out. It was Phil Tuck that had ridden Burrough Hill Lad at Cheltenham, yet John Francome regularly rode the horse (holding an unbeaten partnership of four races prior to Newbury), and the jockey had only ridden Brown Chamberlin in the Gold Cup because of a deep loyalty to trainer Fred Winter, despite acknowledging beforehand that Burrough Hill Lad was the better horse, and it was Francome that was back on board in the Hennessy. Understandably for a horse of his status, Burrough Hill Lad was allotted top weight of 12st in a soft-ground Hennessy, far more weight than any other horse. Despite the weight burden, Burrough Hill Lad started the well-backed 100/30 favourite, with Mrs Pitman extremely confident of success.

As well as the previous year's runner-up Gaye Chance and the Grand National-bound stayer Lucky Vane, the main challenge to Burrough Hill Lad looked likely to come from Canny Danny, Everett, Earl's Brig and Drumlargan. Trained by Jimmy Fitzgerald, Canny Danny had won the Sun Alliance Chase at the 1983 Cheltenham Festival while Everett – a horse still plagued by jumping problems – had scorched home by fifteen lengths on his seasonal reappearance at Kempton in October and was attempting to give trainer Fulke Walwyn an incredible eighth Hennessy win. One of the less-exposed runners in the field was the big, dark-brown gelding Earl's Brig, trained by Scottish permit holder William Hamilton. Earl's Brig had made his name as a brilliant hunter-chaser and had begun the season with victory at Newcastle, giving his stable the confidence to pitch the horse in against top-level competition at Newbury, where he would have 2st less to carry than Burrough Hill Lad. The Irish hope Drumlargan had not been too far behind Burrough Hill Lad when third in the Gold Cup, and he would now be receiving 11lbs from the same horse. Trained by Edward O'Grady, Drumlargan had a touch of class, yet the two chief factors that

The brilliant Burrough Hill Lad jumps the water on his way to Hennessy glory.

Jenny Pitman stands with her Hennessy winner Burrough Hill Lad.

poorly, although his partnership with jockey Sam Shilston was maintained despite numerous mistakes, and the horse was able to stay in touch with the leaders as the second circuit began.

Burrough Hill Lad had been travelling nicely within himself, the large weight seemingly not affecting his ability to keep in touch with the leaders, and Francome had him settled in the middle of the pack as the field came to the fifteenth. Here the favourite made a mistake and, although not critical, it prompted Francome into sending his horse forward as they approached the end of the back straight.

Having jumped the cross fence, the field turned into the home straight as both Everett and Kumbi started to fade. With Drumlargan having run most disappointingly, the race lay between four horses – Canny Danny, Gaye Chance, Phil The Fluter and Burrough Hill Lad. By the third last, all four were in line yet, flying the last ditch in tremendous style, it was Burrough Hill Lad that set about stamping his authority on the race. Touching down following his breathtaking leap three out, Burrough Hill Lad was set free by Francome, encouraged to roar onwards and, in a matter of strides, his raw power and drive had taken the favourite clear.

Forging even further ahead after the second last, Burrough Hill Lad was now demonstrating his full arsenal as his stamina, power and class were evident for all to see and, flying the last fence with a grace rarely associated with such an imposing animal, he received a rapturous reception on the run to the line as the Newbury crowd acknowledged the fact that they had seen the best chaser in the land destroy an above-average Hennessy field.

In receipt of over a stone, Canny Danny was able to close a little on the favourite as the line drew near, but it was mere consolation as the four-length margin of victory was as convincing as could be, while the tired but game Gaye Chance was a long way back (twenty lengths) in third ahead of the never-threatening Fortina's Express, Kumbi and the staying-on Lucky Vane, a horse better suited to a distance of six miles! Everett's jumping had failed to stand the rigorous test of the Hennessy and he trailed home seventh, while Drumlargan's performance was hard to fathom given the conditions, and he was ultimately pulled up.

Burrough Hill Lad had joined an elite group courtesy of his Hennessy win. Only he, Mill House and Arkle (twice) had won the Hennessy as defending Cheltenham Gold Cup winners, a true sign of a horse at the peak of its powers. True, Bregawn and Mandarin had both won the Hennessy before their respective Gold Cup wins, yet to win the Newbury

elevated him to 11/2 second-favourite on the day were the presence of his beloved soft ground together with his most recent performance at Fairyhouse, where he had given a fair horse named Sicilian Answer a huge 22lbs and still won by a neck.

As a huge Newbury crowd looked on in excitement, the thirteen-strong field were sent on their way, with the pattern of the 1984 Hennessy established early on. As they would for the bulk of the race, Gaye Chance, Phil The Fluter and Canny Danny – wearing a sheepskin noseband – took up order in the front rank. Kumbi, a nine-year-old ridden by Kevin Doolan, was also prominent, but the youngster Tracy's Special and the one-paced Lucky Vane were two that were soon struggling as the race found its rhythm. The first horse to go was Earl's Brig, when the promising individual committed a bad error at the eighth fence and unseated amateur rider Peter Craggs. Everett, as he so often did, was jumping race after seems an even greater achievement, given the Hennessy is a handicap and the Gold Cup winner is almost certain to be giving huge amounts of weight away. It should also be noted that Kerstin won the Hennessy in 1959, almost twenty months after winning the Gold Cup at Cheltenham. Other Cheltenham Gold Cup winners either before 1984 or after it have run in the Hennessy without success. To this day, the list of Gold Cup winners that failed to win the Hennessy when they ran reads as follows: Gay Donald, Linwell, Pas Seul, Woodland Venture, What A Myth, L'Escargot, The Dikler, Master Smudge, Charter Party, Garrison Savannah, Jodami and The Fellow. The fact that no former or future Cheltenham Gold Cup winner has run in the Hennessy since Garrison Savannah was well beaten in 1993 surely illustrates the brilliance and magnitude of Burrough Hill Lad's winning performance, rated as one of the finest runs of the modern era.

Burrough Hill Lad was a horse that Mrs Pitman always had the utmost faith and confidence in, predicting that he would win the Welsh National the season before and producing the horse spot on for Cheltenham and Newbury to win two of the chasing's most important races. It was a first Hennessy success for Pitman and the second consecutive for the masterful Francome, and both were quick to offer support for Phil Tuck, unfortunately jocked off the horse despite having won the Gold Cup. Francome was both a brilliant jockey and fine sportsman. He would later partner Burrough Hill Lad to victory in the King George VI Chase and the horse surely would have enjoyed further success in the major chases but for his career being cruelly interrupted by injury.

1984 HENNESSY COGNAC GOLD CUP RESULT

FATE	HORSE	AGE/WEIGHT	JOCKEY
1st	BURROUGH HILL LAD	8.12.0	J. FRANCOME
2nd	CANNY DANNY	8.10.7	P. SCUDAMORE
3rd	GAYE CHANCE	9.10.10	S. MORSHEAD
4th	Fortina's Express	10.10.0	K. Jones
5th	Kumbi	9.10.0	K. Doolan
6th	Lucky Vane	9.10.3	J. Burke
7th	Everett	9.11.2	S. Shilston
8th	Phil The Fluter	9.10.0	S. Youlden
9th	Tracys Special	7.10.5	Steve Knight
Pulled Up	Sointulla Boy	9.11.3	Mr T. Houlbrooke
Pulled Up	Drumlargan	10.11.3	Mr F. Codd
Pulled Up	Cobley Express	8.10.2	C. Brown
Unseated Rider	Earl's Brig	9.10.0	Mr P. Craggs

24 November 1984
Going – Soft
Winner- £14,081
Time – 6 mins 56.2 secs
13 Ran
Winner trained by Mrs Jenny Pitman at Upper Lambourn, Berkshire
Winner bred by Mr R.S. Riley
Winner owned by Mr R.S. Riley

Betting – 100/30 Burrough Hill Lad, 11/2 Drumlargan, 6/1 Everett, 13/2 Canny Danny & Earl's Brig, 8/1 Gaye Chance, 11/1 Tracys Special, 12/1 Lucky Vane, 14/1 Fortina's Express, 28/1 Phil The Fluter, 50/1 Sointulla Boy, 100/1 Cobley Express.

1985

GALWAY BLAZE

Every runner in the 1985 Hennessy Cognac Gold Cup was new to the race. As it transpired, however, some of the finest staying chasers of the mid-1980s would emerge from the race, many of them just beginning to enter their prime. Indeed, the likes of Charter Party, Run And Skip, By The Way, Maori Venture, Door Latch and Rhyme 'N' Reason would all play their part in some of the most important races of the era.

Favourite on this occasion was the Monica Dickinson-trained By The Way, a seven-year-old chestnut considered to be at the peak of

Richard Rowe goes to post aboard the well-fancied Door Latch in 1985.

his powers. The withdrawal of his stablemate, the dual King George VI winner Wayward Lad, at the overnight stage had left By The Way to carry top weight, the weights rising by 8lbs, meaning the favourite shouldered 11st 7lbs. By The Way was a horse compared to former Hennessy winner Bregawn for the way he had made a significant and powerful surge to the top end of the handicap for, after joining the Dickinson stable from Ireland, the horse had won the Whitbread Gold Cup at the end of the previous season and had concluded that campaign with a facile twenty-length success at Wetherby. On his reappearance in the current season, By The Way had carried 12st 2lbs to victory, albeit against moderate opposition, to set up a crack at the big Newbury race. A natural, free-flowing jumper that appreciated the quick conditions present in 1985, By The Way started at a price of 11/4.

One of the most interesting runners in the field was the Jimmy Fitzgerald-trained chestnut Galway Blaze. The Fitzgerald yard was brimming with confidence following the recent success of their Forgive 'N' Forget in the Cheltenham Gold Cup in March and, in Galway Blaze, they had something of a dark horse, despite him being a nine-year-old. Galway Blaze had been an above-average novice but had then missed the following season through injury. The horse had shown he had retained plenty of ability when finishing an encouraging third at Market Rasen in early November, staying on strongly at the end of the race. The main concern Fitzgerald had for Galway Blaze (a horse that notoriously suffered from sore shins) was the presence of quick ground, and it was only after the late withdrawal of Wayward Lad that the trainer elected to let the horse take his chance.

Both Maori Venture – who had won the Mandarin Chase over course and distance the previous season – and the bold front-runner, Run And Skip, were talented horses, yet both were prone to jumping errors, while youngsters Rhyme 'N' Reason, Elmboy, Door Latch and Charter Party were each worthy of consideration. Only a six-year-old, Rhyme 'N' Reason had won the previous season's Irish Grand National, while the bay Elmboy had been the top hunter-chaser of the season before. Door Latch, a progressive stayer trained by Josh Gifford, would be good enough to feature prominently in future Cheltenham Gold Cup and King George VI chases, while Charter Party – another yet to fully master the art of jumping – would eventually win a Cheltenham Gold Cup, his finest hour arriving in March 1988. The presence of this half-dozen made the 1985 field deep and strong.

Jumping the water from left to right: Rhyme 'N' Reason, Elmboy, Don Sabreur and Glyde Court.

The fragile Galway Blaze enjoyed his finest hour in the 1985 Hennessy.

Run And Skip set off like a rocket in front, determined to provide an electric pace. The grey horse Tom's Little Al, Door Latch, By The Way, Galway Blaze and Glyde Court were all close to the leader early on, as was Maori Venture, until a mistake sent him backwards somewhat at the eighth fence. Run And Skip, despite making a mistake at the twelfth, continued to lead on at a cracking pace until just headed by the smooth-travelling chestnut Door Latch at the fifteenth and, as the field prepared to turn into the home straight for the final time, many still held a chance, although the outsiders Cobley Express, Mount Oliver and Integration had always been struggling and were out of contention, while Tom's Little Al, although prominent on the first circuit, succumbed to lack of stamina and was pulled-up at the fourth last.

Sweeping for home, Door Latch held the edge over Run And Skip, while Galway Blaze travelled beautifully for jockey Mark Dwyer just behind. Elmboy and the favourite By The Way had run well, but now both began to tire and it was Charter Party, Rhyme 'N' Reason and Glyde Court that improved the most to challenge the leaders in the straight. Charter Party had made the most significant move as the leaders came to four out, pestering Door Latch for supremacy jumping the fence. But it was here where his jumping problems resurfaced and he came down agonisingly. The favourite By The Way was next to go a fence later but, unlike Charter Party, By The Way was a beaten horse when he fell, crumbling to the ground extremely tired as the crowd groaned. When Glyde Court made a mistake severe enough to ruin his chance at the second last, the field had suddenly carved up dramatically.

Having blazed a trail, Run And Skip could give no more and neither could Rhyme 'N' Reason, as Door Latch hung on grimly in front. But Galway Blaze had travelled better than any other horse throughout the race, jumping magnificently and, swallowing up Door Latch approaching the last fence, he remained on the bridle, simply cruising under Dwyer. Taking the last with authority, the chestnut came home gracefully to record one of the easiest victories in Hennessy history, beating Run And Skip handsomely by twelve lengths with Door Latch a further five lengths away in third. The breakneck gallop supplied by Run And Skip had resulted in Galway Blaze clipping 1.2 seconds off the race-record time set by Approaching in 1978.

Galway Blaze, jointly owned by Beverley Formby and Georgina Tulloch (who had also owned the good hurdler Pollardstown), emphatically fulfilled his potential in the Hennessy, providing another big-race success for the blossoming talent that was twenty-two-year-old Dwyer, a former apprentice with Liam Browne. Dwyer had won the Gold Cup in March on Forgive 'N' Forget.

The manner in which Galway Blaze travelled and stayed cast him boldly as an ideal candidate for the 1986 Grand National, a race for which Fitzgerald immediately targeted the horse. Sadly, Galway Blaze never made it to Aintree, further injuries curtailing his season. In fact, injuries deprived the horse of much of the next two seasons, running only three more times before a second crack at the Hennessy in 1987. It was a real shame that a racehorse as clearly talented as Galway Blaze should suffer such misfortune, yet at least he was able to show his true worth at Newbury in 1985, convincingly dismantling a cluster of the sport's finest chasers to land the Hennessy Cognac Gold Cup.

1985 HENNESSY COGNAC GOLD CUP RESULT

FATE	HORSE	AGE/WEIGHT	JOCKEY
1st	GALWAY BLAZE	9.10.10	M. DWYER
2nd	RUN AND SKIP	7.10.9	S. MORSHEAD
3rd	DOOR LATCH	7.10.8	R. ROWE
4th	Glyde Court	8.10.2	S. Sherwood
5th	Rhyme 'N' Reason	6.11.2	G. Bradley
6th	Elmboy	7.10.12	A. Webber
7th	Maori Venture	9.11.1	Steve Knight
8th	Cobley Express	9.10.0	R. Millman
9th	Mount Oliver	7.10.0	M. Williams
Fell	By The Way	7.11.7	R. Earnshaw
Fell	Charter Party	7.10.2	P. Scudamore
Pulled Up	Gallaher	9.10.13	K. Mooney
Pulled Up	Tom's Little Al	9.10.12	C. Brown
Pulled Up	Integration	11.10.5	H. Davies
Pulled Up	Don Sabreur	8.10.0	R. Dunwoody

23 November 1985
Going – Good to Firm
Winner – £17,474
Time – 6 mins 29.5 secs
15 Ran
Winner trained by Jimmy Fitzgerald at Malton, Yorkshire
Winner bred by Mrs W. O'Malley
Winner owned by Mrs B. Formby & Mrs W. Tulloch
Galway Blaze, chestnut gelding by Little Buskins – Grace's Gold

Betting – 11/4 By The Way, 5/1 Charter Party, 11/2 Galway Blaze, 6/1 Elmboy, 7/1 Run And Skip, 9/1 Door Latch, 10/1 Rhyme 'N' Reason, 16/1 Gallaher & Glyde Court, 20/1 Maori Venture, 25/1 Don Sabreur & Tom's Little Al, 33/1 Integration, 40/1 Mount Oliver, 50/1 Cobley Express.

Jockey Mark Dwyer and trainer Jimmy Fitzgerald share a joke following their Hennessy win.

1986

BROADHEATH

The 1986 Hennessy Cognac Gold Cup – the thirtieth running of the race – threw forward a competitive mix of seasoned handicappers, improving young chasers and interesting outsiders. It may not have been the classiest Hennessy in the race's history, but the open, competitive feel of the 1986 renewal was strong and vibrant, with many former or future big-race winners in the line-up.

Top weight and the class horse in the field was the David Nicholson-trained Charter Party, a horse that had looked set for at least a place in the 1985 race but for falling four fences from home. It had long been a desire of Nicholson's to win a Hennessy. Indeed, the trainer had finished second in the race as a jockey aboard Rough Tweed in 1962 as well as leading over the last on Bassnet in 1967. The early part of Charter Party's chasing career had been littered with jumping problems and, at the time of the 1986 Hennessy, he had yet to shift his label of 'suspect jumper'. However, signs that the eight-year-old was starting to improve came in the 1986 Ritz Club Handicap Chase at the Cheltenham Festival, where the horse jumped immaculately, and this was followed by a return to Cheltenham in April where he trounced the subsequent Whitbread Gold Cup winner, the Fred Winter-trained Plundering (also in the 1986 Hennessy field) by twenty lengths in the Golden Miller Chase. An encouraging fourth on his seasonal reappearance promised better still to come, and with testing conditions in the horse's favour at Newbury and with jockey Richard Dunwoody on a personal high having won the Grand National on West Tip in April, followers of Charter Party had every reason to believe the horse could win the Hennessy, and he began the race as favourite at 5/1.

As well as the next Grand National winner in Maori Venture, the 1985 Hennessy third Door Latch, Plundering and the three-time winner

of Kempton Park's Charisma Gold Cup in Everett, the tall and rugged Broadheath featured among the seasoned chasers in the field. Trained by David Barons in Devon, Broadheath was a bulky, bay horse with enormous heart and deceptive speed. The horse had run in the Mackeson Gold Cup at Cheltenham a fortnight earlier and was running well when brought down six fences from home. He then reappeared at Wincanton a week later, winning easily to elevate his position in the Hennessy betting. The problem for Broadheath, according to his jockey Paul Nicholls, was the ground, as it was thought the horse required genuinely good going to be at his best, rather than the sluggish conditions present at Newbury in 1986.

From a useful band of seven-year-olds that included the jet-black Stearsby, the imminent Welsh Grand National winner trained by Jenny Pitman, and the Northern raider The Langholm Dyer, trained in Cumbria by Gordon Richards, two that seemed armed with the right credentials to win the Hennessy were Strands Of Gold and Church Warden. Strands Of Gold – a full brother to the 1984 Hennessy runner-up Canny Danny – was attempting to give trainer Jimmy Fitzgerald a second consecutive Hennessy victory. Despite the horse's reported dislike of softer conditions and an apparent tendency to make hard work of his races, Strands Of Gold was a very talented horse and got into the race on a low weight of 10st 3lbs, a weight that looked all the more appealing following a victory at Newcastle a week before the Hennessy in which he beat the veteran Silent Valley. Church Warden, sidelined for much of the previous season, was perhaps the dark horse of the race. Trained by David Murray-Smith, Church Warden had won at Ascot the week before the Hennessy and was a horse that possessed good stamina and a liking for cut in the ground, although he was officially 5lbs out of the handicap.

The fact that the weights had not risen after the top weight Run And Skip had been withdrawn was to come into focus after the race. Run And Skip had been accidentally left in by connections at the four-day stage but was not an intended runner and was pulled out on the morning of the race, benefiting those towards the top of the handicap.

It was The Langholm Dyer that set the pace for the first two miles, albeit sedately, but when the grey horse Two Coppers displaced him in front the race was given a vital injection of urgency. Two horses struggling were Church Warden and Charter Party. Church Warden had appeared somewhat out of his depth in such a contest and was never able to get into the race. Something may well have been amiss with Charter Party, for he was having an off day and, according to Dunwoody, the horse went

Hennessy favourite Charter Party stands at the start under jockey Richard Dunwoody. In the bottom right of the picture is the horse's trainer, David Nicholson.

out like a light at the seventh last fence. In dire trouble, he was eventually pulledup, much to the disappointment of the large number in the crowd that had backed the horse.

At the cross fence five out, Door Latch put in an enormous leap to briefly take command but the game Two Coppers – 19lbs out of the handicap – had regained the lead by the first in the home straight. A number of horses remained in contention over the final fences, with Two Coppers and Door Latch hanging on in front of the steadily improving Broadheath, while Plundering, Maori Venture and Strands Of Gold were still in touch but getting increasingly tired on the holding ground. The Catchpool, an outsider that had run with credit, travelling with the leaders for most of the way, also began to fade away as the race intensified from the fourth last.

Three fences out Broadheath made a mistake, pitching on landing and sending Nicholls rocketing forward in the saddle. However, the partnership remained intact as the stout Broadheath recovered admirably, losing no ground and marching on bravely. Not so lucky was Door Latch. Having run a solid race, the Josh Gifford-trained chestnut was held in fifth place when putting in a short stride and coming down.

Broadheath held the advantage over Two Coppers, Plundering, Strands Of Gold and Maori Venture over the last two fences, yet the final push to the line seemed to run in ultra-slow motion, with all the runners exhausted and virtually walking. As it was, it was to be Broadheath that emerged the bravest, plugging on to hold the surprising Two Coppers at the line by a length and a half. Two Coppers, trained by Les Kennard, would have been in receipt of 3lbs extra from Broadheath had the weights risen, yet the sporting Kennard refused

Trainer David Barons (left) with his Hennessy winner Broadheath.

to offer this as an excuse for his horse's defeat, stating that Two Coppers ideally desired an absolute mudbath to be at his best, while the going at Newbury – though clearly leaving the horses tired – was officially good to soft. Next home came Maori Venture and Plundering, the pair staying on resolutely at the finish, serving indication as to their Grand National aspirations, which in the case of Maori Venture turned into sweet triumph at Aintree the following April. Strands Of Gold finished fifth but showed that, if conditions suited, he was capable of holding his own in the important staying chases.

Nicholls – a future trainer of the highest standard – was delighted with the progress Broadheath had made since joining the yard from David Nicholson in 1985, with his solid jumping and rugged determination key to his success. Nicholls, who had moved to Barons' yard following spells at the stables of Josh Gifford and Kevin Bishop, had only been made the stable's number one jockey at the start of the season, and it was by far the biggest win of his career to date.

Broadheath had now won eight times for Barons and, while the horse was never destined to be a true superstar like some of the horses that recently preceded his Hennessy win, such as Bregawn and Burrough Hill Lad, Broadheath had proved to be the toughest horse on show at Newbury in 1986, battling his way home to become the thirtieth winner of the Hennessy Cognac Gold Cup.

1986 HENNESSY COGNAC GOLD CUP RESULT

FATE	HORSE	AGE/WEIGHT	JOCKEY
1st	BROADHEATH	9.10.5	P. NICHOLLS
2nd	TWO COPPERS	11.10.0	B. POWELL
3rd	MAORI VENTURE	10.10.13	STEVE KNIGHT
4th	Plundering	9.10.12	P. Scudamore
5th	Strands Of Gold	7.10.3	M. Dwyer
6th	Stearsby	7.10.9	G. McCourt
7th	The Catchpool	7.10.0	K. Mooney
8th	The Langholm Dyer	7.10.3	P. Tuck
9th	Tracys Special	9.10.0	L. Harvey
Fell	Door Latch	8.11.1	R. Rowe
Pulled Up	Charter Party	8.11.7	R. Dunwoody
Pulled Up	Everett	11.11.7	S. Shilston
Pulled Up	Arctic Beau	8.10.5	H. Davies
Pulled Up	Church Warden	7.10.0	C. Brown
Pulled Up	Quick Trip	7.10.0	Mr D. O'Connor

22 November 1986
Going – Good to Soft
Winner – £17,448
Time – 6 mins 55.8 secs
15 Ran
Winner trained by David Barons at Woodleigh, Devon
Winner bred by P.J. McGee
Winner owned by Mr & Mrs M.L. Marsh
Broadheath, bay gelding by Master Owen – Lady Conkers.

Betting – 5/1 Charter Party, 6/1 Broadheath, 13/2 Door Latch, 15/2 Stearsby & Strands Of Gold, 9/1 Church Warden, 10/1 Plundering & The Langholm Dyer, 16/1 Everett & Maori Venture, 20/1 Arctic Beau, 25/1 The Catchpool, 33/1 Quick Trip, 40/1 Tracys Special, 50/1 Two Coppers.

1987

PLAYSCHOOL

The top two novice chasers from the previous season became the two market leaders for the 1987 Hennessy Cognac Gold Cup. Despite a cluster of competing veterans, including the two most recent Hennessy winners, Galway Blaze and Broadheath, it appeared that both the Toby Balding-trained Kildimo and the David Barons-trained Playschool were a cut above their rivals in the 1987 renewal, the pair boasting talent and class as well as rich potential.

Kildimo had been, for some time, the clear ante-post favourite for the Hennessy following an outstanding novice season in which his victories had included a seven-length success in the Sun Alliance Chase at the Cheltenham Festival. A tough, sure-staying seven-year-old, Kildimo had begun the current campaign with victory over Playschool at Cheltenham. The downside of that win was that Kildimo returned home with a thorn in his foot and, although the horse did not miss any work because of it, Balding did admit that the Hennessy favourite had been suffering somewhat. In spite of this, both Balding and big-race jockey Graham Bradley were ultra-confident that Kildimo would win the Hennessy, with the betting public agreeing, sending the horse off a strong 2/1 favourite.

Playschool, a tough, stocky, bay horse with a white face, had similarly been a fine novice chaser, although he had seen his colours lowered by Kildimo in the Sun Alliance Chase. Playschool's main strengths were terrific stamina coupled with the ability to gallop relentlessly, and Newbury's flat track and the Hennessy's distance were expected to suit the youngster greatly. Playschool, purchased in New Zealand as a three-year-old by Barons, was partnered by Paul Nicholls, who had ridden the stable's Broadheath to victory twelve months previously and who rated Playschool a superior prospect to the 1986 hero. Playschool started the

race four points behind Kildimo at 6/1, partly because of the absence of his preferred soft ground but mainly because it was hard to envisage – on all known form – Playschool outgunning Kildimo, his nemesis on more than one occasion in the past, despite an advantage at the weights.

Newcomers to the race included West Tip, Gainsay and Durham Edition. West Tip, a brilliant jumper and a most reliable and consistent performer, was one of the most popular horses in training. From the yard of Worcestershire trainer Michael Oliver, West Tip had won the Grand National in 1986 and was a specialist in that particular race, while he also had enough class to compete in many of the top chases including the Cheltenham Gold Cup, a race where he had finished fourth behind The Thinker in March. Gainsay was trained by Jenny Pitman and owned by Hot Chocolate singer Errol Brown. Despite being a talented horse, the front-running Gainsay came from an out-of-form stable, although

Contradeal goes to post under jockey Kevin Mooney.

Playschool has the lead over Contradeal at the second-last fence.

in the Hennessy the horse would be receiving weight from the likes of Run And Skip, West Tip and Kildimo. Durham Edition was a big, raking chestnut that hailed from the yard of Arthur Stephenson. A superb jumper and thorough stayer, Durham Edition had made his name in lower-class company in the North, but the feeling was that he was a horse capable of landing one of the season's major staying chases, whether it be the Hennessy or another contest.

As expected, Run And Skip and Gainsay set about their normal front-running tactics, yet it was the presence of a third horse, Midnight Madness, that really contributed to a whirlwind early pace, a gallop so searching that a thorough test of stamina was assured. The front three had begun the race with such recklessness that a let-down in the pace seemed inevitable,

with the likes of Playschool, Kildimo and the Fulke Walwyn-trained Contradeal (second in April's Whitbread Gold Cup), patiently waiting their turn to attack.

With the rank outsider Sam Da Vinci having fallen at the fourth, the field reached halfway with the pace having taken its toll on a number of runners. Golden Minstrel and Broadheath were struggling badly, while it was especially sad to see the 1985 hero, the injury-plagued Galway Blaze, losing touch and tailing off, eventually being pulled up before the sixteenth fence. West Tip and Durham Edition, although valiantly chasing the leaders, seemed taken off their feet and, when the three early leaders gradually began to fade from the sixteenth, the main players were Playschool, Contradeal and Kildimo.

Playschool sets sail up the run in having safely negotiated the final fence.

Playschool jumped emphatically to the front at the cross fence, the horse having found his rhythm ominously well under Nicholls yet, at the same fence, the favourite Kildimo virtually extinguished his chance with a terrible blunder. Consequently, straightening for home, the race lay between Playschool and Contradeal. Contradeal was brave and resilient, yet Playschool had travelled superbly throughout, jumping with delightful precision and, when Contradeal made an error three out, the race was Playschool's to lose.

The dynamic early pace had benefited Playschool immensely. Here was a horse that greatly appreciated a thorough test of stamina and, thwarting a renewed effort from Contradeal in decisive fashion, Playschool was driven out strongly by Nicholls and won by five lengths. Following the front two home was Durham Edition, staying on bullishly to take third, and he, like

West Tip, would develop into a fine Grand National specialist, finishing an agonising second to Rhyme 'N' Reason in 1988 having led over the last fence, and filling the same position in a breathtaking, race-record-time-breaking duel with future Hennessy contestant Mr Frisk in 1990. Kildimo had been somewhat disappointing and had to settle for fourth, having been out-jumped and out-fought on this occasion by his old rival Playschool.

The result did not deter Balding from stating that he hoped Kildimo would win the Gold Cup at Cheltenham the following March yet, in the months between Newbury and Cheltenham, it was to be Playschool that established himself as the horse to beat in the Blue Riband event. Defeating the Welsh Grand National field in December, Playschool then won the Irish Gold Cup at Leopardstown and, when the ground came up soft at Cheltenham in March,

Mr and Mrs Cottle with their Hennessy winner Playschool.

1987 HENNESSY COGNAC GOLD CUP RESULT

FATE	HORSE	AGE/WEIGHT	JOCKEY
1st	PLAYSCHOOL	9.10.8	P. NICHOLLS
2nd	CONTRADEAL	10.10.12	K. MOONEY
3rd	DURHAM EDITION	9.10.5	S. SHERWOOD
4th	Kildimo	7.11.5	G. Bradley
5th	Midnight Madness	9.10.0	D. Morris
6th	West Tip	10.11.8	R. Dunwoody
7th	Golden Minstrel	8.10.1	R. Rowe
Fell	Sam Da Vinci	8.10.1	D. Dutton
Pulled Up	Run And Skip	9.11.10	P. Scudamore
Pulled Up	Galway Blaze	11.11.1	S. Smith-Eccles
Pulled Up	Gainsay	8.10.13	M. Pitman
Pulled Up	Broadheath	10.10.11	H. Davies

28 November 1987
Going – Good
Winner – £29,498
Time – 6 mins 46.8 secs
12 Ran
Winner trained by David Barons at Woodleigh, Devon
Winner bred by R.J. Poole
Winner owned by Mr R.E.W. Cottle
Playschool, bay gelding by Valuta – Min Tide

Betting – 2/1 Kildimo, 6/1 Playschool, 13/2 Contradeal, 7/1 Gainsay & Run And Skip, 10/1 Durham Edition, 16/1 Galway Blaze & West Tip, 20/1 Midnight Madness, 25/1 Broadheath & Golden Minstrel, 33/1 Sam Da Vinci.

he looked destined for the ultimate prize. Unfortunately for Playschool, it all went wrong on the day, with the horse running so miserably that Barons insisted something had happened to affect the horse's performance. However, post-race tests showed nothing, although Barons remained adamant that his horse had been 'got at', and Playschool's 1988 Gold Cup run – a race won by former Hennessy favourite Charter Party – remains one of the most baffling and mysterious of any in the modern era of the sport.

Despite what happened to him at Cheltenham, Playschool was one of the outstanding Hennessy winners of the 1980s, giving Barons and Nicholls consecutive victories in the race, a feat no trainer/jockey combination had achieved since Tom Dreaper and Pat Taaffe with Arkle in the 1960s, and the fact that the 1986 and 1987 triumphs had been achieved with different horses spoke volumes about the abilities of both men. In 1991, with Nicholls then part of the training team at Woodleigh in Devon, Barons saddled Seagram, another New Zealand-bred horse, to win the Grand National in what was the trainer's finest hour. It was not long after that race that Nicholls applied for a training licence of his own and, in a very short space of time, he established himself as one of the best young trainers in the sport. Although Derek Ancil had trained and ridden Knucklecracker to success in 1960, by 2003, Nicholls had also trained a Hennessy winner, making him only the second trainer (Andy Turnell was the first in 1993) to win the race having previously won it as a jockey.

1988

STRANDS OF GOLD

When he had finished fifth behind Broadheath in the 1986 Hennessy, the talented bay chaser Strands Of Gold had been trained by Jimmy Fitzgerald in Yorkshire. However, since that time, the horse's career had petered out somewhat into a series of disappointing runs, and when Strands Of Gold finished last in a race at Market Rasen in January 1988, his chasing career was at a crossroads. Deciding that the horse needed a change of scenery, owner Steve White opted to remove Strands Of Gold from Fitzgerald's stable and place the horse in the yard of the Somerset-based Martin Pipe, one of the most rapidly ascending trainers in the business. Unfortunately for Fitzgerald, he was on holiday at the time of the transaction and, on returning to Yorkshire, the trainer was understandably annoyed to find Strands Of Gold's box empty. However, the move had the desired affect, as Strands Of Gold seemed rejuvenated at Pipe's stable. Pipe quickly discovered that the horse had been suffering from arthritis in his leg, and was able to correct this sufficiently by putting the horse through hours of beneficial swimming sessions. By the end of that season, the horse ran three times for Pipe, including in the Grand National where, travelling like the winner, he tipped up in the lead at the second Becher's Brook. That bold run at Aintree was followed by an excellent third to the brilliant grey Desert Orchid in the Whitbread Gold Cup at Sandown. The good ground at Newbury for the 1988 Hennessy Cognac Gold Cup was thought to be ideal for Strands Of Gold and, even though it was his first run of the season (the horse had won first time out the previous three years), he carried much support in the betting market, starting at 10/1 with the Champion Jockey Peter Scudamore in the saddle.

Favourite for the 1988 Hennessy was the eight-year-old Cavvies Clown. The horse was trained by the reigning Champion Trainer, David Elsworth, who could boast that he trained the 1988 Grand National winner Rhyme 'N' Reason and the imminent Cheltenham Gold Cup hero Desert Orchid.

In retrospect, Cavvies Clown should have given Elsworth a first success in the Gold Cup in March, but the horse had blundered the second-last fence very badly, relinquishing a winning position and virtually gifting the race to Charter Party. Cavvies Clown was a thorough – albeit sometimes sluggish – stayer that really appreciated the mud, so it was somewhat of a surprise, despite his talent, that he started favourite, given his big weight of 11st 9lbs and the presence of genuinely good ground.

Joint top weights with 11st 13lbs each were Kildimo, the previous year's favourite, and the French challenger Nupsala. Trained by Francois Doumen, Nupsala had stunned many when winning the King George VI Chase at Kempton, beginning a fine sequence in that particular race for his trainer. The horse then ran in the Gold Cup at Cheltenham, but found the soft ground against him there, while he also went winless in five subsequent races in France due to similar conditions. Ridden by André Pommier, Nupsala carried the extreme confidence of Doumen, who claimed the nine-year-old to be in better form than ever as he attempted to become the first French-trained winner of the Hennessy.

The Hennessy favourite Cavvies Clown and jockey Russ Arnott.

Well-fancied, High Edge Grey was a faller during the race.

As well as Kissane, one of the top staying novices from the previous season, and the sound-jumping Handy Trick from the yard of Arthur Stephenson, Mr Frisk and High Edge Grey were others to command attention. A front-running chestnut, Mr Frisk was one horse expected to love the top of the ground. Trained by Kim Bailey and ridden by Richard Dunwoody, the nine-year-old had won a three-mile amateur handicap chase at Ascot recently. High Edge Grey was trained in Scotland by Ken Oliver, who compared the horse favourably to his 1979 Hennessy winner Fighting Fit. Only a seven-year-old, High Edge Grey had been used to running in lower-class races in the North, but a recent Wetherby success over the talented Yahoo had temporarily placed him at the top of the ante-post market for Newbury, and he entered the race unbeaten in three runs during the season.

As expected, Mr Frisk set the early pace, pressed hard by Midnight Madness and Kissane, with Strands Of Gold handily placed just in behind these. At the sixth fence, runners seemed to bunch together and jumping room became tight. The chief victim of this incident was Kildimo, who was badly hampered. Struggling thereafter, Kildimo was eventually pulled up by jockey Jimmy Frost at the thirteenth. A fence after Kildimo's exit, High Edge Grey became the next casualty. Having jumped well for the most part, the Scottish raider was in touch with the leaders when he came down frustratingly, while struggling towards the rear was the French horse Nupsala, and he failed to make any impact on the second circuit.

Jumping the cross fence five out and turning for home, it was Mr Frisk that remained in the lead, but Scudamore was beginning a forward move on Strands Of Gold, overtaking the weakening pair of Handy Trick and Kissane as they faced up to the first in the home straight. Having jumped with great enthusiasm throughout the race, Strands Of Gold came to join the long-time leader Mr Frisk at the third last and, with another immaculate leap, seized the lead for good with two to jump.

From that moment, the race was over. Scudamore kept Strands Of Gold going strongly, the horse displaying the fine fitness that would become a trademark of Pipe's skills as a trainer and, staying on stoutly to the line, Strands Of Gold became the first horse since Diamond Edge to win the Hennessy on his seasonal debut. Handy Trick, who had rallied past Mr Frisk over the final fences, was six lengths back in second having jumped like a giant throughout, while third-placed Mr Frisk was quickly earmarked for the Grand National by Bailey, a race that the brilliant front-runner would eventually capture on blazing fast ground in 1990. Despite again looking lazy on ground just too quick for him, Cavvies Clown proved his stamina by staying on doggedly for fourth while Nupsala was a real disappointment, trailing in last.

It was the biggest success of Martin Pipe's training career at that point, and was followed a month later by a victory for Bonanza Boy in the Welsh Grand National, the first of five winners that Pipe has trained in that race, in addition to a further two Hennessys, three Whitbread Gold Cups, two Champion Hurdles and a Grand National, to merely name but a few of his big-race successes. Once tagged solely as a trainer of hurdlers, it was the classy chestnut Beau Ranger – third in the 1988 Gold Cup – that really kick-started Pipe's career training chasers. Now that Strands Of Gold had set the standard for future success, there would be no stopping Pipe and his revolutionary training methods, his team in Somerset swelling to army-like status during the next fifteen years as he targeted, and predominantly conquered, every major race in the land with a huge squad of talented, ultra-fit horses that helped to make Pipe the most successful trainer of his era – and, some would argue, through sheer volume alone, the greatest of all time. Pipe eventually retired at the conclusion of the 2005/06 season, handing the reigns of his powerful stable to son David.

Strands Of Gold jumps the last fence en route to victory.

Peter Scudamore rode his first Hennessy winner in 1988.

1988 HENNESSY COGNAC GOLD CUP RESULT

FATE	HORSE	AGE/WEIGHT	JOCKEY
1st	STRANDS OF GOLD	9.10.0	P. SCUDAMORE
2nd	HANDY TRICK	7.10.2	M. HAMMOND
3rd	MR FRISK	9.10.2	R. DUNWOODY
4th	Cavvies Clown	8.11.9	R. Arnott
5th	Midnight Madness	10.10.0	Mr R. Greene
6th	Bucko	11.10.2	M. Dwyer
7th	Gala's Image	8.10.0	B. Powell
8th	Nupsala	9.11.13	A. Pommier
Fell	High Edge Grey	7.10.5	T. Reed
Pulled Up	Kildimo	8.11.13	J. Frost
Pulled Up	Kissane	7.10.13	T. Morgan
Pulled Up	On The Twist	6.10.0	G. Landau

26 November 1988
Going – Good
Winner – £29,543 50p
Time – 6 mins 37.8 secs
12 Ran
Winner trained by Martin Pipe at Nicholashayne, Somerset
Winner bred by D. Turnbull
Winner owned by Independent Twine Mnfct. Co.
Strands Of Gold, bay gelding by Le Coq D'Or – Sweet Fanny

Betting – 7/2 Cavvies Clown, 11/2 Kildimo, 6/1 Handy Trick & Nupsala, 7/1 High Edge Grey, 10/1 Strands Of Gold, 11/1 Mr Frisk, 12/1 Kissane, 14/1 Bucko, 18/1 Gala's Image, 20/1 Midnight Madness, 200/1 On The Twist.

1989

GHOFAR

The presence of lightning-quick ground at Newbury due to an extended dry spell led to the field for the 1989 Hennessy Cognac Gold Cup cutting up considerably. Come the day of the big race, only eight horses faced the starter, the majority of which were fast-ground specialists. Despite the small size of the field, 1989's renewal was by no means a weak edition; in fact, many of the runners were at the peak of their powers having either recently won, or were soon to win, some of the most important chases in the National Hunt calendar.

Quite rightly, the favourite was the hugely talented Brown Windsor, a rapidly improving little bay horse from the yard of Nicky Henderson. The seven-year-old was in his first season removed from novice company and was a young horse fast becoming a major force to contend with. Brown Windsor had taken to chasing brilliantly as a novice, winning on his debut at Newbury and following that up with a win at the 1988 Hennessy meeting, beating the gifted but tragically ill-fated David Elsworth-trained prospect Sir Blake. Having placed third in the Sun Alliance Chase at the Cheltenham Festival, Brown Windsor was having only his sixth outing over fences when winning the Whitbread Gold Cup from 5lbs out of the handicap in April to really announce his arrival on the chasing scene. Now the horse was in a position to join an elite group consisting of Taxidermist, Arkle, April Seventh and Diamond Edge, as horses that had captured both the Whitbread and the Hennessy in the same calendar year. His chance appeared golden following a twenty-length success on his seasonal debut at Sandown and, with Richard Dunwoody in the saddle, Brown Windsor began the race the red-hot 7/4 favourite.

Among the fast-ground specialists in the field were Mr Frisk and Durham Edition, two veterans of Hennessys past. Despite being principally aimed

at the 1989 Grand National, Mr Frisk had been withdrawn from that race by trainer Kim Bailey because of heavy ground yet, on his favoured quick going, the front-running chestnut was a match for any horse, despite a hefty weight of 11st 8lbs. Durham Edition had, however, run in the 1989 Grand National and, despite running a fine race for the second consecutive year, the big horse simply could not quicken on the surface in the closing stages, eventually finishing fifth behind surprise winner Little Polveir. Durham Edition had looked as good as ever at the beginning of the current season, running really well to win the respected Charlie Hall Chase at Wetherby, defeating good horses such as Hennessy top weight Ballyhane and the Cheltenham Gold Cup runner-up Yahoo, and Durham Edition proved very popular on the day of the Hennessy, with Arthur Stephenson's big chestnut starting at 5/1 joint-second favourite.

The 1989 field also contained Ballyhane, the bottom weight Solidasarock, the useful Gala's Image, the most recent Scottish Grand National winner Roll-A-Joint and the six-year-old Ghofar. Having recently lost a talented young horse in Sir Blake, trainer David Elsworth was very confident in the ability of Ghofar, a chestnut with a big white face. Ghofar had won three times as a novice chaser and was a reliable jumper for a horse so young. Having most recently finished second to Man O' Magic over two-and-a-half miles at Ascot, Ghofar was expected to relish the extension in trip in the Hennessy, as well

David Elsworth, trainer of Ghofar.

Mr Frisk (2) jumps the final fence in the lead from Brown Windsor (blue cap, sleeves) and the hidden Ghofar.

The white-faced Ghofar emerged victorious from a titanic struggle for the 1989 Hennessy.

as the fast ground. Partnering the horse was Welshman Hywel Davies, called up after Dunwoody opted to ride Brown Windsor and regular pilot Brendan Powell chose Roll-A-Joint out of loyalty to trainer Chris Popham.

There had been some tremendous battles for Hennessy glory throughout the history of the great race, yet the finish that lay in store for the 1989 renewal was perhaps the most enthralling to date. As Roll-A-Joint – a prolific winner from the year before – and Mr Frisk set about blazing a furious trail right from the get-go, the first casualty came at the opening fence when Solidasarock sent Peter Scudamore clattering to the Newbury turf, a fall that somewhat impeded the following Ballyhane.

The seven remaining runners continued to race at a heart-thumping pace, Roll-A-Joint and Mr Frisk showing the way to the blinkered youngster Ghofar, with Durham Edition, Brown Windsor, Ballyhane and Gala's Image all well placed in behind and fencing well. By the time the field had reached the fifth from home, the gallop had receded somewhat in its ferociousness, yet this failed to stop Roll-A-Joint feeling the strain of the contest as Mr Frisk boldly jumped into the lead and set sail for home with a confident swagger, although every horse in the race still held a chance of winning.

Mr Frisk increased the tempo again in the straight, hard pressed by the dangerous-looking duo of Brown Windsor and Ghofar, while gradually the hopes of Durham Edition, Ballyhane, Roll-A-Joint and Gala's Image ebbed away over the closing fences as the front three displayed uncommon zest and appetite for both the conditions and the battle. Mr Frisk still led at the last but he had 5lbs more to carry than Brown Windsor while Ghofar shouldered just 10st, and the latter two were snapping menacingly at the leader's heels like hungry wolves once on the flat.

Brown Windsor was the first to pass Mr Frisk and, as he did so, a huge roar erupted from the army of favourite-backers in the crowd. But there was more to come as, in behind and waiting patiently was young Ghofar and, halfway up the run-in, Davies sent him surging past the front two. In a pulsating, three-horse finish, the youngster prevailed by a mere neck from the game Brown Windsor and the gallant Mr Frisk in what was a thoroughly riveting conclusion to a top-class race, with the winning time faster by more than a second than Galway Blaze's record set in 1985.

Following the efforts of Mandarin, Taxidermist, Mill House, Spanish Steps and Bright Highway, Ghofar became the sixth six-year-old to win the Hennessy, with great credit going to Elsworth. It was the trainer that realised Ghofar was both a very lively character and also a slightly hesitant jumper when he first started his chasing career, and the fitting of blinkers proved an instant success and helped mould the horse into a fine chaser.

Extremely confident in his horse's jumping and staying ability, Elsworth immediately touted the 1990 Grand National as Ghofar's main target for the season. With Powell back on board, Ghofar was one of a sextet of runners from the 1989 Hennessy to run in the National (Ballyhane and Solidasarock did not), with the ground at Aintree exceptionally firm. Despite handling the big spruce-covered fences well, Ghofar never seriously threatened to become the first seven-year-old since Bogskar in 1940 to win the National, as Mr Frisk won a thrilling race from old adversary Durham Edition in a race where the record time for the Grand National was emphatically shattered. Brown Windsor, with a win in the Cathcart Chase at the Cheltenham Festival preceding his run at Aintree, came fourth, demonstrating the rich form of the 1989 Hennessy, form that was shown again a few weeks later when Mr Frisk concluded his season with another memorable performance to win the Whitbread Gold Cup at Sandown.

1989 HENNESSY COGNAC GOLD CUP RESULT

FATE	HORSE	AGE/WEIGHT	JOCKEY
1st	GHOFAR	6.10.0	H. DAVIES
2nd	BROWN WINDSOR	7.11.3	R. DUNWOODY
3rd	MR FRISK	10.11.8	MR M. ARMYTAGE
4th	Durham Edition	11.11.2	A. Merrigan
5th	Ballyhane	8.11.10	R. Rowe
6th	Roll-A-Joint	11.10.8	B. Powell
7th	Gala's Image	9.10.6	J. Shortt
Fell	Solidasarock	7.10.0	P. Scudamore

25 November 1989
Going – Good to Firm
Winner – £30,271 50p
Time – 6 mins 29.5 secs
8 Ran
Winner trained by David Elsworth
Winner bred by M.Channon
Winner owned by Mr D. Taffner & Sir Hugh Dundas
Ghofar, chestnut gelding by Nicholas Bill – Royale Final

Betting – 7/4 Brown Windsor, 5/1 Durham Edition & Ghofar, 6/1 Ballyhane, 13/2 Roll-A-Joint, 14/1 Gala's Image & Solidasarock, 16/1 Mr Frisk.

1990

ARCTIC CALL

The number of American chasers that had graced the British National Hunt scene in modern times was not high. Fort Devon had run well in numerous big chases during the 1970s, Ben Nevis had surprisingly won the 1980 Grand National and, most recently, Uncle Merlin had made a bold bid to win the 1990 Grand National, duelling with Mr Frisk until capsizing at Becher's Brook second time. Von Csadek – based at Henrietta Knight's stable – was considered the best American chaser to cross the Atlantic for some time.

Although little known in Britain, Von Csadek had been extremely successful in America between distances of three and four miles, winning five of his six races the previous season, his one defeat arriving when unseating his rider when clear in the famous Maryland Hunt Cup. In the autumn of 1990, Von Csadek was carefully introduced to British racing, winning against weak opposition at Uttoxeter and Worcester. Undeniably, his venture into a higher class in the 1990 Hennessy Cognac Gold Cup carried with it some degree of uncertainty, and many – Knight included – wondered if the horse may struggle for speed against trailblazers such as Mr Frisk and Arctic Call, with the ground, as it had been the year before, on the fast side. However, Von Csadek jumped and stayed well and, in the days leading up to the race, disputed favouritism at the top of the betting market with the Oliver Sherwood-trained Arctic Call.

With the David Nicholson stable in tremendous form, the horse that would ultimately start as favourite was the Richard Dunwoody-ridden Sam Da Vinci, a faller in the 1987 Hennessy. Formerly trained by the since-retired John Blundell, Sam Da Vinci was now an eleven-year-old and had run well in the previous two Whitbread Gold Cups – finishing second to the late charge of Brown Windsor in 1989 and then fifth to

Mr Frisk in 1990. With a fair racing weight of 10st 10lbs and fresh from a debut victory for the Nicholson stable earlier in the season at Cheltenham, Sam Da Vinci began the race as 4/1 favourite.

Mr Frisk (still in inspired form following a recent Ascot win but with a huge weight of 12st 1lb to carry) and old rival Durham Edition were back, as was former runner-up Handy Trick, while among the newcomers were the stamina-packed David Barons-trained chestnut Seagram, Cahervillahow, the leading staying novice chaser from Ireland the previous season, and Arctic Call from the Sherwood yard. Arctic Call had been a very good novice the season before and owned a 100 per cent record at Newbury, having won all three of his races there. Formerly trained by Monica Dickinson, the seven-year-old was considered to be on the upgrade but was a somewhat quirky character and a notoriously difficult ride. He was also inclined to make mistakes in his races and had been fitted with blinkers. The horse came to the Hennessy in good form, having won at Newbury two weeks previously, and partnering him on the day was twenty-three-year-old Jamie Osborne, a jockey rapidly soaring through the ranks.

Arctic Call (blue blinkers) jumps the water ahead of Mr Frisk (red cap).

Arctic Call (6) battles Master Bob in the closing stages of the 1990 race.

Jockey Jamie Osborne with the winning trophy.

Oliver Sherwood, trainer of Arctic Call.

Not since Arkle had a horse carried such a big weight to win the Hennessy, yet Mr Frisk was in sparkling form. Having become the first horse to have won the National and the Whitbread in the same season, he now attempted to become the first National winner to take the Hennessy and, in his customary manner, he dictated proceedings on the first circuit, setting a sensible gallop together with Arctic Call.

Von Csadek, at least on the first circuit, proved he could handle the pressure of the big race by confidently lying up with the early pace, while the twelve-year-old Durham Edition was also prominent. Seagram, the favourite Sam Da Vinci and New Halen were among those struggling on the first circuit, but the only casualty came at the eighth fence when the 33/1 shot Wigtown Bay fell.

Having won the race the year before on Ghofar, Hywel Davies was paired with the virtually unconsidered Master Bob on this occasion. Trained by Nicky Henderson, Master Bob had won the Kim Muir Chase at the Cheltenham Festival in March, and the horse came to challenge the leaders at the halfway point in the Hennessy, briefly leading at the tenth fence before Arctic Call regained control a fence later at the water jump.

By the twelfth, Von Csadek was beginning to feel the pace and lost his position in the front rank, while Mr Frisk too was starting to struggle under his big weight burden. The favourite Sam Da Vinci was another under pressure, ominously receiving reminders from Dunwoody halfway down the back straight. At the cross fence, five from home, Arctic Call – having made a hash of the previous fence – bounded onwards, increasing the tempo from Master Bob and Kim Bailey's second runner, Man O' Magic, who was now travelling far stronger than his tiring stablemate Mr Frisk. Entering the home straight, the once-prominent duo of Von Csadek and Durham Edition were now out of contention.

Arctic Call clattered the fourth last, costing him some ground and, by the next fence, Master Bob was pressing him hard under an influential ride from Davies, while outsiders New Halen and Cahervillahow were staying on from further back. Arctic Call was now to show his resilience and toughness. Despite continuing to make jumping errors as well as being chased relentlessly by Master Bob taking the final fence, the horse was driven strongly by Osborne all the way to the line and, finishing powerfully, he deservedly won the Hennessy by two lengths from Master Bob with Cahervillahow staying on stoutly for third. The favourite Sam Da Vinci made some headway in the straight without seriously threatening and came fourth. Von Csadek had been left flat-footed in the straight and finished eighth, while Mr Frisk eventually finished tenth, pleasing Bailey nonetheless. Of the remainder, Seagram would become the second consecutive horse to run in the Hennessy then win the Grand National, beating the Cheltenham Gold Cup winner Garrison Savannah at Aintree in April in an epic finish.

Arctic Call had maintained his unbeaten record at Newbury despite some careless fencing. Osborne confirmed the horse to be a difficult ride, one that lost concentration during his races, and stated the blinkers were essential to his success. Osborne had every right to be proud of Arctic Call's win, as the jockey – a rising star in the sport – had broken three vertebrae in a fall at Worcester in April and had been sidelined for the best part of six months.

Arctic Call had been hobdayed before he had joined Sherwood's yard and the horse was owned by an eight-strong syndicate of Lloyds Bank brokers. Still an improving individual, Arctic Call was good enough to contest the 1991 Cheltenham Gold Cup. Unfortunately, his tendency to clout the odd fence resurfaced in that race and he hit the eleventh hard, rattling his confidence so severely he was soon pulled up.

1990 HENNESSY COGNAC GOLD CUP RESULT

FATE	HORSE	AGE/WEIGHT	JOCKEY
1st	ARCTIC CALL	7.11.0	J. OSBORNE
2nd	MASTER BOB	10.10.3	H. DAVIES
3rd	CAHERVILLAHOW	6.11.3	C. SWAN
4th	Sam Da Vinci	11.10.10	R. Dunwoody
5th	New Halen	9.10.0	E. Tierney
6th	Man O' Magic	9.11.4	M. Perrett
7th	Ace Of Spies	9.10.0	M. Lynch
8th	Von Csadek	8.10.11	Mr P. Worrall
9th	Seagram	10.10.8	R. Greene
10th	Mr Frisk	11.12.1	Mr M. Armytage
11th	Handy Trick	9.10.7	G. Bradley
12th	Durham Edition	12.11.2	A. Merrigan
Fell	Wigtown Bay	7.10.0	P. Niven

24 November 1990
Going – Good to Firm
Winner – £36,958
Time – 6 mins 34.5 secs
13 Ran
Winner trained by Oliver Sherwood at Upper Lambourn, Berkshire
Winner bred by Mrs Elinor M. Hoyne
Winner owned by Mr B.T. Stewart Brown
Arctic Call, bay gelding by Callernish – Polar Lady

Betting – 4/1 Sam Da Vinci, 5/1 Arctic Call, 6/1 Von Csadek, 13/2 Man O' Magic, 8/1 Mr Frisk, 10/1 Durham Edition, 11/1 Seagram, 16/1 New Halen, 20/1 Cahervillahow, 33/1 Handy Trick, Master Bob & Wigtown Bay, 40/1 Ace Of Spies.

CHATAM

It had been one of the most remarkable training achievements of recent times when Jenny Pitman sent out her attractive dark-bay horse Garrison Savannah to win the 1991 Cheltenham Gold Cup in March. The horse had contested just one race since winning the Sun Alliance Chase at the previous year's Cheltenham Festival, suffering considerably with shoulder problems in the interim period, with Mrs Pitman putting the horse on a course of therapeutic assistance in the run-up to his big day at Cheltenham. Having beaten the young French horse The Fellow (a future Gold Cup winner himself) in a thrilling finish at Cheltenham, Garrison Savannah – partnered by Mrs Pitman's son Mark – very nearly won the Grand National as well, falling to a heartbreaking defeat in the dying strides to former Hennessy runner Seagram, having been well clear at the final fence.

Those performances at Cheltenham and Aintree – where he jumped immaculately on both occasions – had marked Garrison Savannah down as one of the most talented horses of his generation and made him one of the most cherished individuals to pass through the Weathercock House stables of Jenny Pitman, drawing comparisons with legends such as Corbiere and Burrough Hill Lad. What remained to be seen was how much two such fantastic performances had taken out of Garrison Savannah. Understandably, he was given top weight of 12st for the 1991 Hennessy Cognac Gold Cup, with the previous year's winner Arctic Call next on 11st 2lbs. Garrison Savannah was allowed to take his chance in a highly competitive renewal of the race for two reasons. Firstly, the horse had finished second on his reappearance at Wincanton, prompting both Jenny and Mark Pitman to believe the horse to be in top form, and second, the Newbury ground had dried considerably from earlier in the week to leave the going as good; conditions deemed ideal for the horse. Despite

facing a field of improving and intriguing horses, Garrison Savannah started as joint 6/1 favourite for the Hennessy as he attempted to enhance his lofty status among the best in the sport.

In something of a surprise development, it was the nine-year-old improver Gold Options that shared favouritism with the Gold Cup winner. Trained by Jimmy Fitzgerald, the horse was the subject of a huge ante-post gamble that saw his odds tumble from 25/1 to 10/1 and ultimately to his 6/1 starting price. Gold Options had plenty of speed and had regularly run over far shorter distances in his younger days. However, it was a winning performance over three miles and a furlong at the Grand National meeting in April that led many to believe Gold Options to be capable of landing one of the major staying chases of the season. Gold Options began the season with a three-length second to his talented stablemate Phoenix Gold at Uttoxeter and, with Mark Dwyer in the saddle, proved a very popular selection on the day.

Among the more interesting prospects in the fifteen-strong field were Docklands Express, Party Politics, Rawhide and Chatam. Docklands Express, trained by Kim Bailey, had been one of the most consistent chasers of the previous season, winning both the *Racing Post* Chase at Kempton and the Whitbread Gold Cup at Sandown, although the latter was on a disqualification having initially finished second to former Hennessy runner Cahervillahow. Docklands Express had also fallen, uncharacteristically, at the first fence in the Grand National won by Seagram. Docklands Express had risen dramatically through the weights from the beginning of the previous season yet, despite his small build, the horse possessed tremendous heart and determination. An absolute giant, the brown seven-year-old Party Politics was the biggest horse in training. Considered to be one of the rising young stars of the game, Party Politics had twice won at Newbury the season before yet had looked a little unpolished when running in Garrison Savannah's Gold Cup. With a summer of strengthening behind him, Party Politics – trained by Nick Gaselee – looked primed for a big run in the Hennessy, as he was well-weighted in addition to being a superb jumper. Rawhide, another smallish gelding but one with fine stamina, was the latest Hennessy representative seeking to end Ireland's drought in the race that had begun following Bright Highway's win in 1980. A useful stayer and with the assistance of the golden boy of Irish racing in the saddle, Charlie Swan, the worry for Rawhide was the going, as the horse was far better on soft ground. Trained by Martin Pipe, Chatam was not a tall horse, but was stocky and powerful.

Cheltenham Gold Cup winner Garrison Savannah waits at the start of the 1991 Hennessy.

A bay gelding with a white nose, Chatam had won the Cathcart Chase at the 1990 Cheltenham Festival but had not seen the racecourse for 233 days prior to the Hennessy. Chatam was not a graceful horse to watch, sometimes appearing untidy, and came with a quarrelsome temperament, yet he possessed rich drive and tenacity, capable of grinding out a finish with any rival and, with Pipe a master of bringing a horse back to full fitness after a long lay-off, Chatam was respected on the day. Well-weighted and with Peter Scudamore on board, Chatam carried with him the bullish confidence of Pipe into the race.

As the race got under way, Scudamore and Chatam were prepared to bide their time in mid-division as the leaders set a breakneck early pace,

tearing into the first few fences with Cuddy Dale showing the way to Arctic Call, Master Bob, What's The Crack and Party Politics. It was the first two home in the 1990 race, Arctic Call and Master Bob that were the chief components in the fierce gallop. Master Bob led from the fourth to the eighth before Arctic Call, again partnered by Jamie Osborne, stripped him of the lead.

As well as Rawhide and the unreliable jumper Rowlandsons Jewels (placed in the 1990 Welsh Grand National), the horse that was really struggling on the first circuit was Garrison Savannah. Something seemed badly amiss with the Gold Cup winner as he began to lose touch from the sixth fence. The horse made an error at the seventh and later clouted

Party Politics and jockey Andy Adams return having finished second to Chatam (behind).

the fourteenth, a mistake that convinced Pitman to pull up the normally sure-footed gelding. It had been a hugely disappointing run from Garrison Savannah, made all the more confusing since the horse had been working tremendously well beforehand and, mysteriously, Mark Pitman reported him to be fine afterwards. A blood test was ordered by the stewards and, although Garrison Savannah competed for a number of years more, the horse was never to recapture the form of his finest runs at Cheltenham and Aintree, races where he gave everything he had.

With Arctic Call back in command and still going well, there appeared every chance that the 1990 hero could become the first consecutive Hennessy winner since Arkle. But the race started to go wrong for Arctic Call at the eleventh, a ditch, as the horse began to make a strange noise, giving Osborne serious concern. The horse hit the twelfth fence and weakened coming into the home straight, eventually pulling up three out.

With Arctic Call in distress, it was Cuddy Dale – forcefully ridden by Adrian Maguire – that took up the running and led as the home straight loomed. In behind, Scudamore had quietly guided Chatam into a challenging position while Party Politics, Dockland's Express, What's The Crack and Espy all remained in the hunt, but Gold Options lent even more disappointment to favourite backers as he tired rapidly in the home straight, having jumped the cross fence five out with every chance of winning. As the outsider Cuddy Dale slowly began to weaken, Scudamore sent Chatam through on the inside and, with a fine leap, gathered the lead at the third last. Party Politics, Docklands Express, What's The Crack and Espy tried their best to stay with the leader, but Chatam was ploughing home like a steam train, not stopping and, despite jumping left over the remaining fences, the horse's advantage was decisive.

Continuing with a relentless charge to the line, Chatam reached the post a four-length winner over the staying-on Party Politics, with Docklands Express a further seven lengths away in third. Both the placed horses would go on to enjoy fine seasons. With Welshman Carl Llewellyn standing in for the injured Hennessy jockey Andy Adams, Party Politics ran out a thoroughly convincing winner of the Grand National, barely touching the big Aintree fences en route to a fantastic win. As for Docklands Express, he proved a model of consistency, finishing in the frame in each of the King George VI, Gold Cup and Grand National.

Chatam had not jumped with any great flair, that was simply not his style, but he was a solid jumper and had travelled ominously throughout, becoming the fourth second-season chaser in five years to win the Hennessy.

Trainer Martin Pipe stands with his Hennessy victor Chatam.

1991 HENNESSY COGNAC GOLD CUP RESULT

FATE	HORSE	AGE/WEIGHT	JOCKEY
1st	CHATAM	7.10.6	P. SCUDAMORE
2nd	PARTY POLITICS	7.10.5	A. ADAMS
3rd	DOCKLANDS EXPRESS	9.11.0	A. TORY
4th	What's The Crack	8.10.0	B. Dowling
5th	Espy	8.10.3	G. Bradley
6th	Cuddy Dale	8.10.1	A. Maguire
7th	Boraceva	8.10.3	J. Frost
8th	Kirsty's Boy	8.10.0	M. Bowlby
Pulled Up	Garrison Savannah	8.12.0	M. Pitman
Pulled Up	Arctic Call	8.11.2	J. Osborne
Pulled Up	Gold Options	9.10.6	M. Dwyer
Pulled Up	Rowlandsons Jewels	10.10.1	D. Murphy
Pulled Up	Master Bob	11.10.1	R. Dunwoody
Pulled Up	Buckshee Boy	9.10.0	D. Tegg
Pulled Up	Rawhide	7.10.0	C. Swan

23 November 1991
Going – Good
Winner – £37,462
Time – 6 mins 34.5 secs
15 Ran
Winner trained by Martin Pipe at Nicholashayne, Somerset
Winner bred by Alec Head
Winner owned by Dr B. Nolan & Mr A. Nolan
Chatam, bay gelding by Big Spruce – Cristalina

Betting – 6/1 Garrison Savannah & Gold Options, 13/2 Arctic Call & Docklands Express, 7/1 Party Politics, 9/1 Rawhide, 10/1 Chatam & Master Bob, 11/1 Boraceva, 14/1 What's The Crack, 20/1 Espy & Rowlandsons Jewels, 25/1 Cuddy Dale, 100/1 Buckshee Boy & Kirsty's Boy.

While his win was somewhat overshadowed by the poor performances of Garrison Savannah and Gold Options, Chatam had beaten his opposition with the minimum of fuss in a workmanlike fashion.

The result once again demonstrated the quality of trainer Martin Pipe, as Chatam became the second horse he had prepared to win the Hennessy on a seasonal debut. Chatam had been bred by former Derby-winning trainer Alec Head in the USA and had been bought by Pipe out of Criquette Head's stable as a three-year-old. Chatam was something of a character (his mule-like behaviour would worsen with age), yet Pipe always believed in the horse and knew he had a big chase in him, faith that was proudly rewarded as Chatam became the newest Hennessy hero.

SIBTON ABBEY

Looking back from the present day through the rich and exciting history of the Hennessy Cognac Gold Cup, it would be fair to say that the field for the 1992 renewal was one of the classiest ever assembled. Among the thirteen-runner line-up were many horses that had already captured some major chases, while there were also a number of younger horses that would, in time, reach the highest peaks of National Hunt racing.

Those already established in the sport's upper echelon included Chatam, Party Politics and Twin Oaks. As in the year before, Chatam would be having his first run of the season as he looked to join Mandarin and Arkle as a two-time Hennessy winner. Despite the fact that Chatam had 12lbs more to carry than in 1991, the irresistible combination of Martin Pipe and Peter Scudamore ensured the defending champion was well backed, starting joint-second favourite at 9/2. Seemingly well weighted with just 10st 13lbs to carry was April's Grand National hero, the freakishly gigantesque Party Politics. The 1991 Hennessy runner-up had been mightily impressive when winning at Aintree and many believed his ability to front-run and jump precisely could lead to Hennessy glory and a potential bid for the Cheltenham Gold Cup. Despite being lightly raced and best when fresh (as he was at Newbury), a major problem for Party Politics was the state of the ground. The huge horse had come through two wind operations and good ground was seen as imperative to his success yet, for him, the going had unfortunately turned soft on Hennessy day. Another big, bold-jumping mammoth of a chaser graced the race in the form of the popular Northern raider Twin Oaks. Trained by Gordon Richards, Twin Oaks was a twelve-year-old but, because of injury in the middle of his chasing career, the horse was very lightly raced for his age. Twin Oaks was a Haydock Park specialist, but had enough class to

have run in the 1991 Cheltenham Gold Cup, while a victory in the Peter Marsh Chase at Haydock had led to a run in the 1992 Grand National where, despite an enormous weight, he ran well to finish fifth. Unlike Party Politics, Twin Oaks adored soft ground and this led to a gamble on the horse the day before the race as he tried to become the first of his age to win the Hennessy.

While the most recent Scottish Grand National winner Captain Dibble and the injury-riddled but gifted David Nicholson-trained chestnut Gambling Royal had their admirers, the two most interesting – and potentially brilliant – chasers in the 1992 field were The Fellow and Jodami. The Fellow, trained in France by Francois Doumen, had already finished runner-up in a pair of Cheltenham Gold Cups, the first in heartbreaking fashion to Garrison Savannah in 1991 when only a six-year-old, and the second in a blanket finish to Cool Ground in March. A powerfully built bay horse, The Fellow possessed a fine cruising speed and jumped majestically, and had twice won in France in the build-up to the Newbury race, although he too was a horse at his best on good ground. A big, old-fashioned, dark-bay chaser, Jodami had risen merrily through the ranks as a novice the season before under the guidance of trainer Peter Beaumont. A fine jumper, the horse had won nine of his sixteen races and loved soft ground. Having made an encouraging reappearance at Haydock, the lightly weighted Jodami (10st 2lbs) was backed into 100/30 favourite as he attempted to continue the trend set recently by the likes of Playschool, Ghofar, Arctic Call and Chatam; all second-season chasers that won the Hennessy.

After his horse had won at Cheltenham a fortnight before the Hennessy, owner Geoff Hubbard had warned people not to write off his soft-ground loving Sibton Abbey (trained by Ferdy Murphy), yet his advice had fallen on deaf ears, as the horse was allowed to start at 40/1. However, directly from the start, jockey Adrian Maguire set about maximising Sibton Abbey's stamina by keeping the horse in the front line of challengers, with the imposing figures of Party Politics and Twin Oaks also right up with the pace.

With Newbury having taken a pounding from the rain in the weeks leading up to the Hennessy, the ability to thoroughly see out the trip was an absolute necessity on this occasion and the early gallop had a few in trouble immediately, notably Nicky Henderson's runner Sparkling Flame, while Captain Dibble and Mr Boston were also closer to the rear than the lead, as Jodami and The Fellow settled comfortably in mid-division. Party

The chestnut Gambling Royal at the start of the 1992 race.

Politics, Sibton Abbey and Twin Oaks remained in control on the second circuit but there were plenty of horses plotting challenges and, despite hitting the fourteenth, Chatam soon took much closer order, together with Gambling Royal, the cruising Jodami and the French hope The Fellow.

Twin Oaks – with a mighty leap – wrestled the lead from Party Politics five fences out and, from here, the Grand National hero began to struggle, weakening on the unfavourable soft ground and eventually pulling up in the home straight. Twin Oaks only held the lead momentarily however as, by the next fence, the feisty Sibton Abbey was back in front, a move that appeared to demoralise Twin Oaks, and he too began to struggle, and he was fading rapidly when he clouted the second last, pulling up shortly after.

The challenges of both Chatam and Gambling Royal had failed to materialise and, as Sibton Abbey churned onwards, it was Jodami that emerged as the strongest and most threatening of the chasing pack. Jodami had quietly moved forward on the second circuit, stalking the leaders before Mark Dwyer sent him closer after the seventeenth and, as the jockey sat motionless over the final fences, Jodami looked a certain winner.

But Sibton Abbey was brave and warrior-like and, having jumped the last, battled relentlessly to fight Jodami's seemingly inevitable procession towards victory. Realising he was in a dogfight, Dwyer tried to rouse Jodami but, surprisingly, the horse found little and, never giving up under a courageous ride from Maguire, it was Sibton Abbey that held on to become the longest-priced Hennessy winner in history, repelling Jodami by three-quarters of a length, with The Fellow staying on well to take third – despite the soft ground – with Chatam fourth.

The form of the 1992 Hennessy Cognac Gold Cup proved rock solid. Jodami eventually confirmed his undoubted potential by winning the Cheltenham Gold Cup in March, with The Fellow fourth, Sibton Abbey fifth and Chatam eleventh, while The Fellow himself would finally claim a Gold Cup crown of his own, winning emotionally for connections at Cheltenham in 1994.

Sibton Abbey's victory had come as a real surprise but had been confidently predicted by Hubbard himself, and the horse had jumped wonderfully, stayed courageously and relished the conditions on the day. It was the biggest win to date for the Suffolk-based trainer Murphy, and the gripping finish gave further evidence of the unflinching nerve, steely determination and fine horsemanship of Maguire, a man who, on

Above: Sibton Abbey (13) takes the water in the lead from Jodami (7) and Latent Talent (pink).

Below: Northern raider Twin Oaks jumps the water.

Jockey Adrian Maguire holds his Hennessy winner Sibton Abbey. To the left is trainer Ferdy Murphy and right is owner Geoff Hubbard.

Cool Ground, had out-battled the more fancied pair of The Fellow and Docklands Express to win the Gold Cup in March. True, Sibton Abbey was 2lbs out of the handicap, but the horse thoroughly deserved his Hennessy success and, in his future races, proved consistent against, and worthy of facing, the finest chasers in the land.

1992 HENNESSY COGNAC GOLD CUP RESULT

FATE	HORSE	AGE/WEIGHT	JOCKEY
1st	SIBTON ABBEY	7.10.0	A. MAGUIRE
2nd	JODAMI	7.10.2	M. DWYER
3rd	THE FELLOW	7.11.13	A. KONDRAT
4th	Chatam	8.11.4	P. Scudamore
5th	Gambling Royal	9.10.0	R. Dunwoody
6th	Rowlandsons Jewels	11.10.0	D. Gallagher
7th	Captain Dibble	7.10.4	C. Llewellyn
Pulled Up	Twin Oaks	12.11.6	N. Doughty
Pulled Up	Party Politics	8.10.13	D. Murphy
Pulled Up	Sparkling Flame	8.10.6	J. White
Pulled Up	Mr Boston	7.10.0	S. Turner
Pulled Up	Latent Talent	8.10.0	J. Osborne
Pulled Up	Bishops Hall	6.10.0	N. Williamson

28 November 1992
Going – Soft
Winner – £36,160
Time – 7 mins 1.3 secs
13 Ran
Winner trained by Ferdy Murphy at Woodbridge, Suffolk
Winner bred by Richard & David Ferguson
Winner owned by Mr G. Hubbard
Sibton Abbey, bay gelding by Strong Gale – Bally Decent

Betting – 100/30 Jodami, 9/2 Captain Dibble & Chatam, 5/1 The Fellow, 13/2 Gambling Royal, 11/1 Twin Oaks, 12/1 Latent Talent & Party Politics, 25/1 Bishops Hall, 40/1 Sibton Abbey, 50/1 Mr Boston, Rowlandsons Jewels & Sparkling Flame.

COGENT

The Friday of the 1993 Hennessy Cognac Gold Cup meeting was lost due to fog. Happily, come the Saturday, conditions were ideal, with the ground riding on the quick side of good. Another high-calibre field had been assembled for the thirty-seventh running of the race and, while it was a small group numerically at just nine, not one of the runners was without a lively chance in a fascinating renewal.

Jetting into England from their home in Los Angeles, California were Sir Andrew Lloyd Webber and his wife Madeleine, the reason being to view their recent purchase, the favourite for the 1993 Hennessy. The horse in question was the classy but fragile Black Humour, trained by Charlie Brooks. Despite being a third-season chaser, Black Humour was a relatively unexposed individual, and a horse that did not stand a lot of racing. A half-brother to the 1983 Hennessy runner-up Gaye Chance, Black Humour certainly had the potential to figure prominently in one of the season's big chases, but was equally as liable to commit costly errors during his races, such as falling three fences from home when well-positioned in the Cheltenham Gold Cup in March, and it was those kind of mistakes that saw Black Humour labelled a sketchy jumper and a horse that flattered to deceive. Even so, he remained a talented chaser, and the horse had impressed mightily when winning the Charisma Gold Cup at Kempton on his seasonal reappearance, a performance that earned him 7/2 favouritism for the Hennessy.

Although Merry Master (partnered by the first female to ride in the race, Gee Armytage) was the outsider of the field at 20/1, the horse had finished an excellent second in the most recent Scottish Grand National at Ayr, while the remaining seven runners in the race all held solid claims, headed by race newcomers Whispering Steel, Zeta's Lad and Rolling Ball.

Whispering Steel, a natural, fluent-jumping seven-year-old from the yard of Gordon Richards, was attempting to become the first Northern-trained horse to win the Hennessy since Galway Blaze in 1985. With the exception of Black Humour, Whispering Steel was perhaps the most naturally gifted horse in the field, unbeaten in his previous six races, and had been, as a novice, a three-time winner over Haydock's difficult drop fences. The concern regarding Whispering Steel was whether the horse was ready for a test such as the Hennessy, having only recently returned to the racecourse (winning over an insufficient two-and-a-half miles at Ayr) following a nine-month lay-off. Zeta's Lad had been one of the most improved chasers of the previous season, landing a series of staying chases, including the *Racing Post* Chase at Kempton that helped propel him to the top of the Grand National betting market. Tough and a solid jumper, Zeta's Lad was trained by John Upson, who had radiated confidence for his horse before the 1993 Grand National at Aintree, a race that was famously declared void following two false starts, and that confidence remained strongly intact after the horse had finished third in the Irish Grand National

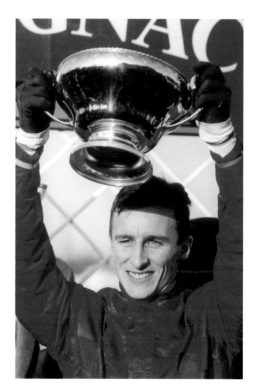

Winning jockey Danny Fortt lifts the trophy.

Whispering Steel (noseband), Cogent (red) and Garrison Savannah jump the water.

at the end of the previous season and then second at Cheltenham on his seasonal reappearance. Having previously saddled both Strands Of Gold and Chatam to win the Hennessy on their seasonal bows, Martin Pipe now tried to do the same with his French import Rolling Ball. Despite being well-weighted, Rolling Ball's task seemed immense, given the fact the horse had not run for nearly two years because of leg trouble, and had only ever run three times over fences. What made Rolling Ball so intriguing was the fact that he had won all three of those chases, including the 1991 Sun Alliance Chase at the Cheltenham Festival.

The field was completed by Garrison Savannah, his stablemate Royal Athlete (third in the 1993 Cheltenham Gold Cup), Cahervillahow and Cogent, a nine-year-old, second-season novice trained by Andy Turnell. Cogent had finished second at Newbury two weeks prior to the Hennessy and was a horse that had 7lbs taken off his back after the appointment of twenty-year-old jockey Danny Fortt as a replacement for Simon McNeill.

It was Merry Master and the extremely keen Rolling Ball that set off at a stupendous pace. Rolling Ball was running very fresh and gave the first two fences a considerable amount of air but, at the third fence, the horse simply never left the ground, running straight into the obstacle and coming down hard. Rolling Ball's exit allowed Gee Armytage to extend her lead, pushing Merry Master ten lengths clear of the pack and, by the fifteenth, the horse still held command from the chasing Whispering Steel, Garrison Savannah and Cogent. Royal Athlete had become the race's second casualty by that time, falling at the thirteenth.

Coming to take the fifteenth fence, Merry Master was showing signs of slowing down and, when the horse made a mistake at the fence, the chasing group smelled blood. By the next, the long-time leader had been engulfed by a glory-hungry pack. Merry Master tried grimly to stay among the leaders but his efforts were to no avail and, with a fine jump at the seventeenth, it was Whispering Steel that took the lead, sending ripples of expectancy through the Newbury stands as the Northern horse sailed effortlessly over the cross fence. At the same fence, both Garrison Savannah and the improving Cahervillahow received reminders, but Black Humour committed a monumental error that saw him touching down sideways, virtually reduced to a walk. The error by Black Humour was all the more frustrating for his followers considering he had jumped immaculately until that moment. Despite losing around six lengths, his race was not over, and jockey Graham Bradley soon had the horse back with the leaders as the field bunched together coming to the first in the home straight.

Whispering Steel remained in the lead but, having looked so dominant at the cross fence, the horse suddenly came under pressure as the race reached boiling point, with Cogent, Cahervillahow, Zeta's Lad and the rallying Black Humour all breathing down his neck. Whispering Steel held a fractional lead over the fourth last but, at the next, Cogent overtook him, as the Northern raider's nine-month absence appeared to have caught up with him. By the second last, Whispering Steel had faded badly, while Zeta's Lad similarly could find no extra, and it was left to Cahervillahow and the favourite Black Humour to try and claw back Cogent.

Black Humour was now looking the strongest of the three as they approached the last, but here the favourite made another critical mistake, jumping wildly out to his left, costing him vital ground. Cogent seized his chance and, powering admirably to the line, the horse held off the threat of Cahervillahow to win by two-and-a-half lengths. The Irish-trained Cahervillahow could be considered one of the unluckiest horses in training. Solid and consistent, the horse had now been placed in two Hennessys, been disqualified after winning the 1991 Whitbread Gold Cup at Sandown, run the whole race in the 1993 Grand National and finished second only for the race to be declared void and also finished as runner-up in the high-profile Ritz Club Handicap Chase at the Cheltenham Festival. Black Humour had contributed much to an eventful race, finishing a further three lengths back in third but returning home lame on his off-fore, although happily Brooks reported the horse to be sound the next day. Zeta's Lad had run a solid race under a big weight, while Richards refused to be downcast over Whispering Steel's somewhat tame finish, suggesting the ground may have been on the quick side for his horse, although the talented chaser was destined never to carve his name onto the roll of honour of one of the sport's big chases.

Cogent had surprised many of the chief contenders by winning the Hennessy. The horse was not especially gifted athletically, but took his fences economically and with assured precision, and had been willing to battle when Fortt asked him for his effort over the final fences. It would be the biggest win of Fortt's career and arrived four years after the jockey – the former captain of the British Junior Showjumping team – had joined Turnell's yard.

Turnell normally used Simon McNeill to partner Cogent (owned by Americans Jim Chromiak and Richard Gilder) but realised that Fortt being able to claim 7lbs would be of huge benefit in a competitive race, and so it proved as Cogent enjoyed a nice weight advantage as he

Cogent (7) has the edge over Black Humour at the final fence.

battled Cahervillahow and Black Humour, both of whom were carrying 11 stone.

Turnell showed true sportsmanship after the race as he spared a thought for Jeremy Glover, the trainer who had done a lot of the work with Cogent only to see the horse transferred to Turnell's yard because it was nearer to the vets where Cogent was at the time receiving treatment for a shoulder injury. Despite pouring much credit upon Glover, Turnell could feel justifiably proud of his achievement, as Cogent's success meant he was now only the second man to have ridden (April Seventh) and trained a winner of the Hennessy, although the first man, Derek Ancil, had ridden and trained the same horse, Knucklecracker in 1960.

1993 HENNESSY COGNAC GOLD CUP RESULT

FATE	HORSE	AGE/WEIGHT	JOCKEY
1st	COGENT	9.10.1	D. FORTT
2nd	CAHERVILLAHOW	9.11.0	A. MAGUIRE
3rd	BLACK HUMOUR	9.11.0	G. BRADLEY
4th	Zeta's Lad	10.11.4	R. Supple
5th	Whispering Steel	7.10.4	N. Doughty
6th	Merry Master	9.10.0	Gee Armytage
7th	Garrison Savannah	10.10.13	B. Powell
Fell	Royal Athlete	10.11.10	J. Osborne
Fell	Rolling Ball	10.10.3	R. Dunwoody

27 November 1993
Going – Good
Winner – £35,152
Time – 6 mins 33.1 secs
9 Ran
Winner trained by Andrew Turnell at East Hendred, Oxon
Winner bred by J. Griffin
Winner owned by Pell-Mell Partners
Cogent, bay gelding by Le Bavard – Cottstown Breeze

Betting – 7/2 Black Humour, 4/1 Whispering Steel, 11/2 Zeta's Lad, 13/2 Rolling Ball, 7/1 Cahervillahow & Royal Athlete, 10/1 Cogent, 16/1 Garrison Savannah, 20/1 Merry Master.

ONE MAN

In a sense, the 1994 running of the Hennessy Cognac Gold Cup was a major chance for one of a batch of emerging horses to propel itself towards the upper levels of chasing's hierarchy. Although a sprinkling of old favourites returned, such as the three most recent Hennessy heroes Chatam, Sibton Abbey and Cogent, plus former Scottish Grand National winner Captain Dibble, the sixteen-strong field for the 1994 race focused more on candidates capable of competing with the very best staying chasers in the land. The 1994 Hennessy arrived at a time when steeplechasing was in need of an injection of fresh, captivating talent, for there seemed somewhat of a dearth of top-class chasers over three miles plus. Although The Fellow had won the most recent Cheltenham Gold Cup, he was now in the veteran stage of his career, while previous winners of the sport's Blue Riband event Garrison Savannah and Jodami appeared on the downgrade. Others such as the tough, consistent chestnut Young Hustler and the stamina-rich Grand National winner Miinnehoma were good horses that had enjoyed some fine moments, yet hardly set the heart aflutter, and even though the rapidly improving grinder Master Oats would jump and gallop his way to a total domination of his rivals over the course of the coming season, the Kim Bailey-trained chestnut was not yet fully established as a Cheltenham Gold Cup-class horse at the time of the Hennessy, and was not even in the field for Newbury. With that in mind, the stage was set for a number of others to make their mark, and into this category fell Dubacilla, Lord Relic, Deep Bramble, Fighting Words, Martomick, Commercial Artist and One Man.

No mare had won the Hennessy since the resolute Kerstin in 1959, but Dubacilla was considered to be one of the finest of her sex to have graced the sport for some time. Dubacilla was a horse on the rise, one that had won nine of thirteen completed chases. With stamina very much her main weapon (she was a half-sister to the dour 1994 Grand National runner-up Just So), Dubacilla had transferred from the yard of her permit-holding owner Henry Cole to the stable of David Nicholson at the start of the season and had readily impressed her new trainer and stable jockey, Adrian Maguire, as she won her first start for them at Sandown three weeks before the Hennessy. Despite having 11st 9lbs to carry, the Sandown win was impressive enough to see Dubacilla start favourite in a very open Hennessy, her odds being 3/1.

The New Zealand-bred Lord Relic was one of three challengers from Martin Pipe's yard (Chatam and the outsider King's Curate were the others). Lord Relic had been a fine staying hurdler two seasons previously but, though undoubtedly talented, was an inexperienced and clumsy chaser. The horse had fallen in two of his three chases, including at Ascot the week before the big race, yet some confidence could be attached to the fact that Champion Jockey Richard Dunwoody chose to partner the young horse in preference to Chatam.

Having been trained in Ireland the season before, Deep Bramble had shown enough progress to run in the 1994 Cheltenham Gold Cup but, on his first appearance for his new Paul Nicholls stable, the horse had disappointed in the Charlie Hall Chase at Wetherby and was considered to have much to prove, while Fighting Words, a good-quality eight-year-old, hailed from the Josh Gifford stable and had won the Kim Muir Chase at the 1994 Cheltenham Festival.

Martomick was the second mare in the field and was a very consistent bay seven-year-old trained by Kim Bailey. Martomick had finished second in the 1994 Sun Alliance Chase and was well weighted with 10st 10lbs, while the Irish hope Commercial Artist – trained by Victor Bowens – had run well in the recent Mackeson Gold Cup at Cheltenham, staying on strongly at the end to finish fourth. But the most intriguing contender to line up for the 1994 Hennessy was the ultra-athletic, spring-heeled grey horse One Man, trained in Cumbria by Gordon Richards. A six-year-old with just 10st to carry, One Man had shot to prominence as a novice, disposing of the majority of his opponents with ease to win his first six chases. One Man then went to the Cheltenham Festival heavily backed for the Sun Alliance Chase, only for the weakness in his game to be ruthlessly exposed, as the final climb up the famous Cheltenham hill seemed to wrench the stamina out of the horse, and he finished exhausted having been well beaten. The doubts remained over One Man's stamina,

Fighting Words (red) and Lord Relic go to post for the 1994 Hennessy.

The wonderful grey horse One Man jumps the last fence on his way to victory.

and some recounted his stablemate Whispering Steel's poor finish of the year before, yet there was a feeling that the grey had unlimited potential, and was more than capable of surviving a three-mile-plus trip around Newbury's flat track, a circuit totally different to Cheltenham's severe undulations. Most were prepared to ignore One Man's performance at Cheltenham, giving the horse the benefit of the doubt, and a huge ante-post gamble on the grey saw his price come tumbling down from 20/1 to 9/4, a price that eased slightly to 4/1 when the ground came up good to soft on Hennessy day.

It was Captain Dibble that was the early leader in the race, showing the way to Cogent, Deep Bramble, Capability Brown, Fighting Words, Commercial Artist, Country Member and One Man while, at the sixth fence, the previous year's winner Cogent assumed control. Towards the rear early on were King's Curate, the held-up Lord Relic and the favourite Dubacilla.

Owner John Hales punches the air in delight following One Man's success.

It was a race of very little incident for much of the way, as Cogent continued to make a strong bid for repeat glory throughout the second circuit, belittling his somewhat offensive odds of 33/1, while, quietly, One Man was running a fine race, jumping very well and perfectly poised behind the leaders under a beautiful tactical ride from Tony Dobbin, one of the fast-rising jockeys in the North. Having blundered the twelfth fence, Dubacilla found herself in serious trouble, for she was already behind and the mistake further separated her from the main pack. It was an error the favourite – normally a very good jumper – was unable to recover from and, although she negotiated the remaining fences safely, the Hennessy would prove a disappointment for Dubacilla and her followers, and she eventually finished seventh.

Having taken the cross fence in front, Cogent was soon pressed by a band of challengers as the field entered the home straight. Although both

Deep Bramble and Fighting Words had begun to struggle after the fifth last, One Man, Commercial Artist, Lord Relic, Chatam, Country Member and Martomick were still in contention.

Martomick was the first to crumble after violently hitting the fourth last, while Chatam and the chestnut Country Member failed to quicken sufficiently, but One Man, having travelled imperiously throughout, was there to throw down the challenge to Cogent three out, chased by Commercial Artist and Lord Relic, the lattermost having made steady headway throughout the second circuit, avoiding his jumping mistakes of previous races.

But this was to be the day One Man announced his talent to the sport with thumping emphasis. Albeit with a featherweight of 10st, the grey horse went clear at the second last and, despite Lord Relic's valiant attempt to stay with him, One Man jumped the final fence in fine style and came home an impressive winner to rich applause. Lord Relic was two lengths back in second with the outpaced Commercial Artist a further five lengths away in third. Cogent had covered himself in glory carrying a hefty 11st 5lbs, running a most spirited race and finishing fourth ahead of another former winner, Chatam. The favourite Dubacilla had disappointed mightily, but she, along with One Man and another race disappointment, Deep Bramble, would be the stars to emerge from the 'new batch' that graced the 1994 Hennessy, with the mare developing into one of the most consistent chasers of the season, finishing second in the Cheltenham Gold Cup and fourth in the Grand National, both times coming from way off the pace to display bravery and stamina.

One Man had shown both his finesse and raw potential on the day, silencing those that had doubted him as he delivered a superb exhibition to point himself towards the top end of the chasing division. His victory gave Gordon Richards a first Hennessy victory from eight attempts, having been well represented in the past through the likes of Playlord, Tamalin and Whispering Steel.

As for One Man (only the second grey to win the race following Stalbridge Colonist in 1966), the 1994 Hennessy signalled the beginning of a long and emotional relationship with the National Hunt scene and the racing public, as he became the most recognisable racehorse of the next four years. Despite his Hennessy-winning season ending with a crushing fall in the *Racing Post* Chase at Kempton, the horse would taste stardom. He was virtually unbeatable for the rest of his career between two-and-a-half and three miles, especially at flat, fast courses like Kempton where he

Winning jockey Tony Dobbin lifts the trophy.

won one of his two King George VI Chases (the other came in the rerouted 1995 race at Sandown) in glorious style. Yet Cheltenham would prove his nemesis. Twice he was heavily fancied for the Gold Cup, including when regarded as a certainty for the 1996 race, but both times the horse failed to last home, as One Man twice deflated from a horse travelling with apparent venom to one running on empty, and the sight of a brutally tired grey ghost clambering over the final fence like a drunken cowboy was almost too much to watch for those that were either connected to the horse or that simply loved and admired his talent. For these episodes, One Man became the great enigma of chasing, a horse clearly with as much natural talent as any that had graced the scene since Arkle, yet blatantly destined never to win the ultimate crown the sport has to offer. Finally, in 1998, One Man buried his Cheltenham hoodoo, but not in the Gold Cup. Instead, quite rightly not wishing to subject his stable star to any more heartbreak in the Gold Cup or incur any more vicious attacks by some sections of the media that had verbally lambasted the horse for his previous Cheltenham endeavours, Richards opted to run One Man in the Queen Mother Champion Chase, the season's top prize for two-milers. In a strongly run race, One Man was able to jump with exuberance and flair, scorching up the finishing hill that had blunted his aspirations so many times before and, fittingly, the reception he received on winning was worthy of a true champion.

But, in the cruellest of twists, One Man was killed at Aintree a few short weeks later, an incident that left Richards speechless. The grey departed racing as one of the most captivating, intriguing, talented and popular of all horses to have graced the sport in the twentieth century, and his name on the list merely glorifies further the inspiring Hennessy roll of honour.

1994 HENNESSY COGNAC GOLD CUP RESULT

FATE	HORSE	AGE/WEIGHT	JOCKEY
1st	ONE MAN	6.10.0	A. DOBBIN
2nd	LORD RELIC	8.10.7	R. DUNWOODY
3rd	COMMERCIAL ARTIST	8.10.11	G. BRADLEY
4th	COGENT	10.11.5	MR C. BONNER
5th	Chatam	10.11.9	G. McCourt
6th	Country Member	9.10.12	L. Harvey
7th	Dubacilla	8.11.9	A. Maguire
8th	Deep Bramble	7.11.8	C. Maude
9th	Sibton Abbey	9.10.10	P. Verling
10th	Tipping Tim	9.11.1	D. Bridgwater
Fell	King's Curate	10.10.0	M. Perrett
Pulled Up	Captain Dibble	9.11.0	J. Osborne
Pulled Up	Givus A Buck	11.10.12	P. Holley
Pulled Up	Fighting Words	8.10.10	P. Hide
Pulled Up	Martomick	7.10.10	N. Williamson
Unseated Rider	Capability Brown	7.10.5	M.A. Fitzgerald

26 November 1994
Going – Good to Soft
Winner – £42,874
Time – 6 mins 37.8 secs
16 Ran
Winner trained by Gordon Richards at Greystoke, Cumbria
Winner bred by H.J. Holohan
Winner owned by Mr J. Hales & Miss L. Hales
One Man, grey gelding by Remainder Man – Steal On

Betting – 3/1 Dubacilla, 4/1 One Man, 11/2 Martomick, 8/1 Captain Dibble, 9/1 Country Member, 11/1 Lord Relic, 12/1 Fighting Words, 14/1 Commercial Artist, 16/1 Tipping Tim, 20/1 Capability Brown, Givus A Buck & Sibton Abbey, 25/1 Deep Bramble, 33/1 Cogent & Chatam, 50/1 King's Curate.

COULDN'T BE BETTER

Two days before the 1995 Hennessy Cognac Gold Cup, the race was shaping up as one of the classiest renewals in recent memory. However, the three horses at the top of the handicap would all be withdrawn before the start of the race. First, trainer Peter Beaumont pulled out his former Gold Cup winner and Hennessy runner-up Jodami forty-eight hours before the race, as he was reluctant to expose his stable star against better-handicapped rivals. Then, when a deluge of rain hit Newbury on the day of the race, Gordon Richards withdrew the favourite, the 1994 winner One Man, and Nigel Twiston-Davies opted not to run top weight Young Hustler, a recent winner of the Becher Chase over the big fences at Aintree.

The defections of the high-profile trio obviously removed a portion of glamour and intrigue from the race, but the eleven horses that remained included some fair horses and, even though the likes of National Hunt stalwarts Cogent, Chatam, Black Humour and Givus A Buck appeared to be somewhat on the downgrade, there were still a number of improving contenders to make the 1995 renewal a most interesting affair.

The pounding Newbury had taken from the elements worked in the favour of Earth Summit, a rugged seven-year-old trained by Nigel Twiston-Davies. Earth Summit was a confirmed mudlark, and the soft going was enough to propel him to favouritism at 3/1. Though the horse was not expected to reach Cheltenham Gold Cup class, Earth Summit was a rock-solid jumper and thorough stayer and had proved his ability by winning the Scottish Grand National when just a six-year-old. With Carl Llewellyn on board, Earth Summit had warmed up for the Hennessy by running with promise at Cheltenham recently.

The nine-year-old bay Rough Quest had, in the past, developed a frustrating habit of throwing away his races, normally through careless fencing. However, there was no doubting Rough Quest had a great deal of talent – as good as any in the 1995 Hennessy field – and was more than capable of winning one of the season's big chases. Trained by Terry Casey, Rough Quest had looked brilliant when cruising to victory in the Ritz Club Handicap Chase at the most recent Cheltenham Festival, and that performance was followed by a win at the Punchestown Festival. Rough Quest was a horse entering his prime, and the 1995/96 season would prove to be the campaign where the horse truly came of age.

Another horse that was considered a soft-ground lover was the progressive eight-year-old Couldn't Be Better. Like Black Humour, Couldn't Be Better was trained by Charlie Brooks, and was generally considered to be the stable's 'second string', a fact backed up by the fact that jockey Graham Bradley opted to ride Black Humour. Bradley's decision puzzled some, however, for Couldn't Be Better had been most impressive when winning the Edward Hamner Chase at Haydock two weeks before Newbury, yet there remained a slight worry over the horse's stamina for the Hennessy because he had, during his career, been recognised as a two-and-a-half mile, horse, a distance that he was certainly quick enough to compete over.

Couldn't Be Better clears the last fence ahead of Rough Quest.

With the weights now headed by the 1994 Sun Alliance Chase winner Monsieur Le Cure, the field were sent on their way. Outsider Bishops Hall was the first to show, with the 1993 winner Cogent also vying for the lead over the early fences. By the tenth fence, Jamie Osborne had steered Rough Quest into the lead, while Grange Brake, Couldn't Be Better and Black Humour were all travelling well in behind. A number of horses were clearly not at their best, such as Givus A Buck (a horse that had originally won the 1993 Whitbread Gold Cup at Sandown only to be disqualified after a stewards' inquiry, giving the race to runner-up Topsham Bay), who hit the sixth and soon became detached, while Cogent blundered the seventh and faded very quickly, eventually pulling up at the twelfth. Bishops Hall, a big, brown gelding, made errors at the twelfth and fifteenth to ruin his chances, while the Jenny Pitman-trained Superior Finish made a mistake at the eleventh and quickly lost his place among the leading group. Yet, of all the strugglers, the most significant was Earth Summit. Despite not being a quick horse, the soft ground had been expected to be in his favour, yet he had been badly outpaced on the first circuit, and he remained towards the rear throughout the race.

Jumping ominously well, it was Rough Quest that led the field over the cross fence, travelling as well as he had when landing the Ritz Club at Cheltenham. Couldn't Be Better was gradually creeping into the race under a patient ride from Dean Gallagher and, heading into the home straight, it was he that challenged Rough Quest for supremacy, tracked most closely by his stablemate Black Humour, with Monsieur Le Cure and Grange Brake next. The top weight Monsieur Le Cure had run a fine race but a mistake at the seventeenth had cost him dearly, losing him ground and momentum and, although Black Humour had jumped immaculately for once, both he and Grange Brake began to fade once in the straight, leaving the race between Rough Quest and Couldn't Be Better.

It was noticeable just how smoothly Couldn't Be Better was cruising through the mud and over the remaining fences; he was able to quicken impressively to edge Rough Quest for the lead by the last. Once Couldn't Be Better had got his head in front, the outcome was inevitable. Rough Quest had run his heart out but his opponent was on top of his game, relishing the conditions and, once on the flat, Couldn't Be Better strode out majestically to become one of the easiest winners in the race's history, carving up the ground to come home a fourteen-length winner from the gallant Rough Quest. Superior Finish stayed on to finish third ahead of Grange Brake and the disappointing Earth Summit. After Earth Summit's

Jockey Dean Gallagher embraces his Hennessy partner Couldn't Be Better following their win.

success at the beginning of his chasing career, the next few seasons would prove most frustrating and, at some points, bleak for him. Later in the season, Earth Summit damaged suspensory tendons when running at Haydock and it was thought the horse would never race again. But after a long, hard road back to fitness, Twiston-Davies' charge stormed back to form at the end of 1997, winning the Welsh National at Chepstow on heavy ground and then, a few months later, beating a future Hennessy hero in Suny Bay in some of the most atrocious ground ever witnessed to win the Grand National at Aintree, completing a marvellous comeback and a heart-warming story.

Couldn't Be Better had indeed proved one of the most routine Hennessy victors of all time, and provided a first win in the race for both Charlie Brooks and Dean Gallagher. Both Couldn't Be Better and Rough Quest

Charlie Brooks, trainer of Couldn't Be Better.

1995 HENNESSY COGNAC GOLD CUP RESULT

FATE	HORSE	AGE/WEIGHT	JOCKEY
1st	COULDN'T BE BETTER	8.10.8	D. GALLAGHER
2nd	ROUGH QUEST	9.10.9	J. OSBORNE
3rd	SUPERIOR FINISH	9.10.0	W. MARSTON
4th	Grange Brake	9.10.0	D. Leahy
5th	Earth Summit	7.10.11	C. Llewellyn
6th	Monsieur Le Cure	9.11.9	J.R. Kavanagh
7th	Chatam	11.10.9	D. Bridgwater
8th	Givus A Buck	12.9.11	A. Procter
Pulled Up	Cogent	11.11.7	S. McNeill
Pulled Up	Black Humour	11.10.5	G. Bradley
Pulled Up	Bishops Hall	9.10.3	P. Carberry

25 November 1995
Going – Soft
Winner – £48,988 80p
Time – 7 mins 3.4 secs
11 Ran
Winner trained by Charlie Brooks at Lambourn, Berkshire
Winner bred by Queenford Stud Ltd
Winner owned by R.A.B. Whittle
Couldn't Be Better, brown gelding by Oats – Belle Bavard

Betting – 3/1 Earth Summit, 4/1 Rough Quest, 5/1 Chatam, 11/2 Black Humour, 15/2 Couldn't Be Better, 8/1 Monsieur Le Cure, 9/1 Superior Finish, 16/1 Cogent, 40/1 Bishops Hall, Givus A Buck & Grange Brake.

continued to run at a high level for the remainder of the season, lending much credibility to the form of the 1995 Hennessy. Couldn't Be Better finished third in the Cheltenham Gold Cup behind the excellent Irish youngster Imperial Call, while Rough Quest proved to be perhaps the horse of the season, finishing second in that same Gold Cup before becoming the most convincing winner of the Grand National in the 1990s, with a brilliant victory at Aintree (Superior Finish was third) under a tactically perfect ride from the up-and-coming Mick Fitzgerald.

COOME HILL

The Grey Monk, a stablemate of the famous One Man at Gordon Richards' yard, was one of the heaviest-backed favourites in the race's history as he took his place in the field for the 1996 Hennessy Cognac Gold Cup. Grey (as his name would suggest), tall and a wonderful, effortless jumper, The Grey Monk – an eight-year-old – had been brought steadily through his novice campaign the season before, winning all six of his chases in low-key company. On his reappearance, the horse demonstrated his progression by putting an albeit ageing Jodami well and truly in his place in the Sean Graham Chase at Ayr, meaning he headed for Newbury unbeaten in seven starts over fences. The horse appeared to have all the attributes of a top-class stayer, and a weak-looking 1996 Hennessy looked ripe for the taking, as The Grey Monk attempted to establish himself as a genuine Cheltenham Gold Cup contender, possibly as an alternative to One Man, who had flopped so badly in that race when favourite in March. Though not as extravagant or as athletic as One Man, The Grey Monk was of a larger build and had more stamina than his illustrious stablemate, and the horse was as safe a jumper as could be found, although he had yet to have that side of his game tested in a top chase. In addition, The Grey Monk had a comfortable weight in the Hennessy, with just 10st 3lbs to carry as he prepared to showcase his talent and climb further up the chasing ladder.

The biggest dangers to The Grey Monk appeared likely to arrive from another pair of youngsters on the rise. Challenger Du Luc, a six-year-old French import to the Martin Pipe yard, was unproven over the Hennessy trip but had responded beautifully to a magnificent Richard Dunwoody ride to win the Murphy's Gold Cup (formerly the Mackeson) at Cheltenham two weeks before Newbury, and the horse now attempted to

become only the third after Bachelor's Hall and Bright Highway to achieve that particular double. Coome Hill, on the other hand, was considered ideal for a race such as the Hennessy; being an improving young horse with plenty of scope and stamina in addition to a low weight. A former point-to-pointer, Coome Hill was trained at permit-holder Walter Dennis' dairy farm near Bude in north Cornwall and was, from all accounts, a lazy worker at home. However, there was no doubting that the seven-year-old was an improving horse and, while most of the hype in the race build-up focused on The Grey Monk, Coome Hill could boast a pair of impressive wins already in the season, including the Badger Beer Chase at Wincanton, and the horse was quietly fancied by many to run a big race at Newbury.

The previous season's Irish Grand National winner Feathered Gale, Lo Stregone – a slow but splendid stayer from Tom Tate's stable – and the consistent grey Dextra Dove were others in the field to attract attention,

Hennessy favourite The Grey Monk goes to post for the 1996 race.

Coome Hill jumps the last fence during his Hennessy victory.

as was the previous year's winner Couldn't Be Better, although he had considerably more weight to carry on this occasion and, on good ground, the runners broke away on their quest for Hennessy glory.

It was Coome Hill, ridden by the winning jockey from 1990, Jamie Osborne, that led, bounding out well over the first six fences, with The Grey Monk, Grange Brake and Lo Stregone in close attendance. Grange Brake and Lo Stregone briefly duelled for the lead but, by the eleventh, Coome Hill resumed control, jumping faultlessly and showing the way in commanding fashion. Jumping like the proverbial stag was the favourite, The Grey Monk. His jockey Tony Dobbin had patiently guided him round the first circuit on the heels of the leaders but, on the second circuit, the horse began to show why so much fuss had been made about him. Jumping with beautiful precision down the back straight, The Grey Monk grabbed the lead at the thirteenth and, by the cross fence five out, the grey looked a certain winner as he travelled superbly with Coome Hill next, followed by Lo Stregone, Midnight Caller, Grange Brake, Dextra Dove and General Crack. One horse that would not be contesting the finish was Challenger Du Luc, the youngster having taken a thunderous fall at the fourteenth, although happily he survived, with a King George VI Chase runner-up place waiting in his future.

Despite a last-fence blunder, Dextra Dove recovered to finish fifth.

Winning trainer Walter Dennis receives the trophy from the Queen Mother.

Sensing his horse was relishing the occasion, Dobbin sent The Grey Monk sailing for home very early in the home straight, as the crowd rose to their feet in anticipation of cheering home a winning favourite. Behind him, Midnight Caller and General Crack had weakened, while Lo Stregone and Dextra Dove were outpaced as the tempo quickened. Grange Brake – totally unconsidered at 100/1 – was hanging on defiantly, and it appeared that he and Coome Hill were the last two threats to the favourite.

Coome Hill was resilient but, having led for a long way, it seemed The Grey Monk had his number, having overtaken him coming into the straight. However, despite being 2lbs out of the handicap, Coome Hill too had stamina in reserve and, although The Grey Monk held the lead over the first three fences in the home straight, the tall grey had not quickened as impressively as had been expected. Approaching the last, it was evident that, although not overly tired, the favourite was merely galloping at one pace.

Driven hard by Osborne, Coome Hill responded brilliantly, stalking The Grey Monk two out and, when he surged past the favourite with an impressive burst on the run to the last, the race was his, as those in the crowd that had backed the Cornish raider elevated their support, much to the disbelief of favourite backers, who only a number of fences earlier had seemed sure of celebrating a win for The Grey Monk.

Grange Brake was held in third place when he blundered and unseated David Walsh at the final fence, as Coome Hill flew the last out in front and, churning up the run-in, ran out a four-length winner following a tenacious fight-back. The Grey Monk had done little wrong and had jumped without error the entire race but, having had the others in trouble after making his bid for glory, he had appeared to lack the quickness of a real superstar and, while he had galloped all the way to the line, he had unfortunately been matched against a horse at his peak – and one that possessed slightly more speed over the Hennessy distance – in Coome Hill. Though his colours had been lowered on this occasion, The Grey Monk remained one of the most talented and popular chasers in the game for a number of years. Though injuries and the horse's dislike for ground faster than soft hampered his trainer's intentions to run The Grey Monk in races such as the Cheltenham Gold Cup and the Grand National, the horse always acquitted himself well when raced (which sadly was all too infrequently), finishing third in the season's Irish Grand National as well as winning the Tommy Whittle Chase at Haydock the following season. Lo Stregone had similarly been unable to quicken in the closing stages, yet that was expected of the dour stayer, and his third-place finish was seen as a fine achievement. Tate was delighted with Lo Stregone's run, and the trainer stated that the Grand National would be the horse's chief target. Lo Stregone had been among the favourites for the 1996 National, only to be withdrawn at the last minute with equine flu, and his run at Aintree in 1997 brought no joy either, pulling up behind the New Zealand-bred Lord Gyllene. Of the others, Couldn't Be Better had disappointed, appearing to sulk towards the rear of the field for much of the way, eventually finishing eighth.

The victory of Coome Hill was a feel-good story for a small stable. With the famous yards of Pipe, Nicholls, Twiston-Davies and Richards all represented in the race, a little dairy farm in Cornwall had produced the newest Hennessy hero. The victory, which naturally filled Dennis with pride, was a real credit to the permit holder, who had bought Coome Hill as a four-year-old in Ireland. Having been patiently guided through the point-to-point arena, Coome Hill now seemed ready to challenge the best in the sport at a time where all the major staying chases were open to improvers and up-and-coming horses. Coome Hill had won the Hennessy with authority, and it was Dennis' belief that the horse could reach the very top. Despite some niggling setbacks, Coome Hill contested the Cheltenham Gold Cup the following March, starting among the favourites at 15/2, running well for a long way and eventually finishing with some credit in seventh behind the rangy chestnut Mr Mulligan, one of the star novices of the season before. The horse also ran in the 1999 Grand National, although injuries he sustained in that race led to the horse ultimately, very sadly, being put down, albeit some time later following an operation. However, Coome Hill had enjoyed his finest moment at Newbury in 1996 and, during his career, the horse competed in many of National Hunt's finest races, realising the dream of Walter Dennis, the dairy farmer from Cornwall.

1996 HENNESSY COGNAC GOLD CUP RESULT

FATE	HORSE	AGE/WEIGHT	JOCKEY
1st	COOME HILL	7.10.0	J. OSBORNE
2nd	THE GREY MONK	8.10.3	A. DOBBIN
3rd	LO STREGONE	10.11.0	C. SWAN
4th	Midnight Caller	10.10.1	M.A. Fitzgerald
5th	Dextra Dove	9.10.1	C. Maude
6th	Feathered Gale	9.10.11	F. Woods
7th	Old Bridge	8.10.0	S. McNeill
8th	Couldn't Be Better	9.11.10	G. Bradley
Fell	Challenger Du Luc	6.10.10	N. Williamson
Pulled Up	General Crack	7.10.0	P. Hide
Unseated Rider	Grange Brake	10.9.12	D. Walsh

30 November 1996
Going – Good
Winner – £48,283 20p
Time – 6 mins 40.6 secs
11 Ran
Winner trained by Walter Dennis at Bude, Cornwall
Winner bred by Mrs S. O'Connell
Winner owned by Mrs Jill Dennis
Coome Hill, bay gelding by Riot Helmet – Ballybrack

Betting – 13/8 The Grey Monk, 11/2 Challenger Du Luc & Coome Hill, 7/1 General Crack, 10/1 Lo Stregone, 12/1 Dextra Dove, 14/1 Feathered Gale, 16/1 Couldn't Be Better, 20/1 Midnight Caller, 25/1 Old Bridge, 100/1 Grange Brake.

SUNY BAY

The most recognisable voice ever to be associated with the sport had selected the 1997 Hennessy Cognac Gold Cup as his final race to call. Sir Peter O'Sullevan, whose rousing and emotive commentaries had for so long brought colour, passion and inspiration to television and radio broadcasts, was retiring, with the Newbury spectacle chosen to be his swansong. O'Sullevan's voice was synonymous with all the top races such as the Grand National, Gold Cup, Epsom Derby and, of course, the Hennessy, and his unmistakable tones were the constant link for viewers or listeners to generation after generation of wonderful horses. In addition, in 1979, O'Sullevan had helped put racing in the spotlight by slamming BBC Television for not screening the Hennessy (won by Fighting Fit) in live format after the race had been slightly delayed, with the station opting instead to show rugby union. For O'Sullevan's final commentary, a highly competitive, fourteen-strong field had been assembled, and it was with much anticipation and excitement that viewers awaited the calling of the forty-first Hennessy.

The early part of the 1997/98 National Hunt season had been dominated by grey horses. Former Hennessy winner One Man had won the Charlie Hall Chase at Wetherby and the Peterborough Chase at Huntingdon, while the surprising but game Senor El Betrutti had captured the Murphy's Gold Cup at Cheltenham at long odds. But by far the most impressive performance prior to the Hennessy meeting had come from the well-built, highly progressive Suny Bay. From the yard of Charlie Brooks, Suny Bay had annihilated his opponents (including Hennessy contenders General Wolfe, a tough and talented chestnut trained by Captain Tim Forster, and the mature French-bred five-year-old Eudipe from Martin Pipe's stable) ten days before Newbury in the Edward Hamner Chase at Haydock,

where he displayed outstanding jumping, a willingness to front-run and a relentless galloping style accompanied by a mean turn of foot that had destroyed his rivals on his favoured soft ground. The horse had galloped his opposition into the ground at Haydock, propelling himself to the head of the Hennessy market. Suny Bay, near white in colour, had finished second to the runaway winner Lord Gyllene in the Grand National in April on unsuitably quick ground, but with conditions on the soft side of good at Newbury, the scene appeared set for the strongly made grey to continue his improvement. One man that considered Suny Bay to have an outstanding chance of winning the Hennessy was his jockey Graham Bradley, who had won on Bregawn in 1982 and was so taken with Suny Bay's ability and progression that he believed the horse to be in Cheltenham Gold Cup class. As it was, Suny Bay was a red-hot favourite for the Hennessy, starting as 9/4 favourite.

Although Suny Bay was the outstanding candidate for the 1997 Hennessy, competition was strong with the likes of Time For A Run, Belmont King, Coome Hill and Barton Bank in the field. Time For A Run, trained by Edward O'Grady, was attempting to become the first Irish winner since Bright Highway, and the horse had been targeted at the race ever since finishing a very close second to King Lucifer in the Kim Muir Chase at the Cheltenham Festival in March. Belmont King, trained by Paul Nicholls, was making his seasonal reappearance, but had looked a horse with a great future when winning the Scottish Grand National at Ayr at the end of the previous season, while the 1996 Hennessy hero Coome Hill was back to defend his title, albeit with 22lbs more to carry and having suffered through an interrupted preparation. Top weight was Barton Bank, a horse that had been competing in National Hunt's finest races for many years. Despite winning the 1993 King George VI Chase at Kempton, Barton Bank had always been considered to be a dodgy jumper, similar in that respect to his trainer David Nicholson's former Hennessy favourite Charter Party. But, as the horse had grown older (Barton Bank was now eleven), his jumping had slowly improved, and a splendid second to Mr Mulligan in the Gold Cup in March had proved to many that the old horse had plenty yet to give.

With dark clouds hovering over the course, Suny Bay instantly jumped out in the lead as the race began, bounding out quickly and employing the same tactics that had served him so well at Haydock, with Yorkshire Gale, Barton Bank, Coome Hill, Grange Brake and Trying Again the closest to the grey.

Barton Bank (green) and the grey Suny Bay take the water in the lead.

Suny Bay was a brilliant winner of the 1997 Hennessy.

Having jumped the first three fences in fine style, Suny Bay, one of the best jumpers of his era, had given no indication of what was to happen at the fourth. In what would become one of the most memorable moments in the modern era of the Hennessy, Suny Bay simply walked straight into the fence, chesting it hard and blundering with such severity that it seemed a certainty that Bradley would be unseated, the shocked gasps hailing down from the packed crowd a measure of the unexpected incident. It is fair to say that, on most occasions, the error that Suny Bay committed would have been enough to end a horse's race yet, through the superb horsemanship of Bradley and the stout determination of the grey to stay on his feet, Suny Bay survived, the partnership somehow remaining intact. Yorkshire Gale and Barton Bank took the lead following the favourite's monumental blunder but, in the style of a horse at the peak of his powers, Suny Bay cruised back up to regain control by the seventh.

Jockey Graham Bradley with Suny Bay after their win.

The Suny Bay incident had left the large crowd buzzing and, as the race progressed, there was a real sense of excitement, the scene set beautifully for a fascinating finale as the second circuit got under way. Barton Bank edged his way in front, yet Suny Bay was travelling imperiously on his inside, finding his jumping rhythm following the early scare. The French horse Ciel De Brion – trained by Francois Doumen – was creeping closer all the time just behind Suny Bay on the inside rail, while Josh Gifford's runner Yorkshire Gale was trying desperately to stay with the leaders. Next came Trying Again (a horse that had been off the track for a year), General Wolfe and Belmont King, while Eudipe and Time For A Run gradually made their respective moves from off the pace. Coome Hill had been hampered as a result of the field bunching together tightly at the tenth and, from that point onwards, the 1996 hero had begun to weaken and was sadly no danger to the principals while, jumping down

Winning trainer Charlie Brooks (yellow) is congratulated by Sir Peter O'Sullevan after Suny Bay's win.

the back straight, the horses really struggling towards the rear were Oh So Risky (the former smart hurdler), Bell Staffboy, Doumen's second runner Djeddah and the fading Grange Brake.

By the time the field reached the cross fence, a thrilling finish looked in store. Suny Bay and Barton Bank remained locked in combat for possession of the lead, although Bradley gave the impression he was merely biding his time aboard the grey. Of the chasing pack, the four biggest dangers were Ciel De Brion, Belmont King, Eudipe and Time For A Run, the latter two having steadily improved throughout the second circuit.

However, even though six horses were tightly packed at the cross fence, once in the home straight there was only going to be one winner. Eudipe's challenge never materialised as he was left flat-footed; Ciel de Brion failed to quicken; Time For A Run hit the first in the home straight and weakened rapidly before pulling up, while Belmont King was easily held in third place when crashing out at the second last. For all Barton Bank fought, Suny Bay was simply relishing his task and, over the last four fences, Bradley increased the pressure on his rivals and the response from

the grey was most impressive. Powering on with strength and authority, Suny Bay began to pull clear of Barton Bank from the second last (the crowd erupting as he did so) and, galloping relentlessly to the line, the grey ultimately had destroyed his rivals, registering one of the most commanding of Hennessy victories ever witnessed, and to rich applause, the horse finished thirteen lengths clear of the game Barton Bank, with Eudipe staying on for third ahead of Ciel De Brion.

Having survived his one uncharacteristic error at the fourth fence, Suny Bay had looked an extremely high-class horse when winning the Hennessy, completing his transformation from very good handicapper the season before to a legitimate Cheltenham Gold Cup contender, and it was for that race that Suny Bay was made favourite (together with the Irish stayer Doran's Pride) after his Newbury victory. Suny Bay had resembled a well-oiled machine in the destruction of his Newbury rivals, looking a real class act and, along with One Man, was the best to have won the race since Burrough Hill Lad had won in similar fashion in 1984.

Suny Bay, whose sire Roselier was also responsible for the 1996 runner-up The Grey Monk, had been fired after a fall in the Reynoldstown Chase at Ascot as a novice and, in 1996, Brooks had convinced Suny Bay's owners to let the horse have an operation that necessitated the cutting of the check ligament behind the knee, an operation that seemed to have worked wonders for the grey.

Both Brooks and Bradley were enjoying their second Hennessy victories and, for Suny Bay, the season still had plenty of excitement left. Though it was not an absolute necessity, Suny Bay – like most offspring of Roselier – appreciated soft ground and, although he was not disgraced in the Cheltenham Gold Cup, he was a little out paced on genuine good ground, finishing fifth behind sound-surface-loving horses Cool Dawn and Strong Promise. In addition, there was a feeling that Suny Bay was best on flat, galloping tracks, and it was to be at Aintree where the nation really took the loveable grey horse to their hearts. On some of the heaviest ground ever witnessed, Suny Bay carried the burden of 12st top weight in the Grand National, yet the horse jumped impeccably all the way round under Bradley as every challenger fell away bar one. That one horse was former Hennessy favourite Earth Summit and, over the final few fences, the pair had the race to themselves, matching each other stride for stride. Cruelly though, Suny Bay had a colossal 23lbs more to carry than his opponent, a horse that simply adored the ground and, ultimately, the fight was an uneven one as Earth Summit pulled clear at the death to win by eleven lengths. However, the sight of the wonderfully brave grey gallantly giving his all right until the end, caked in mud, was a sight to behold, and revealed much about the horse's class and courage.

Suny Bay had won the Hennessy following a dramatic but ultimately clinical performance, and his place as one of the finest winners of the race will forever be assured.

1997 HENNESSY COGNAC GOLD CUP RESULT

FATE	HORSE	AGE/WEIGHT	JOCKEY
1st	SUNY BAY	8.11.8	G. BRADLEY
2nd	BARTON BANK	11.11.13	A. MAGUIRE
3rd	EUDIPE	5.10.13	A.P. McCOY
4th	Ciel De Brion	7.10.0	T. Doumen
5th	Trying Again	9.10.10	R. Dunwoody
6th	General Wolfe	8.10.1	S. Durack
7th	Grange Brake	11.10.0	C. Llewellyn
Fell	Belmont King	9.11.4	T.J. Murphy
Pulled Up	Coome Hill	8.11.10	M.A. Fitzgerald
Pulled Up	Djeddah	6.10.10	D. Bridgwater
Pulled Up	Yorkshire Gale	11.10.1	L. Aspell
Pulled Up	Time For A Run	10.10.0	C. Swan
Pulled Up	Bell Staffboy	8.10.0	Mickey Brennan
Refused	Oh So Risky	10.10.0	P. Holley

29 November 1997
Going – Good to Soft
Winner – £50,248 80p
Time – 6 mins 52.9 secs
14 Ran
Winner trained by Charlie Brooks at Lambourn, Berkshire
Winner bred by Mrs E.M. Codd
Winner owned by Uplands Bloodstock
Suny Bay, grey gelding by Roselier – Suny Salome

Betting – 9/4 Suny Bay, 5/1 Time For A Run, 15/2 Trying Again, 8/1 Belmont King, 9/1 General Wolfe, 11/1 Djeddah & Eudipe, 12/1 Ciel De Brion & Coome Hill, 16/1 Barton Bank, 33/1 Yorkshire Gale, 40/1 Oh So Risky, 66/1 Bell Staffboy & Grange Brake.

TEETON MILL

For the third consecutive season, it was a grey horse that was all the rage for the Hennessy Cognac Gold Cup. Following on from the hype generated by The Grey Monk and Suny Bay, the relatively new name of Teeton Mill was the talk of Newbury prior to the 1998 renewal.

Having enjoyed a fruitful career in the point-to-point and hunter-chase ranks from the age of six under the tutorage of Caroline Bailey (the daughter of former Grand National-winning jockey Dick Saunders), Teeton Mill would be making just his second appearance in a handicap chase when

Teeton Mill goes to post in 1998.

tackling the Hennessy. Having been transferred for the new campaign to the yard of Herefordshire trainer Venetia Williams (on the cusp of joining the top ranks in the training sphere in her third season), Teeton Mill had looked a genuine prospect when winning the Badger Beer Chase at Wincanton on his debut – a win achieved in facile style, albeit beating mediocre stayers Menesonic and Jultara. Some thought the bookmakers had reacted far too severely to Teeton Mill's Wincanton win, with the horse being made a short-priced favourite for the Hennessy, yet his credentials were strikingly similar to those of the 1996 hero Coome Hill, with Teeton Mill well weighted as well as being, on all known evidence, a splendid jumper. What remained to be seen was just how the ascending grey would cope against the sort of opposition typical of a Hennessy field.

As it transpired, a deluge of rain hit Newbury before the race, leaving the ground very much on the soft side. For that reason, the honour of starting as favourite eventually went to the intriguing Seven Towers, a most dour stayer. A bay nine-year-old trained in the north by Mary Reveley, the most recognisable trait Seven Towers possessed was an extraordinarily low head carriage, almost offering the belief that the horse was more interested in plucking at grass than concentrating on his races. This feature was deceptive, however, for two seasons before, the young Seven Towers had been one of the most rapidly improving chasers in the land, winning a number of long-distance races including the Midlands National at Uttoxeter (beating that season's Grand National winner, Lord Gyllene, in the process) and, although he lacked top-class speed over three miles, he was as hard as nails and a thorough stayer. Unfortunately for Seven Towers, the horse had missed the whole of the previous season with injury just as he had appeared to be entering his prime, but had recently made an encouraging return in the current season, finishing a staying-on fifth in the Charlie Hall Chase at Wetherby prior to a win at Ayr. With the ground at Newbury stamina-sapping in 1998, Seven Towers became the subject of a huge raceday gamble, starting the 3/1 favourite.

As well as Teeton Mill, the second lightly weighted, unexposed horse in the race was the James Fanshawe-trained front-runner, The Toiseach. Still only a seven-year-old, The Toiseach had proved prolific in modest company the season before, but had opened the season by dominating far more glamorous opponents – including the most recent Gold Cup winner, Cool Dawn – at Ascot the week before the Hennessy. The fact that Newbury arrived so soon after Ascot was a worry for connections, and there were fears that the horse may have had a rushed preparation at Fanshawe's yard, predominantly consisting of horses that ran on the flat. However, the booking of Richard Dunwoody to replace the injured Tony Dobbin was an encouraging sign, and the horse started as 5/1 joint-second favourite together with Teeton Mill.

Coome Hill was back to compete in his third Hennessy having had a soft-palate operation the season before, while the first, second and third from April's Whitbread Gold Cup – Call It A Day, Fine Thyne and Eudipe – also lined up, as did the progressive mare Fiddling The Facts from the Nicky Henderson stable and the tough little Irish horse Boss Doyle, the latter pair two of the best novices from the previous season.

The first circuit was run at an electric pace with Coome Hill and the blinkered bay The Toiseach jostling ferociously for the lead, with Eudipe snapping at their heels, while just behind, jockey Norman Williamson settled Teeton Mill beautifully on the inside with Fiddling The Facts also well to the fore. As Coome Hill and The Toiseach tore past the stands for the first time, ominous mutterings emerged from supporters of the favourite Seven Towers. Even at this early stage, the horse was struggling mightily and was well behind the main pack and being given stern reminders by Peter Niven, the jockey trying desperately to get the detached favourite back into the action. Even though Seven Towers was a confirmed stayer, he was at least ten lengths behind the second-last horse early on and, as the race progressed, it was obvious he was not going to improve. The favourite was eventually pulled up at the sixteenth having disappointed bitterly.

The frenetic pace continued as Coome Hill, The Toiseach and Eudipe led on to the second circuit and, as they did so, plenty of other horses were travelling well, including Teeton Mill, Fiddling The Facts, Boss Doyle, Call It A Day, Fine Thyne and the big horse from Nigel Twiston-Davies' yard, Mahler. It was at the fourteenth fence that the race started to change, with the field beginning to fragment on the stamina-draining ground. Eudipe had taken over the lead as both Coome Hill and The Toiseach began to pay the price for their early charge, and both early leaders had faded out of contention by the time the home straight was reached. Call It A Day and Fine Thyne both weakened from the fourteenth and, as Eudipe took the cross fence and led into the home straight, it was the grey Teeton Mill that was clearly travelling the best, stalking the leader imperiously while, in behind, Fiddling The Facts, Boss Doyle and Mahler were frantically chasing the front two, trying to stay in touch.

Williamson switched Teeton Mill to the outside on the final turn and, from there, the grey was merely toying with the workmanlike Eudipe.

Jockey Norman Williamson and Teeton Mill after their win.

Sure enough, by the third last, Teeton Mill struck the front and gradually began to pull clear. Over the final fences, the horse turned the race into a procession. Not stopping, Teeton Mill surged all the way to the line in glorious and dominant style, powering home to equal the biggest winning margin of fifteen lengths, receiving rich applause from a knowledgeable crowd who realised they may have witnessed the emergence of a new superstar. Eudipe, Fiddling The Facts and Boss Doyle – all very decent chasers – filled the minor places, while the moody but dour Him Of Praise stayed on to take fifth ahead of Mahler and Sail By The Stars, with the remainder failing to complete.

Teeton Mill's victory was the result that well and truly put Venetia Williams on the map as a trainer, providing her with her biggest win to date of a blossoming career. As a jockey, Williams competed against her

The 1998 Hennessy presentation, including Dick Francis (far left), the Queen Mother, Norman Williamson, Hywel Davies (second right, representing winning owners) and Venetia Williams.

Teeton Mill only enjoyed one season in the limelight, but the impact he made was incredible. As performances go, his victory in the 1998 Hennessy Cognac Gold Cup was outstanding, and he will be remembered as one of the most convincing winners in the race's history.

1998 HENNESSY COGNAC GOLD CUP RESULT

FATE	HORSE	AGE/WEIGHT	JOCKEY
1st	TEETON MILL	9.10.5	N. WILLIAMSON
2nd	EUDIPE	6.10.13	T.J. MURPHY
3rd	FIDDLING THE FACTS	7.10.9	M.A. FITZGERALD
4th	BOSS DOYLE	6.11.7	J.R. BARRY
5th	Him Of Praise	8.10.2	J.A. McCarthy
6th	Mahler	8.10.11	C. Llewellyn
7th	Sail By The Stars	9.10.5	S. Wynne
Fell	The Last Fling	8.10.1	S. Durack
Pulled Up	Coome Hill	9.11.10	J. Osborne
Pulled Up	Addington Boy	10.11.10	Richard Guest
Pulled Up	Seven Towers	9.11.0	P. Niven
Pulled Up	Call It A Day	8.11.0	A. Maguire
Pulled Up	Sparky Gayle	8.10.11	B. Storey
Pulled Up	Indian Tracker	8.10.8	C. Maude
Pulled Up	The Toiseach	7.10.5	R. Dunwoody
Pulled Up	Fine Thyne	9.10.3	G. Bradley

28 November 1998
Going – Soft
Winner – £47,926 48p
Time – 6 mins 51.9 secs
16 Ran
Winner trained by Miss Venetia Williams at Aramstone, Herefordshire
Winner bred by Mrs K.I. Hayward
Winner owned by The Winning Line
Teeton Mill, grey gelding by Neltino – Celtic Well.

Betting – 3/1 Seven Towers, 5/1 Teeton Mill & The Toiseach, 8/1 Boss Doyle, 9/1 Fiddling The Facts, 11/1 Coome Hill & Fine Thyne, 12/1 Call It A Day, 14/1 Eudipe, 16/1 Sparky Gayle, 20/1 Sail By The Stars, 25/1 Mahler, 28/1 Him Of Praise, 33/1 Indian Tracker & The Last Fling, 50/1 Addington Boy.

male counterparts in the Grand National, falling in the 1988 race from Marcolo at Becher's Brook, while she learned her trade as an assistant trainer to both John Edwards and Martin Pipe.

Teeton Mill's slaughter of a strong Hennessy field made him the talk of the sport. His immaculate jumping, ability to settle and sure staying had him initially suggested as an ideal horse for the Grand National but, when he similarly destroyed his rivals in the King George VI Chase at Kempton on Boxing Day and later produced outstanding speed over two-and-a-half miles at Ascot, it was clear he was a most worthy contender for the Cheltenham Gold Cup.

Sadly, it was to be in that very race that Teeton Mill – purchased for £40,000 out of the hunter-chase division by Winning Line Syndicate boss Stephen Winstanley – would sustain a career-ending injury. Starting the 7/2 second favourite at Cheltenham, the grey was travelling well within himself when he made a rare mistake at the seventh fence. It transpired that the horse had slipped a tendon off a hock and, two fences later, he was pulled up. As his injury began to heal in time, there were rumours the horse might make a sensational comeback but, due to the severity of the injury, it was never to happen, and the sensible decision was taken to retire him.

EVER BLESSED

The 1999 Hennessy Cognac Gold Cup was a wide-open contest, containing a plethora of talented, seasoned chasers and a number of the unexposed, second-season horses that historically do so well in the race.

The 1997 hero, Suny Bay, now trained by Simon Sherwood, was back at the scene of his greatest triumph, having disappointed in the Cheltenham Gold Cup in March on unsuitable good-to-firm ground, while the previous year's Hennessy third, Fiddling The Facts, also returned for the Newbury showpiece having made a bold bid to win April's Grand National, running a fine race but coming down at the second Becher's Brook when in contention.

There was a strong challenge from the North on this occasion courtesy of Young Kenny, The Last Fling and Tullymurry Toff. There was no doubting that Young Kenny – a big, strong, relentless-galloping bay chaser from Peter Beaumont's stable – had been the most improved staying handicapper of the season before, meeting the expectations that had been placed upon him for some time. A classically built steeplechaser (rugged, tough and stamina-packed), Young Kenny had reeled off a succession of big-race wins including the Midlands National at Uttoxeter, the Greenalls Grand National Trial at Haydock and, most impressively, an all-the-way win carrying 11st 10lbs in the Scottish Grand National at Ayr. These results singled out Young Kenny as an ideal Grand National contender, yet such was the rapid improvement in the Northern horse that many felt him to be good enough to contest the Cheltenham Gold Cup. If that were to be the case, the 11st the horse was asked to carry at Newbury gave him a terrific chance of playing a major part in the outcome of the Hennessy. Though not as championed as Young Kenny, both The Last Fling, trained by Sue Smith, and Tullymurry Toff, trained by Malcolm Jefferson, were solid

stayers, and the pair had finished first and second in the Edward Hamner Chase at Haydock prior to Newbury.

Earthmover, from the Paul Nicholls yard, had disappointed greatly the season before, sustaining a haematoma in a fall that almost proved fatal and subsequently suffering four defeats in what was expected to be a Gold Cup-contending campaign. However, Earthmover was a talented, prolific ex-hunter that had quietly had his confidence restored over hurdles by an excellent trainer in Nicholls, and the chestnut was well backed on the day, while other useful chasers among the thirteen-strong field included the Duchess of Westminster's horse Step On Eyre and the recent Murphy's Gold Cup winner, the questionable stayer The Outback Way, trained by Venetia Williams.

Yet it was a pair of improving youngsters in Ever Blessed and Spendid that appeared primed to continue the forty-two-year-long theme of lightly weighted, up-and-coming chasers capturing Hennessy glory. Mark Pitman had not long been in charge at Weathercock House stables, formerly run by his mother Jenny, but, in Ever Blessed, he had a horse capable of kick-starting his fledgling career, and one that had always been held in high regard by Mrs Pitman. A seven-year-old, 10lbs out of the handicap,

Trainer Mark Pitman and jockey Timmy Murphy with Ever Blessed after the horse had won the 1999 Hennessy.

Earthmover leads the 1999 Hennessy field over the water jump.

Ever Blessed was inexperienced but had impressed many when winning at Chepstow on his seasonal reappearance and, when rain had softened the ground the night before the race, Ever Blessed was destined for 9/2 favouritism, an honour held until the eleventh hour by the Martin Pipe-trained Hanakham, a winner of the Royal & SunAlliance Chase at the 1997 Cheltenham Festival, withdrawn from Newbury very late because of injury. Because of his imminent retirement, much of the race focus centred on trainer David Nicholson and his contender, the eight-year-old Spendid. Nicholson was due to be replaced at his Jackdaws Castle stables the week after the Hennessy by his protégé Alan King and, in Spendid, he

had a horse that had been one of the top novice chasers the season before, though a horse inclined to make mistakes. Spendid had really shown his potential at Aintree as a novice, winning a big chase in fine style in a race where Ever Blessed had been a late faller.

It was Earthmover that set a hectic early pace under young jockey Joe Tizzard and, despite a shaky moment jumping the sixth fence, the ex-hunter appeared to have left his troublesome experiences of the season before behind him as he boldly led for a good portion of the race. Those that chased Earthmover most prominently included Spendid, Suny Bay, Betty's Boy and Young Kenny, while held up were Ever Blessed (taking

Ever Blessed leads Spendid over the last fence.

a keen hold under Timmy Murphy) and The Outback Way, with Fiddling The Facts, Tullymurry Toff and Macgeorge trailing the main pack, the lattermost making jumping errors at the fourth and fifth fences.

It was in the back straight for the final time that the race really began to develop. Suny Bay and Tullymurry Toff both blundered the thirteenth, the former subsequently fading alarmingly while the latter fell two fences later. Spendid, Fiddling The Facts and The Last Fling all started to make good progress, cutting into Earthmover's advantage, but The Outback Way, having hit the twelfth, also made a mistake at the sixteenth and tailed off soon after. One horse that had quietly crept into contention having been

very headstrong early was Ever Blessed and, as the field came to the cross fence, he was right on the heels of the leaders with many of his rivals beginning to come under pressure.

It was at the cross fence that jockey Richard Johnson sent Spendid through to grab the lead from Earthmover and, having run a fine race, the long-time leader suddenly came under pressure, made a mistake at the fence and began to fade. Johnson and Spendid seized their opportunity to strike for home leaving the back straight, and only Ever Blessed emerged from the pack to challenge him. Coming to the first in the home straight, Spendid and Ever Blessed were set for a duel to the end and had the race virtually to themselves although, behind them, both Fiddling The Facts and The Last Fling were staying on defiantly, albeit at a pace that was of no danger to the leading two.

Spendid led marginally four out, but it was Ever Blessed that was travelling stronger and it was no surprise when he struck the front at the next fence. Spendid threw down a brave challenge, but Ever Blessed had less weight and was in full flow. The favourite jumped slightly to the left two out but it made no difference, and the youngster still had the edge when Spendid thumped the last fence. Running on gamely, Ever Blessed stayed on stoutly to win by three-and-a-half lengths to Spendid and, although the runner-up had failed to present his trainer with the perfect send-off, the horse had run most gallantly in defeat. Fiddling The Facts had again proved her worth, the consistent mare running another creditable race to finish third ahead of The Last Fling and Earthmover. Perhaps the most disappointing horse on the day was Young Kenny, the big chaser never a danger to the principals having run a confusing race.

Not surprisingly, the first big winner of Mark Pitman's training career led to emotional scenes in the winner's enclosure. Both mother Jenny and father Richard, the former Champion Jockey turned television presenter, were on hand, the two having been associated with previous Hennessy winners Burrough Hill Lad and Charlie Potheen respectively. Mark, thirty-three, had admitted to feeling a lot of pressure when the rush of late money made Ever Blessed the favourite, but now he could enjoy the win with a huge sense of pride. Indeed, the victory was even more impressive given the fact that Ever Blessed was an extremely fragile horse to train, never needing to be over-exerted in homework. The main problem with the horse was that he needed constant acupuncture for a recurring muscle problem in his shoulder, and the acupuncturist that worked Ever Blessed had also helped in the preparation of the similarly plagued Garrison Savannah before that horse's 1991 Cheltenham Gold Cup success.

The brittle Ever Blessed continued to suffer from injury throughout the remainder of his career and, despite at least running in the 2000 Cheltenham Gold Cup (he was pulled up), long-term plans for races such as the Grand National were inevitably dashed. Happily, connections of the horse could always recount the 1999 Hennessy Cognac Gold Cup as a vintage moment; the day a young chaser provided the springboard for a young trainer's career.

1999 HENNESSY COGNAC GOLD CUP RESULT

FATE	HORSE	AGE/WEIGHT	JOCKEY
1st	EVER BLESSED	7.10.0	T.J. MURPHY
2nd	SPENDID	7.10.4	R. JOHNSON
3rd	FIDDLING THE FACTS	8.10.9	M.A. FITZGERALD
4th	The Last Fling	9.10.0	S. Durack
5th	Earthmover	8.10.0	J. Tizzard
6th	Betty's Boy	10.10.0	R. Wakley
7th	Young Kenny	8.11.0	R. Supple
8th	Step On Eyre	9.10.0	S. Wynne
9th	Djeddah	8.11.7	T. Doumen
Fell	Tullymurry Toff	8.10.0	G. Lee
Pulled Up	Suny Bay	10.11.10	A. Maguire
Pulled Up	Macgeorge	9.11.6	A. Thornton
Pulled Up	The Outback Way	9.10.4	N. Williamson

27 November 1999
Going – Good to Soft
Winner – £48,880
Time – 6 mins 42.6 secs
13 Ran
Winner trained by Mark Pitman at Upper Lambourn, Berkshire
Winner bred by J.H. Ramsden
Winner owned by The Ever Blessed Partnership
Ever Blessed, bay gelding by Lafontaine – Sanctify

Betting – 9/2 Ever Blessed, 13/2 Spendid & Young Kenny, 7/1 Earthmover & Fiddling The Facts, 9/1 Tullymurry Toff, 10/1 The Outback Way, 14/1 Betty's Boy, Djeddah, Step On Eyre & Suny Bay, 16/1 Macgeorge, 25/1 The Last Fling.

2000

KING'S ROAD

One of the major areas of speculation in the days leading up to the 2000 Hennessy Cognac Gold Cup was which horses from the powerful string of leading owner Sir Robert Ogden would take part in the race. Ogden, whose pink-and-mauve-checked colours were among the most recognisable in the sport, had four candidates for a race that he had never won, three of whom were considered to be leading contenders. With heavy ground lying in wait, conditions were deemed unsuitable for the talented but heavily weighted Marlborough, while the Paul Nicholls-trained outsider Extra Jack was also ruled out. However, the two horses that represented Ogden, Kingsmark and Ad Hoc, held excellent chances.

Kingsmark, small but tough, was attempting to replicate the like of One Man, Suny Bay and Teeton Mill and continue the fine recent record of grey horses in the race. A seven-year-old trained by Martin Todhunter, Kingsmark's form in the early part of the season had been very impressive, especially when winning the Edward Hamner Chase at Haydock in early November, his third consecutive win of the season. Kingsmark was partnered at Newbury by twenty-one-year-old conditional jockey David Dennis, an up-and-coming rider who had led-in his father Walter's Coome Hill when that horse had won the race in 1996. With good form behind him and conditions in his favour, Kingsmark was thought to be well treated on just 10st 4lbs and started the race the 100/30 favourite.

Also well backed was the six-year-old Ad Hoc, trained by Nicholls. Ad Hoc had been marked down as a horse to follow for the season by many leading journalists and his potential was rich, yet, at the time of the 2000 Hennessy, the horse's jumping was sketchy at best and he was prone to clumsy errors, such as when throwing away an obvious winning chance in the recent Badger Brewery Chase at Wincanton, a race won by

his stablemate Flaked Oats. At this stage of his career, Ad Hoc was well respected yet largely unproven and he began the race at 7/1, with jockey Timmy Murphy seeking his second consecutive Hennessy win.

Even with the early morning defection of the winner of the Royal & SunAlliance Chase at the Cheltenham Festival in March, Lord Noelie, the strength in depth among the seventeen-strong field was outstanding, with the likes of Foxchapel King, Beau, Alexander Banquet, Lady Cricket and King's Road all arriving at Newbury with fine credentials and definite winning possibilities. Foxchapel King was the latest horse attempting to break Ireland's long-standing drought in the race, and the Mouse Morris-trained horse had improved greatly over fences since his younger days, as evidenced by a recent victory over a strong field in a Cheltenham handicap. The front-running bay Beau, trained by Nigel Twiston-Davies, had marched to prominence with an emphatic win in the Whitbread Gold Cup at Sandown at the end of the previous season and was the selected ride of stable jockey Carl Llewellyn. Alexander Banquet was another Irish raider and was a soft-ground lover from Willie Mullins' yard that had designs on the season's Cheltenham Gold Cup after the horse had finished second to Lord Noelie in the Royal & SunAlliance Chase in March. The chestnut mare Lady Cricket, trained by Martin Pipe, was stepping up

Winning jockey Jamie Goldstein lifts the trophy. Far right is trainer Nigel Twiston-Davies.

Gingembre (13) and King's Road settle down to battle out the closing stages of the 2000 Hennessy.

considerably in distance but had won by ten lengths in the recent Thomas Pink Gold Cup (formerly the Mackeson and Murphy's), while King's Road, supposedly the second string from Twiston-Davies' yard, had finished second to Flaked Oats in the Badger Brewery Chase – a race that had yielded recent winners Coome Hill and Teeton Mill – and was a horse that carried the full confidence of assistant trainer and former Hennessy-winning jockey Peter Scudamore, who felt the heavy ground would be ideal for King's Road.

Right from the outset, it was clear the 2000 Hennessy was going to be a brutal examination of stamina and courage as horses began their quest in the extreme conditions, and it was Beau that adopted his customary position in front, setting a sensible gallop from the outsider Folly Road, King's Road, Gingembre, Alexander Banquet, Kingsmark and Foxchapel King while, even in the early stages, some horses were finding the experience far too demanding, with Bouchasson, Zaggy Lane and Norski Lad the chief stragglers.

As he had done in April's Whitbread, Beau attempted to make every jump tell, as Llewellyn tried to stretch the field on the front-runner, but Newbury in November 2000 was a far cry from Sandown Park the previous spring and, with 11st 10lbs to shoulder on wretched ground, Beau's task was immense. Even so, the game bay continued to dictate and still led at the sixteenth. However, by the cross fence, he came under

With ground conditions heavy, Foxchapel King (black and white) clears the water from Esprit De Cotte (yellow and green).

pressure as the field began to bunch up, with a whole army of horses still in contention and looking threatening.

King's Road, Gingembre, Alexander Banquet, the chestnut Red Marauder, the little grey Kingsmark and the main Irish hope Foxchapel King were still in the hunt, as was the improving Lady Cricket, but Ad Hoc was the horse making the most eye-catching progress as, having been held up for much of the race, he began to make serious headway under Murphy. But Ad Hoc's jumping was his weakness at this stage of his career and, misjudging the cross fence, he crashed out, frustratingly tumbling to the muddy Newbury turf.

As Foxchapel King weakened, there were six still in with a chance as they turned for home: King's Road, Gingembre, Kingsmark, Alexander

Banquet, Lady Cricket and Red Marauder, yet the picture was about to change swiftly. King's Road had jumped very well for a horse that did not hold the best reputation in that area, while Gingembre – trained by Lavinia Taylor – was also considered a somewhat dicey fencer, yet he too had jumped perfectly against stronger opposition, and it was these two that suddenly forged clear of the other four as they came to the fourth last, a fence where the favourite Kingsmark made an error back in the field, hindering his progress and ruining any remote winning chance he may have had.

It was Gingembre, a tall, athletic chestnut, that narrowly edged ahead under Andrew Thornton – one of the tallest riders in the game – but conditions were absolutely perfect for the smaller, stockier King's Road and, sticking comfortably with Gingembre as the chestnut made his bid for glory, King's Road managed to overhaul his rival over the remaining fences. Ploughing through the mud all the way to the finish, it was he that emerged the five-length winner under jockey Jamie Goldstein. Gingembre had surprised many with his bold performance, especially considering he preferred far better ground, and he would develop into a very good horse, perhaps not Gold Cup-class, but good enough to win a Scottish Grand National and deliver another fantastic effort in a future Hennessy. In third place, some way back, came Alexander Banquet, with Lady Cricket fourth, Red Marauder fifth and Kingsmark sixth. Many of the field, including the hard-luck story of the race, Ad Hoc, had failed to complete the course, with only Foxchapel King and Strong Tel finishing in addition to the top six. Red Marauder, despite blundering four out, had run well in the heavy going and, later in the season, he would win an unforgettable Grand National in conditions even more atrocious than at Newbury.

As well as a first Hennessy win for Nigel Twiston-Davies, it was the biggest victory of twenty-two-year-old Goldstein's career. The jockey's father was Ray Goldstein, a former jockey and a man nicknamed 'Iron Man' in his day for his willingness to ride notoriously dodgy jumpers. King's Road was by no means a dodgy jumper, yet he did tend to land somewhat steeply at his obstacles, meaning that – as Scudamore suggested – the Grand National at Aintree would most likely prove unsuitable for the horse, disappointing many that foresaw King's Road's stamina as an ideal asset for that particular race.

Sadly for King's Road, he missed plenty of time with injury after the Hennessy and never competed in any other major chases. Sadly he died a few short years later, but his mark on the history of the Hennessy had been made, and he will be remembered as a horse that handled heavy going better than most, and certainly better than any rival in the 2000 Hennessy Cognac Gold Cup.

2000 HENNESSY COGNAC GOLD CUP RESULT

FATE	HORSE	AGE/WEIGHT	JOCKEY
1st	KING'S ROAD	7.10.7	J. GOLDSTEIN
2nd	GINGEMBRE	6.10.3	A. THORNTON
3rd	ALEXANDER BANQUET	7.11.3	R. WALSH
4th	LADY CRICKET	6.10.12	A.P. McCOY
5th	Red Marauder	10.10.12	Richard Guest
6th	Kingsmark	7.10.4	D.R. Dennis
7th	Foxchapel King	7.10.8	J.R. Barry
8th	Strong Tel	10.10.13	D.J. Casey
Fell	Ad Hoc	6.10.0	T.J. Murphy
Pulled Up	Beau	7.11.10	C. Llewellyn
Pulled Up	Spendid	8.11.0	R. Thornton
Pulled Up	Windross	8.10.10	R. Johnson
Pulled Up	Zaggy Lane	8.10.4	S. Burrough
Pulled Up	Bouchasson	7.10.3	R. Widger
Pulled Up	Norski Lad	5.10.1	J. Tizzard
Pulled Up	Esprit De Cotte	8.10.0	J.R. Kavanagh
Pulled Up	Folly Road	10.9.11	H. Oliver

25 November 2000
Going – Heavy
Winner – £52,200
Time – 6 mins 59.2 secs
17 Ran
Winner trained by Nigel Twiston-Davies at Naunton, Gloucestershire
Winner bred by Mrs L. Eadie
Winner owned by Mrs Nicholas Jones
King's Road, bay gelding by King's Ride – Live Aid

Betting – 100/30 Kingsmark, 5/1 Foxchapel King, 7/1 Ad Hoc & King's Road, 8/1 Alexander Banquet, Beau & Lady Cricket, 10/1 Windross, 20/1 Gingembre, Red Marauder & Strong Tel, 33/1 Norski Lad & Spendid, 40/1 Bouchasson, 50/1 Esprit De Cotte, 66/1 Folly Road, 100/1 Zaggy Lane.

2001

WHAT'S UP BOYS

It was Paul Nicholls that was very much the trainer of interest in the build-up to the 2001 Hennessy Cognac Gold Cup. Nicholls was responsible for the first two horses listed in the betting market, as he held a strong hand in an attempt to take a first Hennessy crown back to his powerful stables at Ditcheat, Somerset.

It looked a deep, competitive Hennessy field beforehand, and it was testament to the ever-blossoming reputation and stature of the Nicholls yard that both Montifault and Ad Hoc stood above their rivals in the market. Ad Hoc had threatened to win the race the year before only to fall five out and, in truth, that was typical of how much of that season transpired for the horse. As well as his fall in the Hennessy, Ad Hoc had capsized in the Badger Brewery Chase at Wincanton and pulled up in the Great Yorkshire Chase at Doncaster before finally putting in a clear round in the *Racing Post* Chase at Kempton. After a very disappointing start to the previous season, Ad Hoc started to improve dramatically after his confidence-boosting run at Kempton, and he finished a most encouraging second in the Scottish Grand National behind 2000 Hennessy runner-up Gingembre, before finally realising his undoubted potential by winning the Whitbread Gold Cup at Sandown. That last performance obviously marked Ad Hoc down as a serious contender for the top prizes in the 2001/02 season, despite the fact that his Whitbread success had earned the horse a dramatic rise in the weights. With no run prior to Newbury and with Norman Williamson on board, Ad Hoc began the Hennessy as 5/1 second favourite.

The honour of favourite went to Ad Hoc's far less championed stablemate, the French-bred chestnut Montifault, a six-year-old. Montifault's chasing career had really taken off following a soft-palate operation and, three weeks before the Hennessy, the horse had delivered a performance of rich promise with an easy, front-running win in the Badger Brewery Chase at Wincanton, a race fast becoming the key trial for the Hennessy. The concern over Montifault's chance was whether he would cope with the step up in class, especially on soft ground that was far from his ideal surface.

It was a fierce-looking Hennessy field in 2001 with some class horses competing, such as the 2000 Royal & SunAlliance Chase winner Lord Noelie and the 2000 Irish Grand National winner and future Cheltenham Gold Cup runner-up Commanche Court. In addition, the race featured some hardy, sure-staying warriors like former Welsh Grand National winner Jock's Cross, the Ferdy Murphy-trained Streamstown, the consistent chestnut Bindaree, the trailblazing Grey Abbey and the fast-improving Take Control from Martin Pipe's yard. However, two horses of real interest were Behrajan and What's Up Boys. Behrajan was a giant six-year-old, still growing into his massive frame. Quite possibly the biggest horse in training and very similar in appearance to former Hennessy contender The Dikler, Behrajan had been a high-class staying hurdler that had taken well to fences. Trained by Henry Daly, the horse did possess an annoying habit of idling in front, as evident when only finishing third in the recent Edward Hamner Chase at Haydock when looking set to win, yet the feeling remained that he was a horse more

Philip Hobbs, trainer of What's Up Boys.

Streamstown goes to post for the 2001 Hennessy.

than capable of winning an important chase. Possessing a similar career profile to Behrajan was the talented grey horse What's Up Boys, trained by Philip Hobbs. At the 2000 Cheltenham Festival the grey had delivered a most memorable performance when overtaking fourteen horses on the run-in to win the Coral Cup Handicap Hurdle. Despite a shaky start to his novice chase career, What's Up Boys rallied well at the end of the previous season and, although well beaten by Ad Hoc in the Whitbread, the horse held the notable distinction of having won at the Cheltenham, Aintree and Punchestown Festivals, and was considered a horse on the rise.

Right from the start there was a strong pace to the race as Grey Abbey swept the field along, but the first shock arrived at the third fence when the normally sure-footed leader hit the obstacle hard and came down. Thankfully, Grey Abbey was none the worse for his tumble, and would develop into one of the nation's favourite chasers for years to come, enjoying plenty of success along the way. Grey Abbey's fall left Montifault in front and, with the likes of Lord Noelie, Frantic Tan and What's Up Boys pressing him strongly, the favourite appeared to be rushed in his fencing, possibly somewhat wound up by those in behind. Behrajan, Take Control, Bindaree and Ad Hoc were nicely settled just off the pace (the lattermost running on the wide outside), but Commanche Court, Streamstown and Jock's Cross found the pace too strong and were never able to threaten the leaders.

The gallop set by Montifault had been extremely lively and, by the time the field had reached the cross fence five out, the chestnut was under intense pressure, with at least five serious challengers waiting to attack. What's Up Boys and Lord Noelie held prominent positions, Behrajan and Take Control had come through smoothly to make their presence felt and Ad Hoc, although given plenty of daylight, held every chance.

At the cross fence, Ad Hoc made a terrible blunder and almost came to grief at an identical stage to the year before, going down on his nose before Williamson skilfully recovered him. Ad Hoc kept going, but his chance of winning had been ruined and from there he started to fade. Steaming into the home straight, Montifault was about to be engulfed. Headed by What's Up Boys four out, the favourite tired rapidly and, although he had run a bold race, the tactics employed on the soft ground had backfired. When he swerved violently through the third last his race was over, and he was pulled up before the next.

The four-strong group of What's Up Boys, Take Control, Behrajan and Lord Noelie had now pulled well clear of the remainder, and it was Take Control – in a first-time visor – that emerged to lead narrowly having been towards

The grey What's Up Boys dives at the final fence as he prepares to battle Behrajan (leading) and Take Control.

the rear of the field early on. But the menacing figure of Behrajan loomed up to tackle Take Control at the second last and, when the giant delivered a huge jump at the final fence, the prize seemed destined to be won by Henry Daly's charge. However, the Hennessy had been littered with fantastic finishes throughout its history, and the 2001 edition was to be another thriller.

As Behrajan displayed real effort and strength to hold off Take Control, it appeared the big horse had done enough despite jockey Mark Bradburne hitting the front sooner than Daly would have wished. But having been switched to the stands side, What's Up Boys came with one final late drive (similar to when he had won the Coral Cup) and, in the closest of finishes, the grey got up by a neck to deny Behrajan, breaking the hearts of Daly and Bradburne in the process; the pair would surely have thought their horse was going to win just seconds previously. In a brilliantly exciting finish to the Hennessy, Take Control was just two lengths adrift in third with Lord Noelie a mere neck behind him in fourth, the latter receiving huge credit for such a strong run carrying 12st on unfavourable ground. Illustrating the dominance of the first four home, Bindaree was eighteen lengths away in fifth.

Often overshadowed by his Somerset neighbours Pipe and Nicholls, Hobbs had finally won the big race his training record deserved. A most

Winning jockey Paul Flynn chats with the owner of What's Up Boys following the horse's win.

2001 HENNESSY COGNAC GOLD CUP RESULT

FATE	HORSE	AGE/WEIGHT	JOCKEY
1st	WHAT'S UP BOYS	7.10.12	P. FLYNN
2nd	BEHRAJAN	6.10.13	M. BRADBURNE
3rd	TAKE CONTROL	7.10.6	A.P. McCOY
4th	Lord Noelie	8.12.0	Richard Guest
5th	Bindaree	7.10.6	C. Llewellyn
6th	Streamstown	7.10.4	A. Maguire
7th	Ad Hoc	7.11.2	N. Williamson
8th	Hati Roy	8.10.8	A. Thornton
9th	Commanche Court	8.11.10	R. Walsh
10th	Hindiana	6.10.9	D. Gallagher
11th	Jocks Cross	10.10.2	T. Scudamore
Fell	Grey Abbey	7.10.0	B. Harding
Pulled Up	Frantic Tan	9.10.9	T. Jenks
Pulled Up	Montifault	6.10.0	T.J. Murphy

1 December 2001
Going – Soft
Winner – £58,000
Time – 6 mins 48.5 secs
14 Ran
Winner trained by Philip Hobbs at Minehead, Somerset
Winner bred by D. Cahill
Winner owned by R.J.B. Partners
What's Up Boys, grey gelding by Supreme Leader – Maryville Bick

Betting – 11/4 Montifault, 5/1 Ad Hoc, 6/1 Take Control, 8/1 Behrajan, 12/1 Grey Abbey & Streamstown, 14/1 Commanche Court & What's Up Boys, 16/1 Hati Roy, 20/1 Bindaree, 25/1 Jocks Cross, 33/1 Hindiana & Lord Noelie, 40/1 Frantic Tan.

consistent trainer, Hobbs would receive far more attention following the 2001 Hennessy as his career went from strength to strength, highlighted by a win from another of his grey horses, the powerful Rooster Booster, in the 2003 Champion Hurdle.

Paul Flynn had ridden What's Up Boys both in the Coral Cup and in the Hennessy. The twenty-two-year-old Flynn, a County Kildare native, had been standing in for injured stable jockey Richard Johnson at Newbury, although the latter was back on board the grey when the horse ran in the 2002 Grand National. Having been fifth in the Cheltenham Gold Cup, What's Up Boys arrived at Aintree in great form but, in contrast to Newbury, the grey was in the lead jumping the last and looked destined for a memorable victory. However, on the run-in, he was given a taste of his own medicine, as the Hennessy fifth Bindaree flew home to rob What's Up Boys of National glory.

GINGEMBRE

The field assembled for the 2002 Hennessy Cognac Gold Cup was nothing short of splendid. With the now-maximum twenty-five runners taking part, it was the third-largest field in the race's history, and the biggest since Springbok had defeated twenty-six rivals forty years earlier. What made this particular renewal of the Hennessy so special was not only the quantity, but also the sheer quality of the line-up, with many established big-race winners present, together with the usual batch of lightly weighted, potential-loaded youngsters.

The fact that the runaway winner of the Attheraces Gold Cup (formerly the Whitbread) at the end of the previous season, Bounce Back, was favourite, was of less relevance than normal as there were so many horses that held realistic chances of winning on this occasion, while very few could be discounted entirely. Three big, Northern-based raiders fitted the bill as the type of improving young horse that has traditionally fared so well in the Hennessy, and each of Hussard Collonges, Direct Access and Red Striker had the potential to progress further. Trainer Peter Beaumont had come close to winning the 1992 race with Jodami and, in the very promising bay Hussard Collonges, he had a horse capable of winning the Hennessy. A good winner of the Royal & SunAlliance Chase at the 2002 Cheltenham Festival, Hussard Collonges had shown his potential among the top grade with a fine second to the experienced Marlborough in the recent Charlie Hall Chase at Wetherby although, for a relatively inexperienced seven-year-old, he had a big weight of 11st 4lbs to carry at Newbury. The rangy chestnut Direct Access had enjoyed a promising career over hurdles but had always been expected to come into his own over the larger obstacles, and his powerful frame bore some resemblance to former Gold Cup winner Mr Mulligan. Trained by Len Lungo, Direct Access had won

easily on his reappearance at Kelso, and the horse received much support during Hennessy week, despite the fact that the softish conditions were not deemed ideal. Red Striker hailed from the Norman Mason yard, and the horse was a full brother to the 2001 Grand National winner Red Marauder. Red Striker had won the Peter Marsh Chase at Haydock the season before and was said by assistant trainer and big-race jockey Richard Guest to be in magnificent form prior to the Hennessy.

As well as the six-year-old Bounce Back, the selection of jockey Tony McCoy, trainer Martin Pipe ran the Scottish National winner of the previous season, Take Control, the Royal & SunAlliance Chase runner-up Iznogoud and the diminutive but game Stormez, while at the top of the handicap were much-loved veterans Lord Noelie and Marlborough.

No Irish horse had won the race since Bright Highway in 1980, yet the quartet of challengers on this occasion provided reasons for optimism. As well as the Edward Hales-trained Give Over, runner-up in the Irish Grand National in April, and the recent Navan winner Takagi, both Harbour Pilot and Be My Royal ran. Trained by Noel Meade, the sheepskin

Be My Royal is flanked by trainer Willie Mullins (left) and jockey David Casey following the horse's brave Hennessy win. However, Be My Royal would later be disqualified.

The big chestnut Direct Access goes to post in 2002.

noseband-wearing Harbour Pilot was a horse of immense talent, although his jumping remained somewhat questionable. Twice a Grade One winner in his novice campaign, the seven-year-old Harbour Pilot was attempting the Hennessy distance for the first time, although Meade was confident the horse's stamina would prove sufficient. Be My Royal had made an horrendous start to his chasing career, completing just one of eight chases. But the current season – in which the horse was still technically a novice – had seen great improvement from the Willie Mullins-trained eight-year-old, as the horse won three of his four early-season races.

An example of the wonderful strength in depth of the 2002 Hennessy came from the fact that the winner of April's Grand National, Bindaree, and the 1999 Hennessy winner, Ever Blessed, were virtually unconsidered in the betting, while excellent stayers such as the *Racing Post* Chase winner Gunther McBride, the gritty Frosty Canyon from Paul Webber's yard and the former Scottish Grand National winner and Hennessy runner-up Gingembre all had their fair share of supporters.

As the huge field lined up at the start, the atmosphere amongst the large crowd was vibrant and the anticipation tremendous for what promised to be a fantastic Hennessy and, as the twenty-five runners thundered towards the first fence, it was clear that, despite ground on the soft side, the race was going to be run at a hectic pace.

As it transpired, those horses that set about delivering the gallop were also to be among those involved in the finish, and most of the principals come the race's conclusion had travelled in the leading group most of the way. It was Hussard Collonges and Gunther McBride that showed the way, hotly pressed by a whole host of eager challengers including Harbour Pilot, Frosty Canyon, Gingembre, Carbury Cross, Whitenzo and Be My Royal, with the lattermost hitting the seventh fence. Bounce Back, the favourite, was well in touch early on but made a mistake at the tenth, while the likes of Marlborough, Lord Noelie, Red Striker and Direct Access were held up early on as the leaders cut a dynamic pace, with horses such as Southern Star, Ever Blessed, Moral Support and Bindaree soon in trouble.

Towards the end of the back straight on the final circuit, the picture became a little clearer, although there remained a plethora of horses still with chances. Hussard Collonges, despite making a number of mistakes, had duelled with Gunther McBride throughout and by the cross fence the pair were still in command, chased frantically by Harbour Pilot, Whitenzo and Carbury Cross. The cross fence saw Gingembre and Be My Royal lose

their positions as the front five left them flat-footed, while Frosty Canyon began to come under pressure. Bounce Back blundered the cross fence badly and, from there, his chance was over, while Direct Access and Red Striker were now really struggling to stay in touch, and Marlborough and Gola Cher were the only others still in contention.

Gola Cher, an up and coming eight-year-old trained by Alan King and ridden by Robert Thornton, had been well backed in Hennessy week having finished runner-up in the recent Badger Brewery Chase at Wincanton, and he looked as though he may be ready to challenge the leaders in the home straight. However, making a hash of the fourth last, his chance soon evaporated and, unable to reach the front line, he was out of it by the time he crashed down at the last fence.

With Marlborough and Frosty Canyon unable to quicken in the straight, the leading five of Hussard Collonges, Gunther McBride, Whitenzo, Harbour Pilot and Carbury Cross surged on. Having been initially outpaced on the run to the fourth last, Gingembre and Be My Royal battled back majestically to set up an enthralling seven-horse contest over the final obstacles. A talented six-year-old chestnut from the Paul Nicholls yard but generally ignored in the betting, Whitenzo had quietly run a fine race under the guidance of Ruby Walsh, a big-race jockey supreme, and one of the most stylish riders around. Coming to deliver what appeared to be a serious bid for glory, Whitenzo made a terrible mistake at the fourth last and was lucky not to fall; yet the error, most frustratingly, wrecked his chance of winning.

The battle was now ultra-intense and mistakes were inevitable. Gingembre hit the third last, while Be My Royal and Hussard Collonges clattered two out. But such was the determination of those left in contention that all seven, including the rallying Whitenzo, were very much alive as they came to the last. It was Harbour Pilot that moved through to take the narrowest of leads, and the horse looked full of running and ready to take the honours back to Ireland for the first time in twenty-two years. But Harbour Pilot was hardly the most reliable jumper and, diving through the last, he lost his lead and was quickly headed once on the flat.

It was Gingembre, hard driven by Andrew Thornton from the third last, that was first to capitalise on Harbour Pilot's error, and the tall chestnut stormed through on a wave of momentum and took the lead. Be My Royal, who had been travelling beautifully towards the end of the back straight but had been fighting hard to stay in contention since, bravely emerged from the pack of now-tiring horses to throw down the challenge

Hussard Collonges (3) and Gunther McBride fly the water jump.

Harbour Pilot (14) leads a swarming pack of challengers after the last fence, including Gingembre (4).

to Gingembre, with Harbour Pilot, Hussard Collonges, Whitenzo, Gunther McBride and Carbury Cross trying their utmost to get on terms.

With both Gingembre and Be My Royal running as if their very lives depended on it, the finish was mesmerising, and it was the brave Irish horse that emerged victorious by a mere half-length to become the shock winner at odds of 33/1, with David Casey the elated winning jockey. Like the winner, Gingembre had given his all to emerge with tremendous credit in second place, duplicating his finishing position of 2000. The next two home, Harbour Pilot and Whitenzo, had both allowed excellent winning chances to escape them through jumping errors, although Harbour Pilot would develop into one of the finest stayers in the land, twice finishing

third to the brilliant Best Mate in the Cheltenham Gold Cups of 2003 and 2004. Hussard Collonges, with a big weight, won many admirers from his performance at Newbury, eventually finishing fifth ahead of Gunther McBride and Carbury Cross.

No sooner had connections begun celebrating Be My Royal's surprising but enthralling Hennessy win for Ireland than disappointment and sorrow arrived. It transpired that Be My Royal had, somewhere in the back straight, severely injured a tendon in his off-foreleg, which if nothing else proved what a brave horse he was to hold off such strong competition while suffering from the injury. Mullins knew after the race that the injury was serious, and a few days later it was confirmed that, although not in danger of losing his life, Be My Royal had run his last race. Be My Royal, owned by Archie and Violet O'Leary of Florida Pearl fame, was the second horse Mullins had lost in a fortnight after his promising chaser It's Time For A Win had fallen fatally in the Thomas Pink Gold Cup (formerly the Mackeson and Murphy's) at Cheltenham.

Winning jockey David Casey had derived great success in the saddle ever since returning to his native Ireland. Casey used to ride for Lambourn-based trainer Oliver Sherwood but had reportedly been sacked for repeated lateness. Though Be My Royal's win was the biggest of his career, Casey's other notable triumphs had been the Imperial Cup at Sandown, the Charlie Hall Chase at Wetherby and the Grand Annual Chase at the Cheltenham Festival, while among the best horses he had ridden were top Irish chasers Sackville and Foxchapel King.

Despite the agony and ecstasy that surrounded Be My Royal's Hennessy performance, there was more drama to come. It was soon revealed that the horse had failed a post-race drugs test for morphine, the source of which was thought to have been contaminated food. Be My Royal's was one of a number of positive morphine tests that littered racing at the time, and it meant the horse was disqualified from his Hennessy win. A hearing took place at Portman Square some fourteen months after the Irish gelding had triumphed at Newbury and the disqualification stood. Therefore, the 2002 Hennessy Cognac Gold Cup was awarded to Gingembre, trained by Lavinia Taylor and ridden by Andrew Thornton. It was, of course, a most unsatisfactory way to decide such a high-profile race, yet it was the correct decision, with no blame attached to Mullins, and the trainer was not fined.

Out of the grey clouds that had loomed over Be My Royal since he crossed the line first at Newbury in November 2002 came a ray of light. Nursed back to health, the horse, with a new owner and trainer, recovered sufficiently from his injury and, happily, was able to return to the racecourse during the 2004/05 National Hunt season.

2002 HENNESSY COGNAC GOLD CUP RESULT

FATE	HORSE	AGE/WEIGHT	JOCKEY
1st	GINGEMBRE	8.10.13	A. THORNTON
2nd	HARBOUR PILOT	7.10.3	P. CARBERRY
3rd	WHITENZO	6.10.2	R. WALSH
4th	HUSSARD COLLONGES	7.11.4	R. GARRITTY
5th	Carbury Cross	8.10.9	S. Durack
6th	Gunther McBride	7.10.2	R. Johnson
7th	Frosty Canyon	9.10.6	T. Doyle
8th	Marlborough	10.11.9	M.A. Fitzgerald
9th	Give Over	9.10.1	D.N. Russell
10th	Lord Noelie	9.11.12	J. Culloty
11th	Take Control	8.10.11	T. Scudamore
12th	Southern Star	7.10.1	T.J. Murphy
13th	Ever Blessed	10.10.0	P. Flynn
14th	Infrasonique	6.9.9	P.J. Brennan
15th	Bounce Back	6.10.11	A.P. McCoy
16th	Moral Support	10.10.0	B. Fenton
17th	Red Striker	8.10.7	Richard Guest
18th	Stormez	5.10.11	P. Moloney
Fell	Gola Cher	8.10.0	R. Thornton
Fell	Crocadee	9.10.0	B.J. Crowley
Pulled Up	Iznogoud	6.10.11	R. Greene
Pulled Up	Takagi	7.10.5	N. Williamson
Pulled Up	Direct Access	7.10.0	A. Dobbin
Unseated Rider	Bindaree	8.10.11	C. Llewellyn
Disqualified	Be My Royal*	8.10.0	D.J. Casey

30 November 2002
Going – Good to Soft
Winner – £60,900
Time – 6 mins 35.8 secs
25 Ran
Winner trained by Mrs Lavinia Taylor at Lambourn, Berkshire
Winner bred by Jean-Michel Sardyga
Winner owned by Mrs Lavinia Taylor
Gingembre, chestnut gelding by Le Nain Jaune – Teuphaine

Betting – 13/2 Bounce Back, 9/1 Hussard Collonges, 11/1 Direct Access & Harbour Pilot, 12/1 Gola Cher, Gunther McBride & Marlborough, 14/1 Frosty Canyon & Takagi, 16/1 Gingembre & Stormez, 20/1 Give Over, Iznogoud, Southern Star & Take Control, 25/1 Red Striker & Whitenzo, 33/1 Be My Royal, Carbury Cross & Lord Noelie, 50/1 Bindaree, Crocadee, Ever Blessed & Infrasonique, 66/1 Moral Support.

*Be My Royal originally finished first before being disqualified.

STRONG FLOW

With the exception of a cluster of veteran chasers such as Take Control, Royal Predica and Gunther McBride, the 2003 Hennessy Cognac Gold Cup comprised a large field of unexposed youngsters, many of them traditionally low-weighted. While on paper it looked one of the weakest Hennessys for many years, a high number of the entrants were potentially ready to progress into challengers for the season's top chases, with the likes of Strong Flow, Joss Naylor, Hedgehunter, One Knight, Irish Hussar and Sir Rembrandt all seemingly possessing very bright futures.

A most promising six-year-old, the athletic, brown novice Strong Flow shared favouritism at 5/1 with Irish Hussar. Trained by Paul Nicholls, Strong Flow was by the excellent sire Over The River and had taken well to chasing, winning three of his four starts. The horse's only loss had come when he fell in a three-horse race at Aintree in October, and inexperience was the biggest worry in his bid for the Hennessy. It was a huge step up in class for Strong Flow at the current stage of his career, yet Nicholls retained unwavering faith in his horse, insisting the gelding had the makings of a potential Hennessy winner.

Trained by Nicky Henderson and with 4lbs more to carry than Strong Flow, Irish Hussar was the more experienced of the two favourites, yet he too was a lightly raced chaser, only beginning his second season in that sphere. A smart seven-year-old bay, Irish Hussar had finished runner-up to the useful mare La Landiere in the Cathcart Chase at the 2003 Cheltenham Festival, yet had shown his desire for a longer trip when winning over three miles and a furlong at Aintree later that season. Big and rangy, Irish Hussar had clearly strengthened impressively over the summer months and he looked most distinguished in the paddock prior to the race, appearing primed for a major tilt at glory.

Top weight was the winner of the most recent Royal & SunAlliance Chase One Knight, a powerfully built chestnut with a striking white face. One Knight had led all the way when recording his Cheltenham Festival win and had triumphed in four of his five races in his novice chasing campaign. However, the horse from Philip Hobbs' yard had a reputation as a risky jumper, a trait that was highlighted in his only ever chasing defeat. Still, with much power and stamina, he remained a horse to be feared and started at 12/1.

Both Joss Naylor and Sir Rembrandt appeared to have the class to win a race like the Hennessy. A fine horse when fresh – as he was at Newbury – and a horse that appreciated the prevailing soft ground, Joss Naylor had long been opined by many as a potential winner of one of the season's big chases. Small but an excellent fencer, Joss Naylor was a solid stayer that had run in competitive races as a novice and was extremely well fancied to give trainer Jonjo O'Neill a first Hennessy win. A classically built, tall, rugged bay chaser, Sir Rembrandt was a horse with much ability, though one that was prone to injury. Trained by Robert Alner, the

Owner Barry Marshall and his Hennessy winner Strong Flow.

Last fence first time round in 2003. Among those in the group are Irish Hussar (2), Barrow Drive (7), Hedgehunter (19), Joss Naylor (16), Royal Predica (3) and Merchants Friend (21).

horse had shown excellent potential as a novice, winning both his races before sustaining a leg injury, and he was one of the most intriguing and mysterious contestants in the 2003 renewal.

Three relatively unexposed stayers from Ireland, Hedgehunter (who was particularly well treated having made a bold showing in the four-mile National Hunt Chase at the Cheltenham Festival), The Premier Cat and Barrow Drive all had their supporters, while the Nigel Twiston-Davies-trained six-year-old Shardam, had been most impressive when winning over three miles and three furlongs at Cheltenham recently; the youngster took his place in a field of twenty-one that faced the starter following the early morning defections of Haut Cercy and Sudden Shock, the pair withdrawn due to unsuitable ground.

The action flowed thick and fast directly from the start. His big white face beaming like the moon, One Knight was the first to go when he crashed out at the very first fence, sustaining a season-ending injury in the process and hampering Gunther McBride, Shardam and Jungle Jinks, while at the third the fancied Sir Rembrandt, normally a sure and safe jumper, came down unexpectedly. With two of the more fancied horses already out of the race, it was outsiders Native Performance and Tom's Prize that led on at a furious pace, with the likes of Irish Hussar, Barrow Drive and Joss Naylor being patiently ridden in behind.

At the ninth fence, Strong Flow drew gasps from the crowd as he made an horrendous blunder. But, indicative of a very good horse, he recovered quickly and was back in contention on the second circuit. Though Tom's Prize was an amazing fifteen lengths clear at one point on the second circuit, he was eventually caught and, as both he and Native Performance began to fade, the serious players had come to the fore by the time the cross fence was reached. Irish Hussar had not been travelling all that well yet remained in contention, but when he blundered the cross fence, his race was over and, straightening for home, three horses made eye-catching progress from the back, with each of Joss Naylor, Hedgehunter and Strong Flow travelling with serious intent. Both Joss Naylor and Hedgehunter were very lightly weighted, the Irish horse in particular having been treated with lenience by the handicapper and, jumping the first in the home straight, it appeared either could strike for glory at any moment as they marched forward strongly.

But the vast Newbury crowd was about to realise why Nicholls had placed so much faith in his young horse. Edging ahead three out, the way in which Strong Flow accelerated clear to open up a wide margin between

himself and the other two was most impressive. Soaring the last and hitting the ground in stride, Strong Flow roared away to become a most convincing winner, consequently fuelling thoughts of future Cheltenham Gold Cup raids. Joss Naylor had run well but had been unlucky to come up against such a rapidly progressing horse, and the O'Neill runner finished second, although the fourteen-length margin illustrated the authority with which Strong Flow had won. Hedgehunter too had shaped well for a long way, eventually taking fourth; Take Control had passed him on the run-in to grab third. Irish Hussar proved most disappointing of the remainder, eventually pulling up.

It was a winning performance of class and conviction, one made all the more praiseworthy considering Strong Flow's inexperience; the horse was technically still a novice. In addition, the time was electrically fast, despite the ground being good to soft. The victory provided a first Hennessy win as a trainer for Nicholls after his riding exploits aboard both Broadheath and Playschool in the 1980s, while winning jockey Ruby Walsh could

Rolling Stones guitarist Ronnie Wood points to winning jockey Ruby Walsh. Far right is owner Barry Marshall, next to trainer Paul Nicholls.

now add the Hennessy to his growing collection of high-profile victories that had also included the 2000 Grand National on his father Ted's horse Papillon.

There was much speculation after the race as to whether Strong Flow would contest the Cheltenham Gold Cup, but a relieved Nicholls (who had not wanted to rush the youngster and ran the horse in the Hennessy largely at the suggestion of Walsh) suggested that the race would be bypassed later in the campaign in favour of a novice event. However, as the weeks passed, Nicholls and owner Barry Marshall appeared to be swaying towards running in the big race at Cheltenham, a race in which Nicholls had tasted success previously with See More Business. Ultimately, the second-guessing became irrelevant, as Strong Flow cracked a bone in his knee when winning a novice chase at Kempton's Boxing Day meeting, and his season was lost.

Happily, Strong Flow recovered sufficiently and resumed his promising career the following season, though he did not appear quite the same horse, ultimately running in the 2005 Gold Cup and finishing sixth behind the new Irish star Kicking King. Ultimately, his niggling knee injury forced Strong Flow's premature retirement at the beginning of the 2005/06 season. Even though the 2003 Hennessy had looked weak beforehand, subsequent results suggested otherwise. Sir Rembrandt (twice) and outsider Take The Stand were both placed in Cheltenham Gold Cups afterwards, while, after falling at the last fence in the Grand National of 2004 having led all the way, Hedgehunter returned to Aintree to win the National most convincingly in 2005, and finished a gallant second in the 2006 National lending much credit to the young Strong Flow's performance at Newbury in 2003.

2003 HENNESSY COGNAC GOLD CUP RESULT

FATE	HORSE	AGE/WEIGHT	JOCKEY
1st	STRONG FLOW	6.11.0	R. WALSH
2nd	JOSS NAYLOR	8.10.9	B.J. GERAGHTY
3rd	TAKE CONTROL	9.10.9	A.P. McCOY
4th	HEDGEHUNTER	7.10.4	D.J. CASEY
5th	Merchants Friend	8.10.3	N. Fehily
6th	Barrow Drive	7.11.2	J. Culloty
7th	Native Performance	8.10.0	T.J. Murphy
8th	Tom's Prize	8.10.1	L. Aspell
9th	Iznogoud	7.10.13	Mr G. Elliott
10th	Royal Predica	9.11.0	J.E. Moore
Fell	One Knight	7.11.12	R. Johnson
Fell	Sir Rembrandt	7.11.3	A. Thornton
Pulled Up	Irish Hussar	7.11.4	M.A. Fitzgerald
Pulled Up	Arlas	8.11.2	T. Scudamore
Pulled Up	Be My Belle	7.11.0	J.P. McNamara
Pulled Up	The Premier Cat	7.10.13	J.R. Barry
Pulled Up	Gunther McBride	8.10.10	T. Doyle
Pulled Up	Shardam	6.10.10	C. Llewellyn
Pulled Up	Jungle Jinks	8.10.6	A. Ross
Pulled Up	Cruise The Fairway	7.10.4	P. Hide
Brought Down	Take The Stand	7.10.5	S. Durack

29 November 2003
Going – Good to Soft
Winner – £63,800
Time – 6 mins 36.9 secs
21 Ran
Winner trained by Paul Nicholls at Ditcheat, Somerset
Winner bred by P. McCarthy
Winner owned by B.C. Marshall
Strong Flow, brown gelding by Over The River – Stormy Skies

Betting – 5/1 Irish Hussar & Strong Flow, 6/1 Joss Naylor, 9/1 Hedgehunter & Shardam, 10/1 The Premier Cat, 12/1 One Knight & Sir Rembrandt, 20/1 Barrow Drive & Gunther McBride, 25/1 Jungle Jinks & Take Control, 33/1 Take The Stand, 40/1 Native Performance, 50/1 Be My Belle & Tom's Prize, 66/1 Cruise The Fairway, Merchants Friend & Royal Predica, 100/1 Arlas & Iznogoud.

CELESTIAL GOLD

As in 2003, the field for the 2004 Hennessy Cognac Gold Cup was perhaps short of the sort of class usually associated with the race, a fact highlighted by the top weight, the Francois Doumen-trained First Gold, carrying nearly a stone more than the next horse in the handicap, Royal Auclair. But the fourteen-strong field offered a competitive blend of seasoned handicappers and young chasers with plenty to prove, and another exciting contest lay in store.

The favourite was the young Martin Pipe-trained contender Celestial Gold. A six-year-old brown gelding carrying the blue-and-green silks of leading owner David Johnson, Celestial Gold had finished runner-up in the four-mile amateur riders' race at the Cheltenham Festival in March, but had begun the new season in fine style by surprising many with a cracking performance in the Paddy Power Gold Cup Chase (formerly the Mackeson, Murphy's and Thomas Pink) at Cheltenham, jumping with fluency and showing speed and staying power to land the spoils. That win had been the first major victory for jockey Timmy Murphy since he had taken over from Tony McCoy as the number one jockey for the Pipe/Johnson combination and, long regarded as a most stylish of riders and a perfect judge of pace, the season would be an outstanding one for Murphy as he finally took his place among the recognised elite in the sport.

Two other young horses joined Celestial Gold in the field, each attracting his fair share of support. A six-year-old bay trained by Nigel Twiston-Davies, Ollie Magern was developing into a fine novice chaser. Sired by the 1995 Champion Hurdle winner Alderbrook, Ollie Magern was tough, durable and combative, and had won three novice chases before finishing a close-up fourth in the Paddy Power behind Celestial Gold. A year older, but with considerably less chasing experience, was the athletic grey horse

Lord Transcend, running for the ever-ascending team of trainer Howard Johnson and relatively new owner Graham Wylie, an owner who would enjoy a memorable first season of prominence, winning three races at the Cheltenham Festival with his star hurdlers Arcalis, No Refuge and Inglis Drever. Lord Transcend had been a very good hurdler, yet Johnson had always stated that it would be chasing where the grey would become a star, and the horse had won his only novice chase in facile style at Ayr the season before, thrashing another useful grey, Strong Resolve, runner-up in the 2004 Welsh Grand National. A front-runner with plenty of scope but an obvious lack of chasing experience (Newbury would be only his second chase), Lord Transcend came in for much support during the week, eventually starting as 6/1 third favourite.

Sandwiched in between the young chasers in the betting was Royal Auclair, still only a seven-year-old himself but with a tremendous amount of experience; indeed, the French-bred chestnut had won the Cathcart Chase at the Cheltenham Festival as a five-year-old. The horse had slightly lost his way after that win but, now trained by Paul Nicholls having been formerly

Jockey Timmy Murphy returns having won aboard Celestial Gold.

Ollie Magern (red sleeves) battles the partially hidden Celestial Gold and Royal Auclair
(purple cap) in the closing stages of the 2004 Hennessy.

Martin Pipe, jockey Timmy Murphy and owner David Johnson (far right) lift the trophy. Next to Pipe (front) is former jockey turned author Dick Francis.

trained by Pipe, Royal Auclair was a most consistent chaser, and had won the Badger Ales Trophy (won by Coome Hill and Teeton Mill before their Hennessy wins) before Newbury to come into the Hennessy spotlight.

Others in the 2004 field included Frenchman's Creek, a former winner of the William Hill Handicap Chase at the Cheltenham Festival but a horse that had missed the best part of two years with injury, Nil Desperandum, a good novice chaser in Ireland the season before, trained by Frances Crowley and a horse with the same sire (Un Desperado) as triple-Gold Cup winner Best Mate, and Puntal, the front-running winner of the Betfred Gold Cup (formerly Whitbread and Attheraces) at the end of the previous season, trained by Martin Pipe.

The Henrietta Knight-trained outsider Midland Flame was the early leader until the grey Lord Transcend took up the running at the fourth

fence, chased by Ollie Magern, Gunther McBride, Puntal and Artic Jack. Lord Transcend was faring well for his first time in such company and, although he was obviously somewhat erratic at a number of his fences, he maintained a strong early gallop, keenly contesting the lead with Ollie Magern, the latter taking a strong hold on the first circuit. Having been held up towards the rear on the first circuit, the favourite Celestial Gold began to make steady progress at the start of the second and, by the time the field had jumped the cross fence, he had moved smoothly through under Murphy and was on the heels of the leaders.

Lord Transcend had run a brave race and still led into the home straight as the likes of Puntal and Midland Flame began to fade, while Artic Jack blundered four out and was also soon out of contention. Ollie Magern had run with the leading group all the way and it was he, together with

Celestial Gold and Royal Auclair coming from off the pace, that came to challenge the grey three out, a fence where Lord Transcend made his worst mistake of the round.

With the grey horse slowly losing touch, a three-way fight between Ollie Magern, Royal Auclair and Celestial Gold ensued over the remaining fences. The novice just held on to the lead jumping the last, but both he and Royal Auclair were somewhat one-paced once on the flat and, having been strongly driven to challenge at the final fence, it was Celestial Gold that was away the quickest and soon led on the run-in. Fiercely ridden out by Murphy, who again had timed the horse's run to perfection, Celestial Gold held on well to win the Hennessy by a length and a half to Ollie Magern, the novice losing nothing in defeat, with Royal Auclair just over a length further away in third and seven more back to the gallant Lord Transcend in fourth. Ollie Magern proved more than capable of mixing it in top-level competition and was one of the best novice chasers of the season, while Royal Auclair continued his good form throughout the season, running fine races to finish fourth in the Gold Cup and, even more impressively, second under a huge weight in the Grand National. Lord Transcend, though a faller on his next start, showed what a good horse he had the potential to become with more experience by winning the Peter Marsh Chase at Haydock later in the season.

But the day belonged to Celestial Gold, who became only the third horse after Bachelor's Hall and Bright Highway to achieve the Paddy Power/Hennessy double. It was the third Hennessy success for Pipe and thesecond for Murphy, and it continued what would be an unbelievable season for the jockey, as each weekend he seemed to be involved at the business end of all the big races, a huge turnaround in the career of one of the sport's finest jockeys who had unfortunately spent time in prison in the recent past.

Celestial Gold had caught his rivals with a well-timed run and strong finish to win the Hennessy, marking the ninth time a six-year-old had won the race. The horse later ran in the Cheltenham Gold Cup, but unfortunately finished a well-beaten seventh behind the new Irish sensation Kicking King.

2004 HENNESSY COGNAC GOLD CUP RESULT

FATE	HORSE	AGE/WEIGHT	JOCKEY
1st	CELESTIAL GOLD	6.10.5	T.J. MURPHY
2nd	OLLIE MAGERN	6.10.9	C. LLEWELLYN
3rd	ROYAL AUCLAIR	7.10.13	R. WALSH
4th	Lord Transcend	7.10.0	A. Dobbin
5th	Gunther McBride	9.10.0	R. Johnson
6th	Puntal	8.10.12	J.E. Moore
7th	Lord Of The River	12.10.0	M. Foley
8th	Swansea Bay	8.10.3	A. Thornton
9th	First Gold	11.11.12	A.P. McCoy
10th	Artic Jack	8.10.6	D. Elsworth
11th	Midland Flame	9.10.0	P. Flynn
12th	Supreme Glory	11.10.2	L. Aspell
Pulled Up	Nil Desperandum	7.10.8	M.A. Fitzgerald
Pulled Up	Frenchman's Creek	10.10.3	R. Thornton

27 November 2004
Going – Good
Winner – £69,600
Time – 6 mins 30.4 secs
14 Ran
Winner trained by Martin Pipe at Nicholashayne, Somerset
Winner bred by P. Downes
Winner owned by D.A. Johnson
Celestial Gold, brown gelding by Persian Mews – What A Queen

Betting – 9/4 Celestial Gold, 11/2 Royal Auclair, 6/1 Lord Transcend, 13/2 Ollie Magern, 9/1 Nil Desperandum, 11/1 Frenchman's Creek, 14/1 Puntal, 16/1 First Gold, 20/1 Gunther McBride, 33/1 Swansea Bay, 50/1 Artic Jack & Midland Flame, 66/1 Lord Of The River, 100/1 Supreme Glory.

TRABOLGAN

It had been suggested that the 2005 renewal of the Hennessy Cognac Gold Cup was a weak edition. However, the big field of nineteen runners was stocked deep with young, second-season chasers on the upgrade and, as it transpired, the collective performance of this group of horses made for a highly competitive running of the race and gave reason to believe a new batch of stars had emerged.

The Royal & SunAlliance Novices' Chase at the previous season's Cheltenham Festival provided many of the leading contenders, with the first four home in that race featuring prominently in the betting. All four of Trabolgan, Comply Or Die, Cornish Rebel and L'Ami were considered potential Hennessy winners, although all four were required to carry plenty of weight. With 11st 12lbs, the Nicky Henderson-trained bay Trabolgan was top weight. A beautiful-looking horse and a superb jumper, Trabolgan had won the Royal & SunAlliance in fine style and remained unexposed. The worry was that he would have too much weight, yet there was a feeling that if any of the youngsters had the potential to improve considerably it would be Trabolgan. Adding further interest to Trabolgan's challenge was the fact that his jockey, Mick Fitzgerald, had returned to riding just days before, having been sidelined for months with a broken neck. The Martin Pipe-trained Comply Or Die, a six-year-old, had finished second in the Royal & SunAlliance and had the look of a true stayer. Comply Or Die was related to Our Vic, a horse the yard had sent out to win the recent Paddy Power Gold Cup at Cheltenham, while the Paul Nicholls stable – represented in that race by the promising young chestnut Red Devil Robert and the nine-year-old Colourful Life – ran Cornish Rebel, narrow runner-up in the previous season's Scottish Grand National and a full brother to the late triple-Gold Cup winner Best Mate. Of the four, the

dark horse was L'Ami, fourth in the Royal & SunAlliance. Trained in France by Francois Doumen, the big chestnut had won in England before, was a most consistent horse and, at six, was open to further improvement.

Others of note were Joes Edge, Iris Bleu and King Harald. Joes Edge was a thorough stayer trained by Ferdy Murphy and had outlasted Cornish Rebel in a thrilling finish to win the Scottish National the previous season, while the tough chestnut Iris Bleu – also trained by Pipe – had recently won the Badger Ales Chase at Wincanton, traditionally a key trial for the Hennessy. King Harald was another of the promising batch of second-season chasers, the horse having won at the previous season's Cheltenham Festival. Trained by Mark Bradstock, the worry for King Harald followers was that the horse had endured a punishing race at Cheltenham's Paddy Power meeting recently, and some questioned whether the front-running bay had recovered sufficiently.

On a glorious, sunny day at Newbury, Lord Of Illusion set the pace, bounding out majestically from the likes of Ballycassidy and St Matthew, with King Harald rushed along to join the pacesetters, and this group were

Nicky Henderson (left), Mick Fitzgerald and lass Sarah Shreeve with Hennessy winner Trabolgan.

Trabolgan goes to post followed by Cornish Rebel.

Trabolgan (left) and L'Ami take the last fence locked together.

to force the pace for much of the way, with Trabolgan and L'Ami tracking the leading group, Comply Or Die settled in mid-division and Cornish Rebel held up by Ruby Walsh towards the rear.

One horse struggling on the first circuit was Tony McCoy's mount Iris Bleu. The big chestnut undoubtedly had talent, yet too often seemed to run one good race followed by a bad one. The Hennessy was to fall into the latter category and, after hitting the ninth and twelfth fences, was pulled up before the sixteenth. King Harald too was finding proceedings difficult. Having been under pressure to maintain his position, the gelding blundered the fifteenth and unseated Matty Batchelor, while the grey outsider Ross Comm – starting to get into the race – was the only faller of the contest when he came down a fence later.

Lord Of Illusion had set a strong gallop but, at the cross fence the final time, his race was over. Weakening rapidly, he was stripped of the lead by Ballycassidy, who subsequently surged round the turn for home in command. There were, however, plenty of others going even stronger than

the new leader. L'Ami had never been far off the pace and, turning into the straight, he came to play his hand under David Casey, while a roar went up from the crowd as Trabolgan challenged for the first time from four out, closely followed by Comply Or Die, although the latter made a mistake at the fence that slowed his momentum.

Having overthrown Ballycassidy, the final stages of the race soon developed into a fascinating duel between L'Ami and Trabolgan, the two racing neck-and-neck over the final fences. The race could quite literally have gone either way as they came to the last and jumped the fence together, an enormous volume of noise erupting from the crowd. However, it was Trabolgan – carrying 7lbs more – that was away the quicker and, displaying the finishing speed and staying power that had won him the Royal & SunAlliance Chase, the bay justified the faith that Henderson had placed upon him by drawing clear of the young French horse and winning in grand style under top weight by two-and-a-half lengths. L'Ami had run a fine race, smoothly put into the contest by Casey, and the

L'Ami (left) and Trabolgan battle on the run to the line.

youngster's effort was all the more pleasing given that ground conditions were thought to be too quick for him. Cornish Rebel, the favourite, had made up a lot of late ground and stayed on particularly well to be just a length and a quarter back in third. Cornish Rebel had not had an easy passage throughout, having been hampered at the fifteenth before hitting the seventeenth and then losing his position turning for home. Comply Or Die again stayed on well for fourth, just a length and a half back, lending rich credit to the form of the Royal & SunAlliance Chase. Indeed, the first six home were all second season-chasers, while the first seven were covered by less than ten lengths. Seventh-placed Run for Paddy would win the Scottish National later in the season.

But it was Trabolgan that was the star of the show, and confirmed his promise in eye-catching style, becoming the first top weight to win since Burrough Hill Lad. Nicky Henderson had long believed the horse was a real star and Trabolgan proved it at Newbury, immediately being installed among the favourites for the Cheltenham Gold Cup. It gave owner Trevor Hemmings another horse of blessed ability following Hedgehunter's win at Aintree in April's Grand National, while the performance of Mick Fitzgerald demonstrated the unrivalled toughness of the men who ride these beautiful animals.

Owner Trevor Hemmings lifts the Hennessy Cognac Gold Cup, flanked by Nicky Henderson and Mick Fitzgerald.

2005 HENNESSY COGNAC GOLD CUP RESULT

FATE	HORSE	AGE/WEIGHT	JOCKEY
1st	TRABOLGAN	7.11.12	M.A. FITZGERALD
2nd	L'AMI	6.11.5	D.J. CASEY
3rd	CORNISH REBEL	8.11.11	R. WALSH
4th	COMPLY OR DIE	6.11.7	T.J. MURPHY
5th	All In The Stars	7.9.8	D. Jacob
6th	Red Devil Robert	7.10.12	J. Tizzard
7th	Run For Paddy	9.10.13	P. Moloney
8th	Redemption	10.10.11	C. Llewellyn
9th	St Matthew	7.10.9	P. Whelan
10th	Ballycassidy	9.11.6	R. Johnson
11th	Joes Edge	8.11.2	K.J. Mercer
12th	Lord Of Illusion	8.10.13	J.M. Maguire
Fell	Ross Comm	9.10.10	D. Elsworth
Pulled Up	Colourful Life	9.10.8	L. Heard
Pulled Up	Distant Thunder	7.10.9	A. Thornton
Pulled Up	Iris Bleu	9.11.3	A.P. McCoy
Pulled Up	Kandjar D'Allier	7.10.10	R. Thornton
Pulled Up	Tribal Venture	7.10.11	G. Lee
Unseated Rider	King Harald	7.10.9	M. Batchelor

26th November 2005
Going – Good
Winner – £71,275
Time – 6 mins 31.7 secs
19 Ran
Winner trained by N.J. Henderson
Winner bred by Michael Lysaght
Winner owned by Mr Trevor Hemmings
Trabolgan, bay gelding by King's Ride – Derrella

Betting – 11/2 Cornish Rebel, 13/2 Trabolgan, 17/2 King Harald, 9/1 Kandjar D'Allier, 10/1 L'Ami & Red Devil Robert, 12/1 Comply Or Die & Redemption, 14/1 All In The Stars & Iris Bleu, 16/1 Distant Thunder, 20/1 Lord Of Illusion, 25/1 Ross Comm, 33/1 Ballycassidy & St Matthew, 40/1 Run For Paddy, 50/1 Joes Edge, 66/1 Tribal Venture, 100/1 Colourful Life.

HENNESSY COGNAC GOLD CUP ROLL OF HONOUR

YEAR	WINNER	TRAINER	JOCKEY	ODDS	YEAR	WINNER	TRAINER	JOCKEY	ODDS
1957*	Mandarin	F. Walwyn	P.G. Madden	8/1	1982	Bregawn	M.W. Dickinson	G. Bradley	9/4
1958*	Taxidermist	F. Walwyn	Mr J. Lawrence	10/1	1983	Brown Chamberlin	F.T. Winter	J. Francome	7/2
1959*	Kerstin	Major C. Bewicke	S. Hayhurst	4/1	1984	Burrough Hill Lad	Mrs J. Pitman	J. Francome	100/30
1960	Knucklecracker	D. Ancil	D. Ancil	100/7	1985	Galway Blaze	J.G. Fitzgerald	M. Dwyer	11/2
1961	Mandarin	F. Walwyn	G.W. Robinson	7/1	1986	Broadheath	D.H. Barons	P.F. Nicholls	6/1
1962	Springbok	N. Crump	G. Scott	15/2	1987	Playschool	D.H. Barons	P.F. Nicholls	6/1
1963	Mill House	F. Walwyn	G.W. Robinson	15/8	1988	Strands Of Gold	M.C. Pipe	P. Scudamore	10/1
1964	Arkle	T. Dreaper	P. Taaffe	5/4	1989	Ghofar	D.R.C. Elsworth	H. Davies	5/1
1965	Arkle	T. Dreaper	P. Taaffe	1/6	1990	Arctic Call	O. Sherwood	J. Osborne	5/1
1966	Stalbridge Colonist	K. Cundell	S. Mellor	25/1	1991	Chatam	M.C. Pipe	P. Scudamore	10/1
1967	Rondetto	R. Turnell	J. King	100/8	1992	Sibton Abbey	F. Murphy	A. Maguire	40/1
1968	Man Of The West	F. Walwyn	G.W. Robinson	20/1	1993	Cogent	A. Turnell	D. Fortt	10/1
1969	Spanish Steps	E.R. Courage	J. Cook	7/1	1994	One Man	G. Richards	A. Dobbin	4/1
1970	Border Mask	P. Cazalet	D. Mould	7/1	1995	Couldn't Be Better	C.P.E. Brooks	D. Gallagher	15/2
1971	Bighorn	C.J. Vernon Miller	D. Cartwright	7/1	1996	Coome Hill	W.W. Dennis	J. Osborne	11/2
1972	Charlie Potheen	F. Walwyn	R. Pitman	10/1	1997	Suny Bay	C.P.E. Brooks	G. Bradley	9/4
1973	Red Candle	G. Vallance	J. Fox	12/1	1998	Teeton Mill	Miss V. Williams	N. Williamson	5/1
1974	Royal Marshal II	T. Forster	G. Thorner	11/2	1999	Ever Blessed	M. Pitman	T.J. Murphy	9/2
1975	April Seventh	R. Turnell	A. Turnell	11/1	2000	King's Road	N.A. Twiston-Davies	J. Goldstein	7/1
1976	Zeta's Son	P. Bailey	I. Watkinson	12/1	2001	What's Up Boys	P.J. Hobbs	P. Flynn	14/1
1977	Bachelor's Hall	P. Cundell	M. O'Halloran	11/2	2002	Gingembre	Mrs L.C. Taylor	A. Thornton	16/1
1978	Approaching	J. Gifford	R. Champion	3/1	2003	Strong Flow	P.F. Nicholls	R. Walsh	5/1
1979	Fighting Fit	J.K.M. Oliver	R. Linley	15/2	2004	Celestial Gold	M.C. Pipe	T.J. Murphy	9/4
1980	Bright Highway	M.J. O'Brien	G. Newman	2/1	2005	Trabolgan	N.J. Henderson	M.A. Fitzgerald	13/2
1981	Diamond Edge	F. Walwyn	W. Smith	9/2					

*The 1957, 1958 and 1959 races were run at Cheltenham.

If you are interested in purchasing other books published by Tempus,
or in case you have difficulty finding any Tempus books in your local bookshop,
you can also place orders directly through our website

www.tempus-publishing.com